1941

Oberon

A POETICAL ROMANCE

CHRISTOPH MARTIN WIELAND

This engraving by J. F. Bause was made in 1797 after a portrait
painted in the same year by Anton Graff.

OBERON

A Poetical Romance

IN TWELVE BOOKS

TRANSLATED FROM THE GERMAN OF WIELAND

(1799–1801)

By JOHN QUINCY ADAMS

EDITED WITH AN INTRODUCTION AND NOTES

By A. B. FAUST

NEW YORK   F. S. CROFTS & CO.   MCMXL

Preface

JOHN QUINCY ADAMS, while resident in Berlin as United States
Minister Plenipotentiary to Prussia (1797–1801), translated
into English verse what was then the most popular of German
poems, Wieland's romantic epic *Oberon*. This fact was often
recorded, but, since never published, the Adams translation
remained unknown, and its survival was generally questioned.
The editor recently had the good fortune to trace this manuscript to the Archives of the Adams Family, kept in the building of the Massachusetts Historical Society in Boston, not
accessible to the public. Through the kindness of the Trustees
he was permitted to read and study the manuscript, which has
survived in faultless condition, written in the unmistakable,
clear handwriting of the sixth President of the United States.
It was found to be a *complete metrical translation,* of unusual
scholarly and literary merit, remarkable for its fidelity to the
original and its genuine artistry. It takes rank with the few
outstanding metrical translations done by American scholars,
as Longfellow's translation of Dante's *Divine Comedy,* or
Bayard Taylor's *Goethe's Faust.*

The publication of the manuscript is a duty long deferred.
It should be made accessible, however, not alone for its anti-
quarian interest or its connection with a great American name,
but for its own intrinsic literary appeal. As John Quincy Adams
was held under the magic spell of *Oberon* for more than a

v

year of the best, though not of the most prominent, period of his life, during which he wrote and rewrote his English version of the poem at least three times, so it is reasonable to assume, with the translator, that American readers of literary instincts should likewise be fascinated by this German classic, in its type unsurpassed in the world's best literature.

The editor's most grateful acknowledgments are due in the first place to Mr. Henry Adams and Mr. Charles Francis Adams, as Trustees of the Adams Family Archives, for placing in his hands the original manuscripts and securing for him the privilege of publication. He is deeply indebted to them also for supplying valuable references and materials (see Introduction, pp. xlvii–lxxii) relating to John Quincy Adams's residence in Berlin and work on the *Oberon* translation, gathered from the *unpublished* diaries and letters of their distinguished ancestor; also for permission to reproduce the manuscript page in the unique handwriting of J. Q. Adams.

The editor takes much pleasure in expressing his thanks to Miss Harriet Turner of the Enoch Pratt Free Library (Baltimore), Mr. Thomas P. Martin of the Library of Congress, and Mr. Allyn B. Forbes of the Massachusetts Historical Society, for their aid in the quest of the supposedly "lost manuscript"; for their valued co-operation in various ways to Professors A. W. Boesche (Cornell), J. F. Goodloe (Goucher), William Kurrelmeyer (Johns Hopkins), Percy Long (New York), and Heinrich Schneider (Cornell).

For financial assistance toward the expenses of publication of the manuscript the editor wishes to express his sincere appreciation for a substantial grant by the Oberlaender Trust of Philadelphia, negotiated by the Executive Director, Wilbur K. Thomas; for the efficient aid received from a committee of his former graduate students and associates of Cornell University, Gerhard Baerg (De Pauw), Marvin Dilkey (Cornell), O. S. Fleissner (Wells), C. E. Gates (Colgate), E. T. Mohme (Southern California), Walter Mueller (Cornell), Ralph Wood (Princeton), and Edwin H. Zeydel (Cincinnati), chairman, who for some time worked in silence, without the editor's knowledge, to secure a large block of subscriptions sufficient to carry the enterprise through; and last but not least to the publishers F. S. Crofts & Co. for their readiness in recognizing the importance of the publication and launching the volume in an appropriate format.

ALBERT BERNHARDT FAUST

Ithaca, N. Y.
September 28, 1939

Contents

INTRODUCTION

    I. Adams and Wieland   xi

    II. The Translations   xvi

    III. Wieland's Editions of *Oberon*   xxix

    IV. Sources of Wieland's *Oberon*   xxxii

    V. Adams's Four Manuscripts of *Oberon*   xxxvii

    VI. Orthography and Punctuation   xlv

    VII. Extracts (unpublished) from the Diary and Letters of J. Q. Adams   xlvii

    VIII. "Analytical Extracts" from Wieland's *Oberon* by J. Q. Adams   lxxii

TEXT OF ADAMS'S TRANSLATION OF WIELAND'S *Oberon*   3

NOTES TO THE TEXT BY THE EDITOR   315

Illustrations

CHRISTOPH MARTIN WIELAND (an engraving by J. F. Bause after a portrait painted in 1797 by Anton Graff)   *frontispiece*

A PAGE OF ADAMS'S MANUSCRIPT   *facing page* xliii

JOHN QUINCY ADAMS (a portrait painted in 1795 by John Singleton Copley)   *facing page* 3

THE FRONTISPIECE OF THE 1789 EDITION (LEIPZIG) OF *Oberon*   *facing page* 122

Introduction

I. Adams and Wieland

Opposite poles attract one another; otherwise we could hardly understand the extraordinary devotion shown by the American statesman to the amazing task of translating and thrice revising a poem of over 7300 lines, written by a poet who differed from him so widely in character: Wieland, affable and gentle, steeped in the culture of a skeptical, rationalistic, worldly-wise European society—Adams, austere and grave, representing a stern, unbending, narrow type of New England Puritanism. Both men in their youth were under similarly strong religious influences, but the American remained true to his early education, while the German poet yielded, or accommodated his philosophy to changing environments. Adams was ever a fighter, never swerving from the path of duty, right, and justice, unsocial in manner, unpopular in his rectitude, while Wieland compromised between the ideal and the practically attainable, was a favorite of the Graces and grew personally ever more popular.

There never was a more unselfish servant of his people than John Quincy Adams, as United States Minister Plenipotentiary and treaty commissioner in Holland, Prussia, England, France, and Russia, subsequently as United States Senator, Secretary of State under Monroe, and Sixth President of the United States, followed by the most arduous service of his entire political career, when as Congressman, from 1831 to the day of his death in 1848, he held and defended heroically his fearless stand, fighting the battle entirely alone, for the liberty of petition, the right of free speech, of unrelenting opposition to slavery, and through his uncompromising attitude making himself, "the old man eloquent," the best-hated among all American statesmen of his time.

Yet the two men had certain tastes in common: their love of classical literature and their habit of translating from foreign languages, both ancient and modern, and of finding therein a cultural purpose, as Wieland in his pioneer translation of Shakespeare's dramas, Adams in his Thirteenth and Fourteenth Satires of Juvenal. There is an outstanding ideal in Wieland's portrayal of the fidelity of the lovers Huon and Rezia in *Oberon,* while a distinctly didactic trend prevails in his rule for princes, *Der goldene Spiegel,* and its continuation, *Die Geschichte des Philosophen Danischmende.* As tutor of the Weimar princes Karl August and Konstantin, the poet Wieland satisfied an inclination for public service, while the statesman J. Q. Adams felt the lure of literature throughout his long public life, accomplishing what he thought was his best effort in literature at the age of sixty-four with the completion of his historical epic *Dermot Mac Morrogh or The Conquest of Ireland.*[1]

In his diary [2] under date of December 25, 1820, John Quincy

---

[1] Published in Boston, 1832. In the published diary (see footnote 2 below) of J. Q. Adams, under date of April 16, 1831, we find the following entry: "I finished this morning the fair copy of my poem of Dermot Mac Morrogh, and have now the measure of my poetic power. Beyond this I shall never attain." This historical tale, of more than 2000 lines, occupied him for about two months. It left him "with insatiate thirst for accomplishing higher and better things."

[2] Twelve volumes of J. Q. Adams's diary were published by his son Charles Francis Adams: *Memoirs of John Quincy Adams, comprising portions of his Diary from 1795 to 1848,* edited by Charles Francis Adams, 12 volumes (Philadelphia, 1874–1877).

Adams makes the following confession: "Literature has been the charm of my life, and could I have carved out my own fortunes, to literature would my whole life have been devoted. I have been a lawyer for bread, and a statesman at the call of my country. In the practice of the law I never should have attained the highest eminence, for the want of natural and spontaneous eloquence. The operations of my mind are slow, my imagination sluggish and my powers of extemporaneous speaking insufficient. But I have much capacity for, and love of labor, habits on the whole of industry and temperance, and a strong and almost innate passion for literary pursuits. The business and sometimes the dissipations of my life have in a great measure withdrawn me from it. The summit of my ambition would have been by some great work of literature to have done honor to my age and country, and to have lived in the gratitude of future ages. The consummation of happiness has been denied me."

During the years 1798–1801, while United States Minister at the Prussian Court, John Quincy Adams grew very fond of German literature, and, in order to learn the language, he translated various works from German into English, first trying himself in prose on a work then just published by Von Bülow, *Der Freistaat von Nordamerika in seinem neuesten Zustand* (Berlin, 1797), which he started in May and finished in June, 1799, as his diary records. Soon after, he acquired a set of Wieland's works and became deeply interested. In November, 1799, he started abstracting the action of *Oberon,* canto after canto,[3] then very soon began translating, and worked ever more intensely until he had finished the whole poem by May, 1800. But that was not the end, for he revised painstakingly

[3] Printed in this volume; see "Analytical Extracts," Introduction, pp. lxxii–xcii.

for almost another year. Three complete versions and five
cantos of another have come down to us, done in his own careful handwriting. It should be borne in mind that this work was
accomplished fifteen years before the publication of *De l'Allemagne,* the book of Madame de Staël, through which she
opened for England and America the German "kingdom of
the mind." Adams's complete and masterful translation was
unfortunately never published, for reasons which will appear
below, and apparently Adams's friends were not aware of this
work until about thirty years later, when Adams, in a letter to
Charles Follen,[4] congratulating him upon his appointment to
a newly founded professorship of German literature at Harvard,
wrote as follows:

"Thirty years have passed away since a residence of four
years in Berlin, and excursions into Saxony and Silesia, had
given me an enthusiastic relish for German literature. At that
time Wieland was *there* I think decidedly the most popular of
the German poets, and although there was in his genius neither
the originality nor the deep pathos of Goethe, or Klopstock, or
Schiller, there was something in the playfulness of his imagination, in the tenderness of his sensibility, in the sunny cheerful-
ness of his philosophy, and in the harmony of his versification,
which, to me, were inexpressibly delightful. His morals had
too much of the 'quidlibet audendi' of poetry, either for my
principles or my taste; but I, from whom Ovid, and La Fon-
taine, and Voltaire, and Ariosto, and Pope had extorted long
and reluctant admiration, could not subject Wieland to a more
severe scrutiny than they had passed through.

"Among my exercises in learning the German language,

[4] Dated: Quincy, October 24, 1831. Published in *The Life and Works of
Charles Follen* by his wife (Boston, 1842), Vol. I, pp. 306–307. Reprinted sep-
arately in *The Life of Charles Follen,* by E. L. Follen (London, 1845), p. 202.

was a complete translation into English verse of his 'Oberon,' which I should have published, but that Mr. Sotheby got the start of me. When I saw his translation, I was content to keep mine in my *porte-feuille*. My German teacher sent a copy of the first canto of my translation to Wieland himself, and asked him his opinion of it, which he gave with frankness. He compared it with Sotheby's translation, then just published, and gave the palm of poetry to him, and of fidelity to me; a decision which my own judgment fully confirmed."

This letter to Charles Follen, written in 1831 but first published in 1842, has been the main source for our knowledge concerning John Quincy Adams's translation of Wieland's *Oberon*. For nearly a century the record has been handed on, as in Griswold's *Prose Writers of America* (copyrighted 1846); in a Publisher's Note to William H. Graham's posthumous edition of J. Q. Adams's *Poems of Religion and Society* (New York, 1853); in *The National Portrait Gallery of Eminent Americans* (1862), Vol. II; in F. H. Wilkens's *Early Influence of German Literature in America* (1899), where the Follen letter is quoted again; down to the recent book of James Truslow Adams, *The Adams Family* (1930). In most cases the bare fact of the translation's having been made is given. Worthington C. Ford (1913) in *Writings of John Quincy Adams* [5] printed a letter of J. Q. Adams to his mother, Abigail Adams, in which there is a fuller statement concerning the translation of *Oberon*. But Charles Francis Adams in his twelve-volume *Memoirs* (comprising the diary, 1795–1848) of J. Q. Adams, excluded all references to the *Oberon* translation, perhaps as belonging to the "details of common life" that he purposely eliminated. However, these references are of intense interest for our purpose and were kindly supplied

[5] See below, Introduction, pp. lxx–lxxi.

by Mr. Henry Adams for the present volume (see Introduction, pp. xlvii–lxix). There is no doubt that J. Q. Adams fully intended to publish his "complete translation into English verse," but that Sotheby's work pre-empted the ground for him, and that later he lost interest during the great pressure of other duties. There was no good reason, however, for Adams's holding back his translation, for on careful examination it will be found superior in many ways to that which blocked his way and deprived him of the fruits of his great industry.

II. The Translations

1. The Earliest Translations

THE EARLIEST recorded translation into English of Wieland's *Oberon* is that of James Six in 1781.[6] He went to Braunschweig as tutor to J. Stanley, one of the many translators of Bürger's *Lenore*. In 1784 he presented a specimen of his translation from Book IX—saying he had finished ten books (of the fourteen in Wieland's first edition)—to his teacher Eschenburg, who sent some of the stanzas to Wieland. The poet commented favorably, but at that time expressed disapproval [7] of translations of *Oberon,* an opinion which he did not retain when Sotheby's translation was sent to him in 1798. Six's translation seems to have been a very literal imitation of the exact metrical form and content of the original, with many slips in interpretation. No record of publication of any part exists.

Other early translations met a similar fate. Wordsworth spoke of one on his visit to Klopstock in 1790.[8] Another is men-

---

[6] Cf. V. Stockley, *German Literature in England 1750–1830* (London, 1929), pp. 90–100, and W. A. Colwell, in *Modern Language Notes,* XXII (1907), p. 95.
[7] Letters printed in *Schnorrs Archiv,* XIII, pp. 503–506.
[8] See V. Stockley, *op. cit.,* p. 97.

tioned in a review by W. Taylor of *Oberon* in 1806, done by an unknown translator, who used the Chaucerian stanza of seven lines (for Wieland's eight), with no fixed rime-scheme. But the only published translation of *Oberon* into English verse was that of William Sotheby in 1798 (2 vols.), which passed through many editions: a second in 1805, printed for the same London publishers, Cadell and Davies and others; a third in London, from which the American edition of 1810 was printed; then another in London in 1826; and finally one in 1844, proving that the work continued to be popular.[9]

2. Sotheby and Adams

William Sotheby (1757–1833) was highly regarded by his contemporaries as a scholar, poet, patron of poets, and translator of the classics. His translation into English verse of Virgil's Georgics (1800) found particular favor among all critics.[10] Sotheby's first edition of 1798 appeared while John Quincy Adams was writing his translation of *Oberon*, but Adams did not see the Englishman's work until December 4, 1800, more than six months after he had finished his own translation, as his diary entry shows.[11] A study of the two translations reveals very soon that we have before us two masterpieces in the art of translation, of which sometimes the one, sometimes the other seems to have reached the highest possible standard of achievement. The first requirement, that the translator have a com-

[9] The last two editions of Sotheby's translation (1826, 1844) were not available for the editor. They are listed in Professor B. Q. Morgan's *A Critical Bibliography of German Literature in English Translation 1481–1935* (Stanford University Press, 1938), p. 521.

[10] J. Q. Adams was also very favorably impressed by Sotheby's translation of the Georgics. See diary, Dec. 7, 1800. He compares it with Dryden's translation and in the letter to W. V. Murray, January 13, 1801, speaks of it as "one of the most elegantly finished things I ever read." See below, pp. lxviii and lxx.

[11] See Introduction, p. lxviii.

plete control of the foreign language with which he is working, is met by both Sotheby and Adams. There are none of
those glaring misinterpretations which so frequently mar the
value of most translations. Only very rarely can we pick a
flaw, as:

Canto V, *31*, 7–8 [12]

[W] Zwölf Mohren, Riesen gleich, stehn mit gezücktem
     Eisen,
     Die Unberechtigten vom Eingang abzuweisen.
[S] Where with drawn swords twelve moors gigantick wait,
     And piece-meal hack the wretch who steps unbidden
     there.
[A] Twelve moors, like giants stand with falchions bare,
     And to intruders bar all entrance there.

Here the last line in Sotheby's translation looks like a mis-
understanding of the original, while Adams translates correctly.

Canto V, *32*, 2

    [W] Wie er sich der hohen Pforte zeiget . . .
    [S] Huon as he opes the lofty door . . .
    [A] But when the knight before the lofty gate
        Appeared . . .

Here S. mistranslates, while A. is correct. A nobleman
would never open the door himself here.

Canto VI, *16*, 8: Sotheby curiously misses W. *lange Weile*,
while Adams gets it. Even more seldom can we catch Adams
in what seems an error, as in Canto V, *23*, 1, where Adams

---

[12] V, *31*, 7–8 means Canto V, stanza 31, lines 7–8. W. refers to Wieland's
words; S. to Sotheby's; A. to Adams's translation.

translates the German *Flieder* with *alders* (MS IV), *elders* (MS II), instead of *lilacs* as Sotheby correctly interprets, or in Canto V, *24, 1,* where Adams translates W. *Er schlummert ein* with *He slept* (final version). But when we look at MS II we find that Adams wrote more correctly at first: *He dropped asleep.* Nor is Sotheby correct here: *Calm he reposes in unbroken sleep.*

But when we look closely, we find that such errors proceed mostly from the necessity of securing a needed rime, or the temptation of putting a little more color into the picture, not from a lack of understanding. We may draw the conclusion fairly that both translators knew their German and appreciated their original. Only the hypercritical would judge otherwise.

The first striking difference between the two translations is in their metrical form. Sotheby uses a nine-line Spenserian stanza, with the first eight lines decasyllabic, the ninth an Alexandrine; his rime-scheme varies slightly from the Spenserian (ababbcbcc), for he adopts, as his almost invariable type, abbaccddc; there are no feminine rimes as in the German poem. Adams reproduces the eight-line stanza (*ottava rima*) of Wieland, often with freely interlaced rimes like his original, but makes a strong effort (entirely successful in Cantos VIII–XII) to apply a uniform rime scheme, ababcdcd, and adheres to a five-foot line except in the eighth, which is as often an Alexandrine. Wieland by no means follows the rigid form of the Italian *ottava rima* with its eleven-syllable line and fixed rime scheme, abababcc. Wieland's line may be of varied length, from four to six feet; iambic, trochaic, anapestic metrical feet may succeed one another, though the basic scheme is iambic. The number of rimes may vary from two to four in successive stanzas, with a constantly varying rime scheme, as, for example, in Canto VI:

stanza 36, abbaccac (three rimes); stanza 37, abbbaaba (two
rimes); stanza 38, abbacdcd (four rimes). Wieland loved to
be unfettered by rigidity of form, and thought the nature of
the subject and language required freedom. His charming alternation of feminine rimes with masculine his translators did not
or could not imitate. Only Adams has an occasional feminine
rime, as in Canto I, *15* and *44;* IV, *57;* V, *53;* VI, *18,
51, 58, 104* and *107;* X, *31* and *49;* XI, *21.* The English
language does not possess such an abundance of feminine
rimes as the German.

In a comparison of the styles of Sotheby and Adams we
find two divergent conceptions of the translator's aim. Should
we prefer Pope's Homer to one of the translations that give us
a far more faithful reproduction of the naturalness and simplicity of the Greek epic? Sotheby paid more attention to poetic
diction and for this feature was highly regarded by his contemporaries. W. Taylor, writing in 1806, judges: "But if
Sotheby loses something of the easy familiarity and picturesque
precision of the original *Oberon,* he makes ample amends by
smoothness of versification, elegance of phrase and majesty of
diction." [13] Sotheby frequently introduces embellishments that
he may have been forced into by the additional ninth line,
though his temperament quite as frequently carries him in the
same direction. The simplicity of Adams's style generally
stands out against the ornateness of the English translator's.
Undoubtedly contemporary taste favored Sotheby's method,
while Adams's scorn of tinsel and adornment is perhaps more
in keeping with modern preferences. Since the original poem
is not lacking in romantic color and ornamentation, an accen-
tuation of this characteristic is in danger of producing exagger-

[13] Quoted by V. Stockley, *op. cit.,* p. 100.

ations. Beyond any question Adams adheres more closely to the German original and translates more accurately. His diary shows [14] that he took very great pains to interpret faithfully, that he went over completed portions of his work with his teacher, Mr. Catel, in Berlin to test its accuracy. An example will illustrate the fidelity of Adams to his original, the florid touches of Sotheby: [15]

Canto VI, stanza 1

WIELAND
Kaum fing Aurora an, die Schatten zu verjagen,
Und schloß dem Tag mit ihrer Rosenhand
Die Pforten auf, so hielt der Schwanenwagen,
Nicht weit vom seebespülten Strand
Von Askalon, im Schirm von hohen Palmenbäumen,
Auf einmal still. Ein sanfter Stoß
Weckt unser doppelt Paar, dieß aus des Schlummers Schoß,
Und jenes aus der Liebe wachen Träumen.

ADAMS
Scarce had Aurora chased the shades away,
And oped with rosy hand the gates of day,
When from the strand of Askalon not far,
By swans transported thither through the air
Beneath the shade of palm-trees stopped the car,
And by a shock awaked our double pair.
One from the pleasing lap of slumber drove,
The other from the wakeful dreams of love.

[14] See Introduction, pp. lxiii–lxv.
[15] See also *American-German Review*, April, 1939, p. 9; the passage taken there to illustrate is from Canto V, *stanza 40*.

SOTHEBY

Scarce had Aurora chas'd the shades of night,
And with her rosy finger, dipt in dew,
Unbarr'd the gates of day to mortal view,
Than underneath the palm-wood's shelt'ring height,
Not far from Askalon's sea-bounded strand,
Th' aërial steeds descending touch the land!
The rocking wheels with soft vibration shake:
At once from sleep the faithful followers wake,
But these from waking dreams by love's light plumage fann'd.

Canto IX, *stanza* 59

WIELAND

Auf ihr erbärmliches Geschrei,
Das durch die Felsen hallt, fliegt Hüon voller Schrecken
Den Wald herab, zu ihrer Hülf' herbei.
Ganz außer sich, sobald ihm, was es sei,
Die Bäume länger nicht verstecken,
Ergreift er in der Not den ersten knot'gen Stecken,
Der vor ihm liegt, und stürzt, wie aus der Wolken Schoß
Ein Donnerkeil, auf die Barbaren los.

ADAMS

The rocks, resounding with her piteous cries
At last her danger to the knight reveal.
Dismayed, distracted, to her side he flies,
And, soon as intervening trees conceal
No longer what it is, as need inspires,
He snatches the first knotty club at hand,
And swift as from black clouds celestial fires,
Darts down in vengeance on the pirate band.

SOTHEBY

Rous'd by her shrieks, and agonizing groans
That loudly echo'd from each mountain cave,
Down from the wood fierce Huon flies to save,
Mad vengeance roaring in his lion tones;
And when no more the copse that fring'd the bay
Conceal'd the scenes, while darting on their way,
He grasps a knotty club that near him lies,
And like a thunderbolt that rends the skies
Rushes amid the crew that drag their struggling prey.

(The roaring lion, S. line 4, is not in the original; line 9 shows padding to fill up the extra line.)

Canto XI, *stanza* 63

WIELAND

Hier weicht die stolze Kunst der siegenden Natur;
So lieblich girrt der Venus Taube nur!
Die Sprache des Gefühls, so mächtig ausgesprochen,
Der schönen Töne klarer Fluß
Durch kleine Seufzerchen so häufig unterbrochen,
Der Wangen höhers Rot, des Busens schnellers Pochen,
Kurz, alles ist vollströmender Erguß
Der Leidenschaften, die in ihrem Innern kochen.

ADAMS

Here to victorious Nature yields proud art,
The doves of Venus only thus can coo—
So strongly spoke the feelings of the heart!
So clear her voice the beauteous tones ran through!
The frequent, gentle, interrupting sighs,
The reddening cheeks, the panting bosom's toil,
All, all a foaming, dashing torrent flies
Of fiercest passions which within her boil.

SOTHEBY

Art's boastful pow'rs to conq'ring nature yield:
Alone so lovely Venus' doves complain:
Her soul that breathes sensation on the strain,
Warm to his soul her kindling wish reveal'd.
Persuasive tones that clear and clearer spoke,
Sighs that enforc'd the sounds they sudden broke,
Cheeks deeper dy'd, the bosom's quickening play,
Each heightening each, th' omnipotence betray
Of passion's wild excess to thrilling frenzy woke.
(This stanza is found in Sotheby's first edition but was expurgated in the third and last editions.)

Fidelity to his original and conciseness in diction being marked characteristics of Adams's translation, he is very happy in imitating those frequent proverbial expressions and terse popular lines for which Wieland's poem is well known, for example:

Canto I, 27, 4-5
W. Verzweifle Keiner je, dem in der trübsten Nacht
    Der Hoffnung letzte Sterne schwinden.
A (MS II). Let none henceforth despair, though in the
    gloomiest night
      The latest stars of hope should vanish from his
      sight.
A (MS IV, final version, a little less close to the original).
    Henceforth let no one give despair the rein,
      When hope's last star in darkness disappears.
S (takes three lines for it, the last not in W., a case of padding).
    Despair not, man of misery and pain!
    Though hope's last glimmer sunk in darkness dies,
    Again her star to light thy path shall rise.

Canto V, *30,* 1

W. Nichts halb zu tun, ist edler Geister Art.

A (MS II). In doing naught by halves, brave spirits take a
pride.

S. As fays not sparingly their favourites aid—

Canto VII, *41,* 1–4

W. O Liebe, süßes Labsal aller Leiden
Der Sterblichen, du wonnevoller Rausch
Vermählter Seelen! welche Freuden
Sind deinen gleich? (3½ lines)

A. O love! Sweet comforter of human care,
Delicious ravishment of wedded souls!
What other blessings can with thine compare? (3 lines)

S. O love! thou only balm of every woe
That preys on man! intoxicating sweet,
When soul weds soul, and hearts each other meet!
What joys with thine compare, thou heaven below?
(4 lines)

Canto VII, *72,* 8

W. Er prüft nur, die er liebt, und liebet väterlich.

A. He tries but those he loves, and with a father's love.

S. The God that smites the child will soothe to peace again.

Canto VII, *85,* 4

W. Arm kann die Liebe sich mit wenig glücklich schätzen . . .

A. Love deems itself with little blessed, though poor.

S. Though love, devoid of wealth, is richly blest.

Canto VIII, *31,* 5–6

W. Natur, spricht er, bedarf weit minder, als wir glauben;
Wem nicht an wenig gnügt, den macht kein Reichtum
satt:

A. Nature, says he, needs less than we suppose,
   Who pines with little, him no wealth can sate.

S. Nature, he says, my children, covets less
   Than man conceives; ye here enough possess—
   Realms cannot sate whom little fails to please:

Canto VIII, 42, 3

W. Die ungewohnte Hand greift alles schwerer an—
A. The hand unpractised grasps at first with pain—
S (fails to get the meaning of "ungewohnte," unaccustomed).
   Hands to rude toil unus'd but ill succeed.

Canto X, 20, 1

W. Der Erdensohn ist für die Zukunft blind.
A. The future, to earth's children is concealed.
S. Blind to futurity earth's children stray.

Canto XI, 36, 5

W. . . . (wie sich der Zufall
   In alles ungebeten mischt)
A. (For thus in all affairs of mortal men
   Chance, uninvited, meddling, still is seen)
S. And is by Chance (who comes without a call
   And tosses at her will this earthly ball)

Canto XI, 42, 7–8

W. Nur Gold genug, so ist die Welt zu Kauf;
   Ein goldner Schlüssel, Herr, schließt alle Schlösser auf!
A. With gold, Sir knight, the world may all be bought.
   Turned by a golden key all padlocks open fly.
S. But gold enough, the world is at your feet!
   All locks at once fly back when touched by key of gold!

Occasionally Sotheby's mastery of poetic diction takes him quite a distance from the original, tempts him to write a stylistic variation on the same theme, as in the two instances below. Comparing them with Adams's translation found in the text, pp. 119 and 186, we can tell what Wieland wrote, simpler, less ornate. Sotheby is frequently very happy in descriptions of nature, as in the second passage.

Canto V, 82

Far other thoughts inspire the youthful pair,
Whom love with Cytherea's swans conveys—
Whether they speed along unwonted ways,
Wing'd through the pathless regions of the air;
Whether they roll on earth, or swim the main;
Whether with flying course, or flagging rein;
How borne, through rough or smooth, by swan or steed;
What perils threaten, or what scenes succeed;
Of these no transient thought e'er flits across the brain.

Canto VII, 88 (Sotheby's stanza 82)

Sport of rude blasts, the desolated trees
Strew with sear leaf the melancholy shore;
Through naked bows the wintry tempests roar:
And hoary mists, that sweep along the seas,
Veil in dark clouds the sun's meridian light;
In sad confusion air and sea unite:
High o'er the strand tempestuous ocean breaks,
The furious tide its rocky boundary shakes,
Spangling with silver foam the cliff's aërial height.

Though no metrical translation has ever been perfect from beginning to end, satisfying in all its parts the requirements of fidelity, form, and diction, Adams's translation of *Oberon* maintains its characteristic high standard of fidelity throughout, and presents many high spots and larger sections that can silence even the most critical in regard to form, diction, and literary qualities. Such are Canto I, *32–73* (the story of Huon's banishment and what led up to it, the ordeal of battle, Charlemagne's punitive conditions); Canto V, *1–5* (Rezia's search in her dream); V, *17–18* (Rezia arrayed for the banquet); V, *71* (Rezia ready to resign home for love); V, *85–86* (closing stanzas); Canto VII, *41–42* (the grotto); VII, *93* (Huon's despair, especially last two lines); Canto VIII, *80* (the maternal heart); Canto IX, *47–53* (vain search of child by parents); IX, *59–63* (desperate struggle with pirates); Canto XI, *27* (dignity of Rezia); XI, *60–65* (Almansaris' effort to win Huon); Canto XII, *32–38* (Huon and Almansaris, prison scene); XII, *44–45* (Rezia and Almanzor); XII, *57* (lovers ready for supreme sacrifice); and many others might be added.

Another very important difference between the two translations is that Sotheby chooses to expurgate Wieland's *Oberon,* while Adams gives a faithful rendition of every stanza and line, thereby achieving the distinction of furnishing *the only complete translation* of the German classic in the English language. Sotheby's largest omission occurs in Canto VI, where Wieland and Adams have 107 stanzas, Sotheby only 48, omitting 59, with the entire episode of the marriage of January and May. A footnote informs us that this story is "sufficiently known" to the English reader from the "January and May" by Pope (imitated from Chaucer's "Merchant's Tale"). The note also praises the "art and contrivance" of the German poet for interweaving into the story an excellent motivation for the quarrel between Oberon and Titania, leading to their separation. This he concedes is essential to the plot of the whole poem,

yet through the expurgation the action becomes almost unintelligible even to those familiar with the very human and
amusing tale of the marriage of the jealous old man and his
fair young bride, as truthful as the perennial contest between
winter and spring. In this Wieland matches Pope and Chaucer
in the art of story telling, or surpasses them by the elimination
of pseudo-learned obstructing driftwood.

The expurgations in Sotheby's third London edition (from
which the American edition was printed in 1810) are as follows: Canto III, *stanza 24,* and *61,* line 3, to *62,* line 2; Canto
IV, *2;* Canto VI, *32, 35–84, 90–97;* Canto VII, *11, 14, 15,
16, 36, 87;* Canto VIII, *24;* Canto XI, *11, 57, 61, 63;*
Canto XII, *16.* In his first edition of 1798 Sotheby eliminates
nothing until Canto VI, *stanzas 35–84* and *90–97,* then also
Canto VII, *36* and *87,* and Canto VIII, *24,* omitting a total of
sixty-one stanzas, increased to seventy-four in the third edition
or a total of eight per cent of Wieland's 913 stanzas. Perhaps
Sotheby yielded to prudish criticism that attacked his first edition. Yet even in the first edition he had made the largest cut,
the story of January and May, which is more than an expurgation; it is a mutilation of the original. This large block and
twenty-four other important stanzas Sotheby sacrificed on the
altar of respectability, while the rigorously Puritanic Adams
saw no harm in them and reproduced them in English admirable
for its delicacy and refinement. He has given us *the only complete translation* of Wieland's *Oberon* in the English language.

III. Wieland's Editions of *Oberon*

WIELAND was in the habit of revising his works repeatedly,
and especially his *Oberon.* From internal evidence we can
prove that neither translator, Sotheby or Adams, used the

earliest editions, not the first, which appeared in Wieland's *Der teutsche Merkur* in 1780, nor that of 1785. They contained fourteen cantos, which were divided into twelve in subsequent editions, as found in both translations. Sotheby probably used the Weidmann edition of 1792 (possibly that of 1789), while Adams had the advantage of possessing [16] the later Göschen edition of 1796 or last corrected edition, which contained the variant readings of earlier editions, allowing him at certain places to take what he thought was a better though earlier reading, and also affording him the use of the newly added "Glossarium," a brief alphabetical glossary of names and unusual words and phrases.[17] Though Sotheby's work appeared in 1798, it is clearly not based on the edition of 1796, as can be seen by the following evidences:

Canto I, *21,* 5–8
Sotheby takes the reading of *E4,* Adams of *C.* (*Mutter Natur, Felsenkeller.*)

Canto I, *58*
Absence of *Roland's arm* in Sotheby; also see first four lines in *stanza 59.*

Canto V, *38,* 4
E4 reads "Gespenstern gleich," Sotheby "Like ghosts"; *C*

---

[16] See *Diary,* May 17, 1799 (Introduction, p. lvii).

[17] The present standard text edition is that of Professor Wilhelm Kurrelmeyer of Johns Hopkins University: *Wielands Werke:* dreizehnter Band, *Dichtungen II, 1780–1812,* herausgegeben von Wilhelm Kurrelmeyer (Berlin, Weidmannsche Buchhandlung, 1935). Professor Kurrelmeyer has made a critical study of the vast number of *Oberon* editions and gives all variant readings. The edition of 1792 (Weidmannsche Buchhandlung, Leipzig) and that of 1789 (Weidmannsche Buchhandlung, Leipzig) are there designated by the letters *E4* and *E3* respectively. *C* is the symbol for the edition that Adams probably used: *Wielands Sämmtliche Werke,* 22–23 Bd. (Leipzig bei Georg Joachim Göschen, 1796). These symbols will be used here.

changed to "als sähn sie ein Gespenst," Adams "As if they saw a spectre."

Canto V, 48, 3

E3 and *E4* read *Verschnittenen,* which Sotheby correctly translates *eunuchs.* The 1796 edition (*C*) changed the reading to *Kämmerlinge,* which Adams did not adopt because the earlier reading which he found made better sense. Adams translated: *The mutilated crew.*

Canto V, 72, 1

"Wenn dich *die Wage* schreckt." Sotheby, not having had the advantage of the use of the "Glossarium" of *C,* mistranslates "the dangerous flight," while Adams correctly: *risque.*

Canto VIII, 75, 2–4

Different readings in *E4* and *C.* Different in Sotheby and Adams.

Canto X, 2, 5–8

Sotheby uses readings of *E4,* Adams those of *C* (as W. "ein stärkrer Zauber," A. "stronger charm," etc.) See note to X, 2.

Canto XI, 4, 1–4.

E4, Rosenglanz, S. "rosy glance"; *C, Mondesglanz,* A. "moon's mild ray." *C, die Fürstin selbst,* absent in *E4,* therefore not translated by S., but Adams: "if the queen the lovely train adorn." *Dämmerung* in *E4* translated by S. "twilight," not found in *C,* therefore absent in A.

Canto XII, 43, 6

Kurdé mistranslated by S. as "girdle." A. read in the "Glossarium" of *C* (1796) that it meant an oriental garment, and wrote *kurdee.* See note.

Canto XII, 60, 6
Halt! Differing translations due to differences in *E4* and *C*.

Many differences in the renderings of Sotheby and Adams are therefore due to their working with different editions of *Oberon*, Sotheby using an earlier text, very probably that of 1792 (*E4*), while Adams used the last author's revision, the edition of 1796 (*C*), containing also the variant readings in the "Glossarium."

IV. SOURCES OF WIELAND'S *Oberon*

WIELAND made no secret of the fact that he did not invent the fascinating plot of his romantic epic. He even named his sources in the introduction to his last edition of 1796, mentioning three main trends of the action: (1) the adventures of Huon, which he is compelled to seek under the command of Charlemagne; (2) the love-story of Huon and Rezia; and (3) the reconciliation of Oberon and Titania. For the first he gives as his source Count Tressan's (Comte Louis Tressan de la Vergne, 1705–1783) prose abstract of the knightly romance *Huon de Bordeaux,* published in the *Bibliothèque universelle des romans* in April, 1778. This was based upon a French prose romance first published in 1513, which in turn went back to a French *chanson de geste* of the twelfth or thirteenth century. The earlier works were probably not known to Wieland, but the inspiration received from Tressan's narrative in 1778 set the German poet to work immediately on his romance of knighthood, which he published only two years later. The figure of Oberon as created by Wieland differs radically from that of Tressan—he tells us the main influence came from the folklore King of the Fairies and his Queen Titania as found in Shakespeare's *Midsummer-Night's Dream*. These two were his principal sources.

The charming and pathetic episode of the banishment of Huon and Rezia to the desert isle (Cantos VII and VIII) some critics think was in part suggested by a similar idyllic chapter in Schnabel's *Die Insel Felsenburg* (1731–1743), the longest and most popular of the "Robinsonaden." The interlude "January and May" (Canto VI) was obviously derived from Pope's humorous satire of the same name, and its source in Chaucer's "Merchant's Tale." Oberon is not mentioned by that name in either English version; Pope calls him the "monarch of the fairies and his bride" (v. 619 f.), and Chaucer names the pair Pluto and Preserpina (v. 10101–3).

These various epic threads the German poet skillfully interwove in a beautiful pattern rich in color and harmonious in design. He followed the example of the Middle High German court-epic poets Hartmann von Aue, Wolfram von Eschenbach, and Gottfried von Strassburg, who disclaimed originality and referred to "unquestionable" sources for the truthfulness of their plots, but poured into them such an abundance of human experience, reflections, and ethical and social ideals, that their epics became their own. Medieval poets were by no means bereft of poetical imagination, but their powers of invention were directed mainly toward elevating the plot and seeking causation for the action.

Just so Wieland justly claims credit for giving an original motivation for the quarrel between Oberon and Titania. It is the picture of conjugal infidelity between January and May that affects them deeply and causes their quarrel, that leads to their separation (not an Indian boy, as in Shakespeare). Their reconciliation, which king and queen gradually long for, can only be effected by the realization of a moral ideal, the fidelity of two human lovers ready to choose death in preference to their breaking their vows of true love. Hence the continued interest taken by the fairy powers in Huon and Rezia during the last half of the epic.

Wieland eliminates any number of trivialities in the plot of Tressan's abstract: the distracting, tiresome heaping of adventures before the main action at the oriental court (Canto V in Wieland); the multiplication of episodes after the climax, which merely drag on the story; and at the close the unwelcome, disappointing treachery of Huon's younger brother Girard, which, coupled with the inhuman relentlessness of Charlemagne, requires a "deus ex machina" to extricate the heroes. Wieland also screens certain monstrous barbarities of the old plot, such as the extraction of four molars and a handful of the beard of the oriental ruler as required by Charlemagne. This dental operation is performed not by the hand of Huon but by painless fairy magic, not within the sight of Rezia; nor is her father beheaded. Wieland deletes the equally horrible incarnation of the trophies (molars and beard) in the right side of Cherasmin. In these and other eliminations the German poet has shown consummate artistry.[18]

Wieland succeeded in rescuing the character of Charlemagne from something of the scorn with which the abstract of Tressan treats this noble historical figure. Incarnate devils are rare in Wieland's epic; even the great tempters of the conjugal fidelity of our heroes, Almansaris the queen and Almanzor the king of Tunis, are portrayed with very human and at-

---

[18] Düntzer's *Erläuterungen zu Wielands Oberon*, zweite Ausgabe (Leipzig, 1880) gives a complete outline in detail of the plot of Tressan's work. Düntzer's commentary and notes are valuable, also his study of the *ottava rima* as employed by Wieland (p. 153 f.). Cf. also *Das Quellenverhältnis von Wielands Oberon*, von Max Koch, Habilitationsschrift Universität Marburg 17. Dec. 1879 (Marburg, 1879).

tractive traits. Fatme, the faithful maid and confidante of Rezia, is a creation of Wieland. An element of humor, not found in the old French epic, is supplied by Cherasmin (W. Scherasmin) the squire, the most original of Wieland's characters. He is not a knight, as is Tressan's Gérasme, but a faithful retainer, true as steel. He is ready to stake his life at any moment for his lord; yet his heroism is not always that of the ideal medieval knight: foolhardiness is no virtue to him, wisdom and discretion he would have mingled with his master's actions. In fact, this vassal does a lot of thinking for his liege lord. He owns many human weaknesses, as his superstition and his love of the cup, while his story-telling habit reminds some critics of Sancho Panza, the squire of Don Quixote. There are occasional incidents in the epic that remind others of Ariosto and Tasso; yet, while we know that Wieland was very well read in Romance literature, they cannot prove any borrowings. As the Middle High German poets adapted the subjects that they found to their own requirements, so Wieland has made the Huon-Oberon epic his own.

Wieland's superior handling of the action is very evident when we compare his plot with that of the dramatization or libretto written by James Robinson Planché to Karl Maria von Weber's opera *Oberon,* first performed in London, April 11, 1826. The great popularity of this romantic opera, lasting to the present day, is due to the immortal music of the German composer, not to the libretto, which was based in part on Wieland's *Oberon* but also took suggestions from the older versions of the epic.

The greatest of the poets contemporary with Wieland were delighted with his *Oberon,* above all Goethe. Wieland records Goethe's first impressions in a letter to Merck, the severe critic, who thoroughly approved of the work while it was in prog-

ress. Goethe was to sit for his portrait and begged Wieland to
shorten the tedious hours for him by the reading of some finished parts of his epic, which had reached the climax in the
fifth canto. "Never," wrote the author, "in all the days of my
life have I seen anyone so happy over the work of another as
Goethe was at my reading, with all throughout, but especially
the fifth canto." Goethe made an entry in his journal on the
same day (Tagebücher, d. 26sten Juli, 1779): "Es ist ein
schätzbar Werk für Kinder und Kenner, so was macht ihm
niemand nach. Es ist große Kunst in dem Ganzen soweit ichs
gehört habe und im Einzelnen. Es setzt eine unsägliche Übung
voraus" etc., etc. Goethe's praise stimulated Wieland to speed
the poem to its conclusion. When the work appeared in Wieland's journal, *Der teutsche Merkur,* in March, 1780, he could
write to Merck: "My stocks have risen 100 per cent with the
Duke, Goethe, and the Weimar public with this work."
Goethe sent him a laurel wreath, and the older poet was deeply
gratified. Herder wrote to Gleim, "It is a beautiful poem in
matter and form, perhaps the best of its kind," and Gleim was
charmed with it. Lessing was pleased with *Oberon*. There were
critics, to be sure, with little imagination, who had not the
gift of meeting the poet half-way, nor bore in heart Goethe's
well-known maxim: "Wer den Dichter will verstehen, Muß
in Dichters Lande gehen." Among those who viewed the work
rather coldly was Lavater, to whom Goethe presented the case
of *Oberon* in a letter of July 3, 1780, containing the famous
eulogy he gave the poem: "Sein Oberon wird so lang Poesie
Poesie, Gold Gold und Crystall Crystall bleiben wird als ein
Meisterstück poetischer Kunst geliebt und bewundert wer-
den."

A good account of the reception in England of Wieland's
Oberon and also of Sotheby's translation is furnished by the

work already referred to [19] of V. Stockley, *German Literature as Known in England 1750–1830*. The American edition (1810) of Sotheby's two-volume translation of Wieland's *Oberon* contains a preface of ninety-eight pages, written in the extravagantly rhetorical style of that time, highly eulogistic of the German poet and his translator, but of little scholarly value.

A recent investigation of high merit has appeared in the *Review of English Studies* (London, Vol. XV, No. 60, October, 1939, pp. 401–411), by W. W. Beyer, entitled "Coleridge, Wieland's *Oberon,* and *The Ancient Mariner*," in which the author discusses the influence of Wieland's romantic epic upon romanticism in England. He quotes from a letter of Coleridge to William Taylor of November, 1797, in which the English poet refers to his German studies: "I am translating the *Oberon* of Wieland—it is a difficult language, and I can translate at least as fast as I can construe.—I pray you, as soon as possible, procure for me a German-English grammar—I believe there is but one—" etc., etc. The author cites parallel passages in which he finds incidents and "clusters of images" reminding him strikingly of similarities in Coleridge's *The Ancient Mariner,* which first took shape in 1797. Is it possible that Coleridge, like Adams, was deterred from continuing or publishing anything of his translation because of the appearance of Sotheby's translation in 1798? Beyer says of Sotheby's translation that, while "poetical and harmonious, it has often completely obscured Wieland's original imagery."

V. ADAMS'S FOUR MANUSCRIPTS OF *Oberon*

THE FIRST and immediate find in the Adams Family Archives was the neatly bound volume, containing the complete

---

[19] See above, Introduction, p. xvi, and footnote, no. 6.

and final version of J. Q. Adams's translation, entitled: "O B E R O N. A poetical Romance. In twelve Books. Translated from the German of Wieland." The manuscript is immaculate in its state of preservation and the character of the handwriting. In a manuscript of 312 pages, written in the clear, distinct chirography of J. Q. Adams, there is hardly a single blemish that might obscure the meaning (see facsimile facing page xliii). Since this manuscript, bound alone, is unquestionably the final version as J. Q. Adams wished it and wrote it down in his best and exemplary hand, this has been used as the text for the present first publication.

After a search for other materials bearing on the *Oberon* translation, there were found subsequently in the Adams Family Archives two other bound volumes containing fragments of poetry, scraps and longer translations from German and Latin poets mainly, together with what seemed to be sketchy first drafts of *Oberon,* but which on closer examination proved to be much more than that. They contained *three more or less complete earlier versions* of *Oberon,* also in J. Q. Adams's unmistakable handwriting, all of them executed with great care and corrected frequently between the lines. These alterations were adopted in the next version and improved upon again, giving evidence of a degree of industry, zeal, and painstaking devotion to a difficult task that hardly finds a parallel in literary history. It is not difficult to establish the succession of the four manuscripts, and for convenience we shall name them MS I, II, III, IV, and refer to them by number throughout our description in the notes following the text. The final version already mentioned, being the latest, will be given the number IV.

MS I

This, the earliest manuscript, is a complete version of the

poem in all twelve cantos, excepting the first forty-one stanzas of Canto I, stanzas 5–8 and 33–36 of Canto V, and stanzas 44–59 of Canto VII, all of which seem to have been lost, for they are not bound with the rest. The manuscript proves to us with what extraordinary care and conscientiousness Adams went to work. He first wrote down a word-for-word, line-for-line translation into English from his original. Beneath that he placed his first draft of the metrical translation—for example, Canto IV, 43 (the German is given here for comparison, but was not copied by the translator):

Man weiß, daß schon seit Jahren der Khalif,
Auf seine Tochter stolz, nicht selten
An Festen, die er gab, sie mit zur Tafel rief,
Wo schöner Männer viel sich ihr vor Augen stellten.
Allein auch das weiß Stadt und Land,
Daß keiner je vor ihr besonders Gnade fand:
Sie schien sie weniger mit mädchenhaftem Grauen
Als mit Verachtung anzuschauen.

Literal:
It is known, that for years past the Caliph
Proud of his daughter, not seldom
At feasts which he gave, call'd her to table
Where many handsome men shewed themselves to her eyes.
But town and country likewise know
That no one found especial favour in her sight
She seem'd them not so much with maidenly reserve
As with contempt to consider them.

First metrical draft:
For some years past the Caliph it is known
Proud of his daughter, often at his feasts

Has made her come, and there among the guests
Full many a handsome man has to her eyes been shown.
But town and country likewise knew
That none her special favour could obtain
She seem'd them less with bashfulness to view
Than to behold them with disdain.

This first metrical draft was revised and transcribed for the second version, which we shall call MS II.

MS II

This manuscript has survived in complete form through all twelve cantos, without a single gap, written on a larger page more carefully, if possible, and given many new revisions between the lines or written in the margins. The above stanza appears unchanged except the last two lines:

She seem'd them not so much to view
With maiden bashfulness as with disdain.

MS II is bound in a larger octavo volume together with fragments of poetry, translations from the German and Latin (as from Gellert's fables, the first stanza of Klopstock's *Messias*, the Thirteenth and Fourteenth Satires of Juvenal, Elegy from Catullus, etc.), also the excellent prose argument or outline of the action of all twelve cantos written by Adams and printed below in the Introduction, pp. lxxii–xcii. MS II, or the second draft of *Oberon*, is very interesting as a study in the art of translation, but also for another feature. At the close of the cantos or in the margins Adams wrote the date of his completing each section. These dates correspond with the records in his diary, and in many places supplement them. At the beginning of the first canto (or Book, as Adams chooses to call it) he wrote the

date November 14, 1799; at the end, December 15, 1799. Thus
we learn that Canto II was completed December 28, 1799;
Canto III, January 14, 1800; Canto IV, January 27, 1800;
Canto V, February 15, 1800; Canto VI, March 7, 1800 (dates
in the margins show when he worked at particular sections);
Canto VII, March 24, 1800 (noted in the margin); Canto
VIII, begun March 25 and completed April 6, 1800; Canto IX,
begun April 7 and completed April 17; Canto X, begun April
18 and completed April 26; Canto XI, begun April 26 and
completed May 6; Canto XII, begun May 7 and completed
May 22, 1800.

MS III

This manuscript is a fragment, beginning with Canto I
and running through to Canto V, *stanza 37*. There it ends
abruptly. It is based on MS II and contains many revisions
which are not always adhered to in MS IV, the final version.
Sometimes MS IV goes back to MS II by preference. The
revisions in MS III are mostly in the direction of smoothness
of the verse, though often the original force of the earlier reading is thereby sacrificed. Adams attempts to standardize the
rime scheme of his *ottava rima* by adopting a uniform model,
ababcdcd, which is not done in the eight-line stanza of
Wieland, who prefers a more varied and pliant scheme of
rimes, not only ababcdcd, but abbacddc, ababccdd, ababaddc,
aabcbcbc (three rimes instead of four), ababacac (three),
ababbacc (three), and many others, but rarely the rime scheme
of the Italian [20] *ottava rima,* abababcc, only exceptionally as in

[20] The pure form of *ottava rima,* the Italian eight-line stanza with the rime
scheme abababcc, i. e. alternate rimes followed by a couplet, as found in some
of Spenser's minor poems, Byron's *Don Juan,* etc., is not favored by Wieland or
Adams in *Oberon.* Adams, however, adopted the pure form of the Italian model
in his historical epic, *Dermot Mac Morrogh, or The Conquest of Ireland,* written thirty years later, published in 1832.

Oberon.

Book the sixth.

1.

Scarce had Aurora chac'd the shades away,
And oped with rosy hand the gates of day,
When from the strand of Askalon not far,
By swans transported thither through the air
Beneath the shade of palm-trees stop'd the car,
And by a shock awak'd our double pair.
One from the pleasing lap of slumber drove.
The other, from the wakeful dreams of love.

2.

The damsel trembles, in a sweet dismay,
When for the first time, to her eyes ascends
Th' unbounded ocean in the morning ray;
Ranging in unimpeded course extends
O'er all the watery mass her wondering sight:
Before her, boundless space appears to be;
Yet shudderings mingle with her new delight,
In boundless space herself so small to see.

years before, but also by J. Q. Adams, as can be seen by the capital letters and numerous other characteristics, in spite of a trembling hand.

MS IV

This manuscript, written even more neatly than MSS I, II, and III in the clear, firm, easily legible hand of the Sixth President of the United States, is the complete clean, last copy covering the whole of the twelve cantos (or Books), 913 stanzas, or 7304 lines. It is bound in a volume by itself. The *Diary* frequently speaks of his revising, giving "a little polish" to his finished translation, as on May 31, 1800: "But having now finished my translation of *Oberon*"—completed May 22, 1800—"I spend a couple of hours before breakfast in making a copy of it, endeavoring as I proceed to give a little polish to the verse; a point in which it is extremely defective." This polish to the verse consisted mainly in reducing the meter to the standard Adams has adopted for most of his translation: a rime scheme ababcdcd in an eight-line stanza, iambic with but few irregularities, five feet to the line except frequently the last or eighth line with six feet (following in this the preference of Wieland). An example from Canto III, 43, will show the method employed by the translator. It will be seen below that he made a number of verbal changes in MS II, which improve what was already good, but the principal change is from a verse scheme of aabbccdd to ababcdcd and six feet in the eighth line:

MS II

An unknown power which like the magnet's force
Strait on to Babylon directs his course
Seems the sharp edges of his looks to turn

And every charm of Angela to spurn.
In vain her shape is like a beauteous vase
Where Love's own hand its utmost skill displays,
In vain her nose soft rising on her face
Joins the smooth brow, with proud majestic grace.

MS IV

A secret impulse like the magnet's sway
Seems the sharp edges of his looks to turn
Straight on for Bagdad to impel his way
And every charm of Angela to spurn.
In vain her shape is like a beauteous vase
Where Love's own hand its utmost skill has tried.
In vain her nose, soft rising on her face
Joins to the polished brow in majesty of pride.

It is difficult to say which of these versions has greater literary merit; they both match the original and are close reproductions. Wieland has the verse scheme abbacdcd for this stanza; he is not particular about keeping each line of the usual length of five feet, and in this stanza varies with lines of four, five, and six feet; he is most consistent, however, in the alternation of masculine and feminine rimes:

Ein unbekanntes Was, das ihn wie ein Magnet
Nach Bagdad zieht, scheint allen seinen Blicken
Die scharfe Spitze abzuknicken
Und macht, daß jeder Reiz an ihm verloren geht.
Vergebens ist der Wuchs wie eine schöne Vase,
Von Amors eigner Hand gedreht;
Vergebens schließt die sanft erhobene Nase
Sich an die glatte Stirn' in stolzer Majestät.

In MS IV the whole of the first book is uniformly changed to Adams's standard verse and rime scheme, while MS III has been standardized only to Book I, *stanza 28*. Books II–IV are also very regular in MS IV, while Books V and VI are not thus standardized, though we must concede that these cantos are among the very best of Adams's translation. In the last six books there is again a very great regularity of form in accordance with the standard adopted. Though on the whole MS IV shows very considerable improvement upon all his preceding versions, both in purity of form and in aptness and fidelity of expression, still the editor has occasionally observed that an earlier draft was happier, in isolated cases stronger and more beautiful. That is a common experience with manuscripts of writers. Where such few instances have appeared, the editor has called attention to them in the notes following the text. The existence of the four manuscripts of *Oberon* is a monument to the industry, zeal, and scholarship of John Quincy Adams. He furnishes an ideal for all translators, an example worthy of imitation. His fidelity to the original is the result of painstaking, conscientious, repeated effort; his skill in versification, notably in riming, is quite remarkable.

VI. Orthography and Pronunciation

The spelling of a manuscript written 140 years ago exhibits certain archaisms and inconsistencies which are disturbing to the eye of the modern American reader. It would be surprising if there were none in the manuscripts before us. Such instances are: antient (ancient), atchieve (achieve), armour (armor), chace (chase), chuse (choose), Charlemain (Charlemagne), clifts (clefts), cloaths (clothes), colour (color), controul (control), desart (desert), dose (doze), enquire (inquire), extatic (ecstatic), haram (harem), honour (honor), impell (impel), intreat (entreat), nought (naught), shamoys (chamois), shew (show), syren (siren), tyger (tiger), vigour (vigor), untill (until), etc.

On the advice of publishers and interested friends, who believe the primary object in this instance is to meet the wishes of the general reader and to provide a text that may read more smoothly (without doing violence to a single word), in such cases as cited above modern American spelling has been adopted, though the editor confesses to a certain loss of the quaintness of the original spellings.

For the same reason a past tense and a past participle ending in *ed* appear in our text not as Adams wrote them, with *'d,* but with *ed.* When an additional syllable is needed, which occurs very rarely, the text reads *èd,* with a grave accent. Thus: not *astonish'd* but *astonished,* not *hop'd* but *hoped,* not *shun'd* but *shunned,* not *slip'd* but *slipped,* not *span'd* but *spanned,* not *stab'd* but *stabbed,* not *stitch'd* but *stitched,* not *touch'd* but *touched,* not *unfetter'd* but *unfettered,* not *vanquish'd* but *vanquished,* not *past* but *passed* (verb); but *deservèd* (when in three syllables), as in "of victory the well-deservèd meed"; *'r* has been changed to *er* in *prayer,* but *'st* not changed to *est* when part of a single syllable, as in *spok'st* (not *spokest*), *dar'st, gav'st, rav'st, stol'st, etc.* The preposition *towards* was always read in two syllables by Adams, and to aid the reader this word in our text is marked *tŏwards',* so that the line may read metrically correct at once. When accented on the first syllable, it has been marked *to'wards.*

The punctuation in general has been retained as found in MS IV, except in some few cases where an immediate understanding of the line could be achieved by the insertion of a punctuation sign, usually a comma. MS II is frequently more carefully and consistently punctuated than MS IV, and served as a guide in doubtful cases. This goes to show that in his final revision the translator was more interested in diction and rime (carrying through his standard rime scheme of ababcdcd) than in punctuation.

VII. EXTRACTS (UNPUBLISHED) FROM THE DIARY AND LETTERS OF J. Q. ADAMS

IT IS well known that John Quincy Adams was the greatest of American diarists, far surpassing his father John Adams, Second President of the United States, who gave his son the habit of recording his daily acts and thoughts. When Charles Francis Adams published twelve volumes [21] from the diary of his father, he excluded most of the references to his domestic life, also all the passages relating to the translation of *Oberon* and much pertaining to J. Q. Adams's residence in Berlin from 1798 to 1801, when he held the position of United States Minister Plenipotentiary at the Prussian Court. It was during this period, more exactly from November 14, 1799, to May 22, 1800, that he translated Wieland's *Oberon*. There are very interesting entries in the *Diary* relating to *Oberon,* which give a picture of the patient labor bestowed upon this work and the daily progress of the translation. As will be seen, Adams first translated other works from German prose into English in order to learn German, before he took up *Oberon*. This old-fashioned manner of learning a foreign language by translating a larger work had its merits, though modern teachers correctly say that

---

[21] *Memoirs of John Quincy Adams, comprising portions of his Diary from 1795–1848,* edited by Charles Francis Adams, 12 volumes (Philadelphia, 1874–1877). Cf. also *The Diary of John Quincy Adams 1794–1815,* in one volume, edited by Allan Nevins (New York, Longmans, 1928).

this method will never give the student a speaking acquaintance, as Adams found out himself. However, there is much that can be said in favor of cultivating the art of translation for its own sake.

After Adams had started the arduous, engrossing task of translating this long epic of over 7000 lines, he was determined to bring it to a successful conclusion. His appreciation and love of German literature is expressed in the Follen [22] and other letters and aided him to the end. But a very strong will is necessary to carry a translator through a work of such magnitude, and when we consider that J. Q. Adams wrote and rewrote the entire epic more than three times, we moderns can but stand in amazement before the stupendous "capacity for and love of labor" exhibited by this representative man of a vigorous past generation.

The following unpublished records were furnished the editor by Mr. Henry Adams and Mr. Charles Francis Adams after a careful search in the manuscript diaries. They are given in the exact wording found there. The italics and footnotes are the editor's.

Extracts from the Diary of John Quincy Adams, relating to his study of German and translation of Oberon *while Minister to Prussia in Berlin*

1798

March

12. Began an attempt to acquire the practice of reading German. I continually feel the want of it. But know not how I shall proceed. Study the grammar in the morning.

[22] See Introduction, pp. xiv–xv, lxix, and lxx.

23. Making slow progress in the acquisition of the German language.

30. Continue my study of German.

April

8. I continue my study of German, but make in it a very slow progress. Very industrious now upon my study of German.

30. Day—Rise at about 7. Study German till ½ past 9. Breakfast. Write till 2. Walk out till 3. Dine. Pass an hour at the Casino, and the remainder of the evening at home, generally reading Shakespeare. I can perceive some small progress in the acquisition of the German language. I read with more facility than when I first began. Yet it is a dull and tedious kind of application, and it prevents me from obtaining any knowledge more substantial than that of words, by engrossing so much of my time.

May

15. Berlin—Finished reading the second, and began the third volume of the life and actions of Baron Quinctius Heymeran von Flaming,[23] a German novel lent me by Baron Rothkirch, and which I read to acquire the habit of this language. Translated part of Gessner's first Idyll.[24] Walk in the park after dinner with Mrs. A. At the Casino.

[23] *Leben und Thaten des Freiherrn Quinctius Heymeran von Flaming,* von Gustav Freier (pseudonym), four volumes (Berlin, 1795–96; new edition, 1798). This was the work of the German novelist August H. J. Lafontaine, born in Braunschweig in 1758, died in 1831. His voluminous works, some 150 volumes of the then very popular sentimental, "larmoyante" or pathetic type of novel, had best sellers among their number, though now forgotten.

[24] Salomon Geßner (1730–88) was born and lived in Zurich, a poet, painter, and engraver. His idyls were very highly esteemed in his time and at least a generation after. His complete works appeared in 1777–78 in two volumes.

29. I find I can yet understand very little German when spoken.[25]

30. Finished reading the Life and Adventures of Flaming, a German novel in four volumes and began to read Archenholtz's History of the Seven Years War. Found this much more difficult.

June

6. My German studies consume much of my time.

July

31. I have abandoned almost entirely the study of German, and become extremely careless about every other study—of what good is it all?

August

15. Berlin—At the play this evening. Doctor Tunnuccio, a dull thing; and "The Mourning, or Steward Deceived," a farce from the French of Hauteroche, or the English "Ghost." Met the Comte Schall there. I understood somewhat more of the dialogue than I have heretofore. But I still find the difficulties of the language excessive.

16. Buchholz [26] is too dry and uninteresting to learn the language by. There is no attraction that continually draws one to the book. *Flaming* taught me more German in one month,

---

[25] Teachers using the direct method will be delighted at this confession. Obviously the study of grammar and mere reading does not train the ear for understanding the spoken foreign language.

[26] Samuel Buchholz (*Neueste Preußisch-Brandenburgische Geschichte,* Berlin, 1775) does not take rank among German historians. Carlyle in his *History of Frederick the Great,* first edition, Vol. II (1858), pp. 423–424, says of him: "His poor Book is of innocent, clear, faithful nature, with some vein of 'unconscious geniality' in it here and there; a Book by no means so destitute of human worth as some that have superseded it."

than all the rest of my studies since I have been here. I must return to novels. Procured for this purpose Schiller's Ghost Seer [27] and commenced upon it this afternoon. At the Casino. Met there M. de Sartoris.

17. Berlin—Reading this morning the novel of Schiller, and find immediately the difference of application proceeding from a different degree of interest in the book. Read more of it again in the evening.

18. Find one part of my new German book again very difficult. Got over it very superficially. A long argument upon free-will, necessity, and the like metaphysical subtleties, which would be almost unintelligible even if I were master of the language. It takes up 60 or 70 pages. The rest is easy enough.

19. Finished the first volume of the Ghost-seer. Read over again and mastered the metaphysical disquisition which I found so difficult yesterday.

26. Finished this evening the third and last volume of the Geisterseher. The two last are dull and tedious attempts merely to fill the chasms of the first. The object of which is to excite wonder in the highest degree, and leave the whole story covered with a thick veil.

27. Long walk in the park. Began to read the Menschenhass und Reue of Kotzebue.[28] I saw it performed about two years ago at the Hague in low Dutch. It is one of the most celebrated modern German comedies.

28. Finished reading the Menschenhass und Reue this

[27] Schiller's only novel, a pot-boiler, *Der Geisterseher: Eine Geschichte aus den Memoiren des Grafen von O.,* appeared in 1789. *Das philosophische Gespräch,* to which Adams refers August 18 and 19, was deleted in later editions by the author.

[28] The play *Menschenhaß und Reue* of August von Kotzebue (1761–1819) was also very popular on the American stage for more than a generation, and generally was entitled *The Stranger.*

morning, and in the course of the day began a novel called Rudolf von Werdenberg by Lafontaine, the author of Flaming's Life and Adventures.

29. Went to the play this afternoon to see "Oberon, King of the Fairies." [29] But the house was so full we could get no places.

31. At the play this evening: "Two uncles for One," a farce; and "The Village Barber," an opera. Each in one act. Pleasant music. Understood something of the dialogue. (Day) Rise between 7 and 8. Read German till 10. Breakfast. Read and write till 2. Walk. Dine at ½ past 3. Read again after dinner, an hour. At the Casino or in company. Close the evenings as heretofore. I have for the last half of this month resumed my German studies with revived application, and find the facility of reading gradually increase. I find some encouragement in my progress hitherto, and hope to persevere until I can read the language with perfect ease.

September

3. At the play this evening. The performance "Leichter Sinn," Levity, a comedy by Iffland.[30] Pretty well pleased with it, though I understood not much of it.

12. Returned home early in the evening. Began to read a Life of Lessing taken from the circulating library—written by that author's brother.[31]

13. In reading the Life of Lessing this day I met with an

---

[29] Probably one of the numerous dramatizations, or a *Singspiel*, based upon Wieland's epic, as *Hüon und Amanda: Ein romantisches Singspiel in fünf Aufzügen nach Wielands Oberon,* von Friederike Sophie Segler (1789), or *Wielands Oberon in fünf Aufzügen als Dekorations- und Maschinen-Stück,* bearbeitet von Gottfried Busch von Buschen (1794).

[30] August Wilhelm Iffland (1759–1814) shared the popularity of Kotzebue as a playwright and was also famous as an actor.

[31] *Karl Lessings Leben seines Bruders* (Berlin, 1793).

anecdote of which the application was inevitable. Lessing and his friend Mylius at a certain period undertook to learn the Spanish language. They had made some progress, and by way of practicing were speaking it one day as they were walking under the lindens here at Berlin. A Spaniard overheard them and rejoiced at finding persons who, as he supposed, could converse with him in his own language, accosted them and attempted to talk with them, but found they could not understand or reply to a word that he said. His was the language of common life, theirs what they had gathered from books. And so it usually happens (says the biographer) with learned men who in acquiring a language have no other teacher but themselves.

20. Finished the second volume of Meissner's [32] Alcibiades and began upon the third. I doubt the goodness of these historical novels where half is founded upon records and half fiction. It obscures the truth of real history.

October

31. My German reading this month has been small—only a couple of volumes of Lessing and part of Buchholz' [33] last volume which I hope, however, to finish in a few days. I have read him with much more attention than such a miserable historian deserved. But it is the reign of Frederick II that he relates.

November

1. Finished reading Lessing's Emilia Galotti. In this as well as in his Sara Sampson, he has thrown the whole burden of woe

[32] August Gottlieb Meißner (1753–1807), prose writer, was one of the imitators of Wieland.
[33] See above, footnote 26.

upon the virtuous— The detestable characters are not punished. Like most German authors he observes no law of poetical justice at all.

December

8. Berlin—Did not stay to supper, but went to Dr. Brown's [34] where I found Count Brühl [35] with his family; General Descars, a French emigrant, but in the Prussian service. Very talkative, but it is to be hoped he knows more about military service than poetry. He said that he had known Germans who thought KLOPSTOCK superior to all the poets of the world, and that such poets as Homer, and Milton,—and Newton were nothing in comparison with him. Count Brühl is a great musician, and performs remarkably well upon the violin.

1799

February

10. Madame Necker [36] says that by studying a language a quarter of an hour every day, one will make some progress in

[34] Dr. Brown was an English physician of high repute and practice living in Berlin. He was the king's physician there. The names of Dr. and Mrs. Brown and their three daughters appear often in the *Diary*.

[35] "Count and Countess Brühl, and their eldest daughter, passed the evening here— The Count is a son of the famous Saxon minister Count Brühl, so known for his animosity against Frederic II. Yet this one was governor of the present king and is now a general of cavalry. The Countess is the daughter of an English banker who was settled at Amsterdam." Entry in the *Diary* of J. Q. Adams, dated Dec. 18, 1798.

[36] The name thus written applies to Susanne Curchod (1739–1794), socially brilliant wife of the influential financier Jacques Necker (1732–1804), not to their daughter Madame de Staël (Anne Louise Germaine Necker, 1766–1817), then already a well-known writer, subsequently famous for her important work *De l'Allemagne*. After the death of Madame Susanne Necker her husband published her letters, sketches and anecdotes in three volumes, entitled *Mélanges extraits des manuscrits de Madame N.* (Paris, 1798), a work which J. Q. Adams was reading at the time (recorded in his *Diary* Jan. 27, 28, Feb. 4, 14, 17, 1799).

attaining it. I study German between two and three hours at least every day and make scarcely any progress.

March

4. Mr. Catel [37] called on me this morning. He is to give me lessons of German; for after a year's assiduous study without

[37] Mr. Catel was undoubtedly a member of a Huguenot family that came to Germany as refugees in the seventeenth century. The ancestor, Daniel Catel (born at Sedan in 1653, died in Berlin in 1748), was a pewterer by trade (Kurfürstlicher Hofzinngießermeister). His grandson and great grandson became preachers of the French Protestant congregations at Halberstadt (Prussia) and Berlin respectively. J. Q. Adams's teacher was in all probability *Samuel Henri Catel* (born in 1758 in Halberstadt, died in 1858 in Berlin), the son of Jean Henri Catel, French Protestant preacher at Halberstadt. Samuel Henri Catel studied theology at Berlin and had several charges before settling down in the capital city. From 1783 to 1799 he was preacher and teacher at the *École de Charité* of Berlin, since 1792 also Professor of Greek and Regent of the French *Gymnasium,* 1799–1838 preacher at the French *Hospital.* He was very favorably known as a translator of French works into German and German works into French. He wrote on pedagogical, ethical, and historical subjects, and from 1806 to 1822 was on the editorial staff of the influential *Voß'sche Zeitung.* S. H. Catel had many noted pupils, among them the great German dramatist Heinrich von Kleist, who in his tenth year (cf. *Allgemeine deutsche Biographie,* Vol. 16, p. 128) was sent to live in the house of the *Hugenottenprediger Catel,* and there derived his excellent command of French. There is no Catel family record that the American Minister J. Q. Adams received lessons in German from the Huguenot preacher, but the evidence is quite conclusive. The dates correspond exactly. There was no one else by that name who could come into question in Berlin (the name has not survived in Berlin records). S. H. Catel was well known as a language teacher in Berlin when Adams took his lessons, 1799–1800, and an inquiry by J. Q. Adams would have directed him to S. H. Catel at once. Adams, being an excellent scholar in the French language and literature, would have felt personally drawn to so excellent a scholar as the "Huguenot preacher." We read in his *Diary* above (March 31) that Adams translated German into French, which may lead us to suppose that explanations of linguistic difficulties might often have been made in the French language as the best medium common to both teacher and pupil. Catel's interest in Adams's translation of *Oberon,* and his testing its fidelity, gives evidence of a teacher of more than ordinary ability. (The editor is indebted for the biographical data in this note to Mr. Adolf Leisner's assistance in finding for him two descendants of the Catel family living in Berlin, Mr. Kurt Eichelkraut and Major a.D. Julius Weber, who searched their family records carefully and spared no pains in getting all information possible.)

a Master, I still read very indifferently and with great difficulty
—and neither write nor speak it at all. I impute no small part
of the very slow progress I make to the badness of my dictionaries. That which I have, Ludwig's, being one of the very
worst I ever used in my life—which is saying not a little, for I
have long suffered under the curse of bad dictionaries. This
one has not only innumerable faults and omissions of the author—but was doubtless printed by a person totally ignorant
of the English language and never revised. The English side
therefore is almost as often unintelligible as the German.

5. M. Catel came and gave me his first lesson.

7. Second lesson from M. Catel.

14. Lesson of German in the morning.

16. Lesson of German this morning.

19. Lesson of German in the morning.

21. Had a lesson in the morning from M. Catel.

23. Morning lesson of German. (Translating into French
Geßner's letter to Füßlin on landscape painting [*Schriften,* II,
pp. 231–253].)

30. Lesson of German.

31. Berlin—Rise from 7–8. Employ two hours in the study
of German. Three times a week take lessons of M. Catel—
Spend the others in *translating from English into German,* or
from German into French. Breakfast—write letters or journal
till ½ past 2. Walk an hour— Dine— Read a couple of hours
—pass the evening either abroad in company or with company
at home, or read poetry to Mrs. Adams. Sup at 10—and play a
game at chess, until 11.

May

12. Reading Bülow [38] in the afternoon.

[38] D. von Bülow, *Der Freistaat von Nordamerika in seinem neuesten Zustand*
(Berlin, 1797).

13. Translating Bülow's Preface.

14. Lesson of German.[39] Upon looking over Bülow, met a quotation from Cicero, De Natura Deorum. Compared it with the book and thus imperceptibly fell to reading Cicero until the whole morning was passed.

17. *Purchased Wieland's work (s)* and received some other books from the sale.

June

8. Finished the first volume of Bülow and began upon the second.

10. Find my translations more difficult than those of the former volume.

29. Finished the translation of Bülow's book on America.

30. Berlin—Day: Rise irregularly from 6–8. Pursue the study of German until 10. Breakfast. Translate until 3. Walk, half an hour— Dine— Translate again until 7, or read a few pages of German. Take a long walk. Spend an hour at the Casino. Home and sup at 10. Play piquet half an hour with my wife, and retire to bed just after eleven— My translations now cease, as I have done Bülow's book.

July

7. Since finishing my translation I have no particular object upon which to fix exclusively my attention.

31. Töplitz.[40] Finished reading Wieland's Don Sylvio of Rosalva and began his Agathon.

---

[39] J. Q. Adams now (also in the month of April) studied German continuously six days a week, two hours each day. Three two-hour periods were given up to lessons with Mr. Catel; during the others he studied alone.

[40] Teplitz-Schönau, a favorite Bohemian spa, noted for its alkaline and saline springs. Adams resided there during part of the summer for his wife's health.

August

13. (Dresden) Wrote the greatest part of the forenoon. Read likewise part of the 2nd volume of Agathon which is rather tedious. The style of Wieland is far less entertaining than that of Lessing. He is very diffuse and appears to me superficial.

16. (Dresden) Continue to read Wieland's Agathon.

20. Have finished Wieland's Agathon and am reading his Golden Spiegel.

25. (Töplitz) Finished Wieland's Der Goldene Spiegel and began to read his Danischmende.[41] I likewise for some mornings past have generally read a book, or half a book, of his *Oberon*.

30. (Töplitz) Finished Wieland's Danischmende which contrary to the usual course of books, becomes more interesting as it draws toward the end.

September

2. (Töplitz) Read the 6th book of Wieland's *Oberon* into which he has introduced the story of January and May. I have not with me the second volume containing the last six books.

October

27. (Berlin) Finished reading Zimmermann's Anecdotes,[42]

[41] The continuation of *Der goldene Spiegel* is called *Die Geschichte des Philosophen Danischmende*. The name "Danischmende" was given Wieland familiarly by his friends.

[42] Probably one of the works of Johann Georg, Ritter von Zimmermann, famous physician and writer of philosophical essays, born in Brugg, Switzerland, in 1728, died in 1795. Frederick the Great called him to his bedside during his last illness; after Frederick's death Zimmermann published several books that met very severe criticism: *Über Friedrich den Großen und meine Unterredungen mit ihm kurz vor seinem Tode* (Leipzig, 1788) and *Fragmente über Friedrich den Großen* (Leipzig, 1789). The first of these Carlyle called "an unwise book."

and Wieland's Musarion. Read also the seventh book of his
Oberon.

28. (Berlin) Read a German comedy by Großmann [43]
"Nicht mehr als sechs Schüsseln"—and in the evening the 8th
book of *Oberon*.

31. (Berlin) M. Catel at 8 o'clock this morning— With
him I am resuming the study of German. Read in Chaucer the
remainder of the Merchant's and the fragment of the Squire's
Tale. Wieland is mistaken in supposing that Chaucer calls
Oberon and Titania King and Queen of the fairies. Chaucer's
names are Pluto and Preserpina. Pope leaves out the names entirely. [44]

November

3. Berlin—Finished reading *Wieland's Oberon, which is
one of the best things I have read in German.*

8. Berlin—Read the second book of Wieland's Neue
Amadis.

9. (Berlin)—Had a lesson of German this morning. Made
an extract of the first book of Wieland's *Oberon*.

10. (Berlin)—Continuing to make an extract from Wieland's *Oberon*.

11. (Berlin)—Extract from 3rd book of *Oberon*.

[43] Gustav Friedrich Wilhelm Großmann (born in Berlin in 1746, died in
Bonn in 1796) was a very successful actor, writer of comedies, and theater director. He was acquainted with Lessing and began his career with a great hit
in the rôle of *Riccaut de la Marlinière* (Minna von Barnhelm). His outspoken
sympathies with French Revolutionary ideas got him into trouble.

[44] J. Q. Adams's observations are correct. Wieland in his edition of 1796
(Göschen) for the first time wrote a preface, in which the statement occurs:
"Der meinige (Oberon) ist mit dem Oberon, welcher in Chaucer's Merchant's
Tale und Shakspeare's Midsummer Night's Dream als ein Feen- oder Elfen-
könig erscheint, eine und eben dieselbe Person." Here we have another proof of
Adams's use of the Göschen edition of 1796 or a later one of the same publisher.
See Introduction, pp. xxx–xxxii and xxxiii.

14. (Berlin)—Extract from fourth book of *Oberon*.[45]

15. (Berlin)—Still reading and extracting from the *Oberon*.

17. (Berlin)—Finished the introduction to *Oberon*. Made an extract of the 5th book of *Oberon*.

18. (Berlin)—Translated a couple more stanzas from *Oberon*.

19. (Berlin)—Called this morning at the Casino to look in the monthly review for an account of the English translation of *Oberon;* but could not find the reviews themselves. Translated 2 more stanzas.

20. (Berlin)—Translated 3 stanzas of *Oberon*. In the original very fine ones—from the 12th to the 15th.

21. (Berlin)—Two more stanzas of *Oberon*.

23. (Berlin)—Lesson of German. The stanzas of *Oberon* seem to grow more and more difficult—I find it almost impossible with my leisure time to go through two stanzas a day.

29. —I still continue my two stanzas from the first book of Wieland's *Oberon*.

30. —Day. Rise irregularly between 6 and 8. Lesson of German till 10. Breakfast. Spend the forenoon in writing letters— Walk from 2 to 3. Dine— Translate a couple of stanzas from *Oberon*— Evening now for the most part abroad. Bed at about 11.

December

8. Upon coming home found Miss Brown with Mrs. Adams. Read to her the part of the first book of *Oberon* which I have done.

---

[45] MS II tells us that Adams began his translation of the First Book on Nov. 14 and finished it on Dec. 15, 1799, as also stated below in his *Diary* of that date. See also Introduction, p. xli.

12. Lesson in German. It is now merely reduced to an examination of my daily translation from *Oberon*.

13. Made this morning the extract from the 11th book of *Oberon*.

15. Finished this day the *analytical extract* [46] from *Oberon*, and likewise the translation of the first book, and began the second. The Abbé Denina called upon me—and Mr. Arbuthnot spent a couple of hours with me. Read him the last stanzas of my translation.

20. Read the Comte de Tressan's *Huon de Bordeaux* [47] from which Wieland has borrowed almost the whole of his first book. I spend now perhaps too much time upon my translation from *Oberon*.

21. Read this evening the first canto of Spenser's Faery Queen, and the Sixth book of Pope's Iliad.

27. Dined at the Danish Minister, Baron Rosenkrantz's, a company of about twenty persons. M. d'Araujo told me that he had seen Mr. Wieland at Weimar; who showed him the English translation of his *Oberon* by Mr. Sotheby, with which he is much pleased. M. d'Araujo does not like the *Oberon*.

28. Finished the 2nd and began the 3rd book of *Oberon*.

31. Mrs. Adams unwell. Doctor Brown here this afternoon. Evening— Played whist with Countess Moltke, Madame de Zastrow, and Mr. Koblauch. Day: Rise at different hours, from 5–8, generally about 7. [48] German lesson, or translating *Oberon*, till 10. Breakfast. Read or write as I have occasion till 2. Walk. Dine at 3. Translate another stanza from *Oberon*.

[46] These extracts, a summary of the plot of the whole poem, are printed in this volume; see Introduction, pp. lxxii–xcii.

[47] See Introduction, pp. xxxii and xxxiv.

[48] J. Q. Adams was a noted early riser. During his wife's illness he was usually up most of the night and did not get his regular hours of sleep. See *Diary* entry of January 23, 1801.

Read Spenser or Pope's Iliad, or spend the evening out, until 10. Bed at 11.

The year would, in general, have been a pleasant one but for the state of my wife's health, which has been almost continually bad, and concerning which I am now deeply concerned. The subject preys upon my spirits more than I can express. I have written during the year somewhat more than usual. Principally in the months of May and June, when I made the translation of Bülow's book. Since the middle of November too I have amused myself with translating from Wieland's *Oberon*. A book which serves in some degree to withdraw my reflections from painful subjects which have too great a tendency to engross them. I have learnt in the course of the year something more of the German language, which I can read with tolerable facility and I have sufficiently ascertained that I never shall speak it.[49]

1800

January

2. Found Dr. Brown when I came home. The translation of *Oberon* flags—at least as to the success of the work.

4. Had a lesson of German this morning. The *Oberon* grows very tedious.

[49] However, eight months after, we read in his published work *Letters on Silesia*, pp. 154–155, in a letter dated Waldenburg, August 16, 1800, in which the writer gives an account of a Silesian formal dinner party where only German was spoken, the following comment of J. Q. Adams: "For myself I like this much better; it forces me to make trial of my strength in German, and affords me some help in the acquisition of the language." The complete title of this work as published in London in 1804 was *Letters on Silesia, written during a Tour through that Country in the Years 1800–1801*, by His Excellency John Quincy Adams. The letters were written originally to his brother Thomas Boylston Adams at Philadelphia, and were not intended for publication; nevertheless, they appeared in the Philadelphia journal *Port Folio*, from which they were reprinted in England in book form.

7. Miss Brown spent the evening with Mrs. Adams. Read to her the remnant of the first book, the whole of the second, and the part of the third which I have done of the translation of *Oberon*.

14. Berlin. Finished the third book and began the fourth of *Oberon*. Lesson from M. Catel this morning.

21. The translation from *Oberon* now engrosses almost all the leisure time I have. I did this day nothing else; and the practice of writing as yet seems to give no more facility than I had at first.

27. Finished the fourth book of *Oberon*.

28. Began the fifth book of *Oberon*.

February

1. Upon coming home received letters from Mr. King and Mr. Pitcairn with the melancholy tidings of the death of General Washington on the 15th of December, which affected me strongly.

3. The first representation of the 2nd opera, which I did not attend. Passed the evening at home. Read in Spenser the first canto of the legend of Sir Guyon, and found in one of the first stanzas an allusion to Sir Huon and King Oberon.[50] Read likewise a book of the Iliad.

4. Evening at home. Read part of a Book of the Iliad. The translation from the *Oberon* almost entirely prevents me from reading.

15. Mr. Catel this morning. Finished the 5th book of *Oberon,* and begin the 6th.

[50] *The Faerie Queene,* Book II, Canto I, stanza 6:
> Well could he tourney, and in lists debate,
> And knighthood took of good Sir Huon's hand,
> When with king Oberon he came to Faery land.

16. Went through seven stanzas of *Oberon*. No court this evening. Read part of a book of the Iliad.

17. Read in the evening a canto of the Faery Queen, the remainder of the 13th and the 14th books of the Iliad.

March

6. 8 stanzas of *Oberon*. But Mr. Catel criticizes my present performances much more than he did heretofore.

7. The weather continues very cold. Am too much occupied by my translation of *Oberon*. Finished the sixth book, and began upon the seventh. Have now got half through the poem.

11. Had a lesson of German this morning, and found the stanzas of *Oberon* so troublesome that I did nothing else the whole day.

13. The tone and style of poetry in the last half of the *Oberon* differs much from that of the first. It is much more difficult. The labor of it has become nearly insufferable. Read a book in the Faery Queen.

14. Found the *Oberon* again a little more practicable.

15. Lesson for examination of my translation, which is at present all I do. Walked in the park forenoon and afternoon. Read a canto of the Faery Queen in the evening.

16. Read to Miss Brown about a book of my translation.

19. The *Oberon* has now engrossed almost all my time. Read the first canto of the third book of the Faery Queen. The legend of Britomartis or of Chastity.

21. Walked morning and afternoon. Miss Brown spent the evening with us. Read the remainder of the fourth and the 5th book of *Oberon*.

22. My German lessons have become exclusively devoted

to an examination of my translation, and the work my sole occupation. I might likewise almost say my sole amusement.

23. Read a sermon of Tillotson in the forenoon. Did over anew a stanza which teaz'd me yesterday two or three hours and which was after all very ill done. Continued to work on the same book [51] all the afternoon and evening.

24. The weather again cold. Thermometer at 6 below 0. Finished the seventh book of *Oberon,* and read it this evening to Mrs. Adams.

25. Began the 8th book of *Oberon.* I find that with some difficulty I can do six stanzas a day and henceforth shall seldom attempt to do more.

28. Read this evening a canto of the Faery Queen which I began to find tedious—but I read nothing else.

April

2. Mr. Arbuthnot spent the evening with us. Read to him the Seventh book of my *Oberon.* It was so long he probably thought it tedious.

3. Mr. Catel this morning. A long walk before dinner in the park. At least I can take more exercise for being engaged in my present business, which I can do while walking better than when shut up in my chamber.—Yet six stanzas in a day I still find a heavy task.

5. Took a shorter walk than usual. In the afternoon—Burdened excessively with the ungrateful task of my translation, which I have no reason for continuing but that I began it.

6. Finished the 8th book of *Oberon* and began the 9th.

[51] MS II would indicate that Book VI was meant. There, *stanzas 36, 38,* and *40* were entirely rewritten in the margin. Book VII shows no such radical changes.

11. Recovered the time I had lost yesterday in my translation.[52]

15. My time is now so much engrossed by one subject that I have nothing to say upon any other.

17. Finished the 9th book of *Oberon* and began the 10th.

21. Was a little in arrears of my translation yesterday, which I recovered however this day.[53]

24. The weather is again very warm. Walked in the park before dinner and again toward evening. Had in the morning a lesson of German. Read this evening to Mrs. Adams—the 9th book of *Oberon* and a few pages of the mysteries of Udolpho.

26. Finished the 10th and began the 11th book of *Oberon*. Read a little further in the mysteries of Udolpho.

30. Day. Rise generally between 6 & 7 . . . Translate *Oberon* or give Mr. Catel an hour, until 10. Then breakfast. Renew my translation till between 1 & 2. Walk an hour.— Dine— Translate again. Walk an hour or two more. Read in the evening to Mrs. Adams or continue my translation. It engrosses so much my time that I am heartily weary of it; but hope before the end of another month to finish it.

May

6. Finished the 11th book of *Oberon*.

7. Began the 12th book of *Oberon* and busied at it the whole day.

22. *Finished my translation of Wieland's Oberon.*

31. Day—as that of the last months. But having now

---

[52] MS II shows that on April 10 Adams did only four stanzas; on April 11 he translated eight stanzas, recovering his daily average of six stanzas.

[53] MS II shows again that, when the translator had fallen short on April 20 by one stanza, he made up the shortage on April 21 by translating seven stanzas.

finished my translation of the *Oberon,* I spend a couple of hours before breakfast in making a copy of it, endeavoring as I proceed to give a little polish to the verse; a point in which it is extremely defective.[54] After breakfast I write letters; and in my walking hours amuse myself with a Satire of Juvenal.

June

13. I am busied almost exclusively in copying my translations of Juvenal's 13th Satire, and of the *Oberon.*

23. Berlin—Countess Brühl and her daughter Mary took tea, and spent part of the evening with Mrs. Adams. I read to them the first book of my translation of *Oberon,* with which I am wholly dissatisfied. My translation from Juvenal is almost wholly suspended.

30. Berlin—Day: Rise between 6 and 8 very irregularly. Write until nearly ten; either translating or copying off the *Oberon.*—Breakfast— Write letters, or continue to copy or translate until two. Walk an hour in the Park. Dine— After dinner an hour or two of leisure. Walk, two or three hours more in the Park. Home at about 9. Write down the lines I made in walking. Bed at about 11. To this regularity there have been some exceptions this month during five days when we made our tour to Potsdam and Brandenburg; and about ten days together when I had constantly company at home, or dined out myself. In the course of the month I have translated Gentz's [55] essay, and Juvenal's 14th Satire.

(During the interval between the above and the next entry of the diary J. Q. Adams made the tour through Silesia de-

---

[54] See Introduction, p. xliii.

[55] The essay of Friedrich von Gentz (1764–1832), important publicist, was on the "Origin and Principles of the American Revolution, compared with the French Revolution," published in Philadelphia in 1800.

scribed in his *Letters on Silesia,* mentioned above. The first letter states: "On Thursday the 17th July we left Berlin just after three in the morning, and arrived here [Frankfort on the Oder] at about nine the same evening." The last letter of Part One [No. XXIX] was dated Leipzig, September 24, 1800. The letters of Part Two [Nos. XXX–XLIII] were dated Berlin, December 20, 1800, to Berlin, March 17, 1801. A *Diary* entry tells us that Adams returned to Berlin on October 25, i. e. after an absence of a little more than three months.)

December

4. *Saw for the first time Sotheby's translation of Oberon.*
7. I received at length from Mr. Arbuthnot *Sotheby's Oberon* and his Georgics. Read part of the First (Georgic) this evening and compared it with Dryden's translation.—Mr. Sotheby's preface is not remarkable for diffidence, but his performance is such as justifies the consciousness of power which he shows.

10. Finished reading the two translations of the First Georgic. Still working upon my own of *Oberon.*

22. I am likewise busied in writing letters to my brother [56] and in correcting my translation of *Oberon.*

1801

January

23. Rise between 8 & 9. Seldom earlier; for which a partial apology arises from the very frequent bad nights which my wife's state of health occasions.[57] Revise my translation of *Oberon,* about half an hour. Breakfast, dress. Read or write

[56] Thomas Boylston Adams; see *Letters on Silesia* (above).
[57] Cf. the *Diary,* Dec. 31, 1799, and footnote 48.

till 2. Walk an hour. Dine. Spend the evening abroad, or reading to Mrs. Adams—more frequently the latter, until about 10. Take a light supper. Bed at 11.

March

31. Rise at about 8— Correct 1 stanza of *Oberon*. Breakfast at nine. Write letters till 2; walk till 3, dine. After dinner attend to Mrs. Adams. . . . Evening sometimes abroad, but oftener at home.

(This is the last entry concerning *Oberon*, written shortly before J. Q. Adams left for the United States, on the decline of the Federalist Party.)

Letters of J. Q. Adams bearing on Oberon

Among the unpublished letters of John Quincy Adams in the Family Archives not much has been found bearing on the translation of *Oberon*, with the exception of two letters addressed to William Vans Murray. The passages referring to our subject are as follows:

To W. V. Murray, Esq., dated Berlin, November 19, 1799

"I have this day first seen in a Boston paper Humphreys' Sailor Song [58] which, though somewhat watery, will do very well; but should not be read, however, by one who has been recently pampered with the exquisite taste of *Wieland's Oberon*, a poem which my friend Bielefeld [59] used to prize

[58] David Humphreys (1753–1818), one of the poets of the American Revolution, born in Connecticut, aide-de-camp of General Washington, writer of patriotic though mediocre lyrics. Cf. R. F. Griswold, *Poets and Poetry of America*, p. 22.

[59] Bielefeld was chargé d'affaires from Prussia at The Hague while J. Q. Adams was United States minister there (1795–1797). The published diary (*Memoirs of J. Q. Adams*), Vol. I, gives frequent references to the friendly intercourse between Adams and Bielefeld.

as the second masterpiece of the German language, which I now think one of the finest that ever was written."

To W. V. Murray, Esq., dated Berlin, January 13, 1801

"The first draught of my *Oberon* was finished last May, but the labour of curtailing is more tedious and slow than that of the first cast. In its present state it is utterly unfit to be read, and it is doubtful whether I shall ever get through the ungrateful task of finishing it. Ungrateful task I call it, because there is an English translation of *Oberon,* extant, so much superior to what mine would be in its best state, that stanza compared [with stanza] in the two versions, would fill me with mortification, were I desirous of poetical fame. Of this translation I knew nothing, when I began mine, and never saw it until a few weeks ago. It is done by a Mr. Sotheby who has recently published a translation of the Georgics, one of the most elegantly finished things I ever read."

The first letter shows the early enthusiasm with which John Quincy Adams went to work. The second letter exhibits the trials and tribulations of every writer who is conscientiously engaged upon revisions and improvements of his manuscript. Adams was far too modest concerning his accomplishments as a translator. His *Oberon* translation, following the original more closely, is of more lasting value than the poetical translation of Sotheby, for which see the Introduction, pp. xix–xxix.

A section from a letter of John Quincy Adams to his mother Abigail Adams, dated Berlin, May 25, 1800,[60] should find a place here:

"A longer time has elapsed since I wrote you last than I can

---

[60] Published entire in *The Writings of J. Q. Adams,* edited by W. C. Ford, Vol. II, p. 456 f.

apologize for with propriety. It is possible that at some future day I may send you the result of an occupation, which, almost in spite of myself, I have suffered to engross for several months past, not only every moment of my leisure, but even much time which ought to have been devoted to other pursuits. For the present I can only tell you, that it is the translation of a popular German poem, which is so far completed that I promise you it shall not henceforth interrupt the frequency of my correspondence with you. The stagnation of political events during the winter months, together with various other motives, induced me at first to undertake the work as an amusement for myself and a few friends; but what I had taken as a pleasant companion soon mastered me so completely, that for months together I could scarcely snatch from it here and there an hour for any other purpose whatsoever. What is worst of all is that, now I may consider the thing as in a manner finished, I am so ashamed of it in every sense that I hesitate even at promising you a sight of it, and should not now mention it to you, but that the long interval since I wrote you required some excuse on my part, and in this case, as in all others where excuses are necessary, I know of none better than the statement of the naked truth."

In a letter to his father John Adams, dated Berlin, May 16, 1801, when he was about to leave for home, we find the following interesting lines showing John Quincy Adams's thorough and then rare appreciation of German literature:

"I have been packing up my books and the baggage I have determined to take with me. The little library that I have collected here bears no comparison with that I sent home from Lisbon. It consists chiefly of German books, a language in which some of our countrymen think there is nothing like elegant or useful literature. As the Parisian fine lady of whom Montesquieu tells, could not conceive how it was possible to be a Persian."

VIII. "ANALYTICAL EXTRACTS" FROM WIELAND'S *Oberon*

BY J. Q. ADAMS

Book 1

HUON, Duke of Guyenne, after receiving at Rome the Pope's blessing, and recommendation to visit the Holy Sepulchre, as the condition of success in his undertaking, sets out from Rome for Babylon to fulfill the commands of Charlemagne. He lands at Joppe, performs his pilgrimage to the Holy Sepulchre, and then proceeds upon his journey.

He finds in a solitary cavern of Mount Lebanon, Cherasmin, who had sixteen years before accompanied Huon's father Sieguin upon a pilgrimage to the Holy Land, during which Sieguin died, and Cherasmin had ever since lived as a hermit in this cavern. Huon relates to Cherasmin the cause and purpose of his journey. He had been educated by his mother at Court, and upon coming to the proper age, proclaimed Duke of Guyenne at Bordeaux. Charlemagne, instigated by the calumnies of Amory, Baron of Hautefeuille, the enemy of Huon's house, summoned Huon to come and do homage for his fief. Huon accordingly set out, but is waylaid upon his journey by Amory and Charles, second son of Charlemagne, a very wicked youth. Charles assaults and wounds Huon's young brother Gerard, who was in company with him, and had strayed a little out of the way. Upon Huon's coming up, Charles attacked him, calling himself the Duke of Ardennes, and declaring that he would now revenge the injury of his father, whom he says Huon's father had once defeated in a race, by a stratagem. Huon, in defending himself, killed Charles and then continued his journey, and arrived at the Court of Charlemagne.

Amory soon comes with the dead body of Charles, and accuses Huon as his murderer, upon which Charlemagne in great rage, refusing to hear Huon's justification, orders him to be put to death. Huon however appeals to the laws of chivalry, gives the lie to Amory, and challenges him to single combat, to which Charlemagne at length consents, and in which Huon kills Amory. Charlemagne, however, still enraged at the death of his son, pronounces banishment upon Huon, and the confiscation of his estates—but at length promises to pardon him, upon condition that he shall go to Babylon, enter into the presence of the Caliph, when seated at a banquet in his hall surrounded by his Emirs,—cut off the head of the person sitting at the Caliph's left hand, and with a kiss thrice repeated, claim the Caliph's daughter and heiress of the throne, for his bride. Then prostrate himself before the Caliph and request of him, four of his teeth and a handful of his beard, to be presented in token of friendship to Charlemagne. Huon undertakes this achievement, and concludes his narrative by observing, that he was come thus far on his way to perform it.—Cherasmin declares that he will go with him and follow his fortunes. Accordingly, the next morning they proceed upon the journey.

Book 2

Huon and Cherasmin after traveling three days, in descending Mount Lebanon are attacked by a troop of Arabs, many of whom they kill and put the rest to flight. They then come to a village in the plain, where they are hospitably entertained by the good people, who refuse to receive any payment. The travelers continue their journey, and Huon's impatience urging him to take the shortest way to Bagdad, he determines against the advice and entreaties of Cherasmin, to pass through a forest, the abode of an evil reputed Spirit who always transformed into some beast every man who ventured into it. They meet on their way numerous troops of deer, who fly at their approach. After being some time bewildered in the forest, the knight and his companion discover at a distance through the bushes a resplendent castle, the golden gates of which suddenly fly open, and a boy, beautiful as the God of Love, issues from them, sitting in a silver chariot drawn by two leopards, and with the reins in his hand. Cherasmin excessively frightened seizes the bridle of Huon's horse, turns him round and forces him to run with all possible speed away from the dwarf, until they got out of the forest. They were now overtaken by a furious storm of rain, thunder and lightning, in the midst of which they often hear a soft, gentle voice, calling upon Huon to turn back. But Cherasmin prevails upon him not to comply with the invitation.——They continue their flight therefore until they are stopped by the walls of a cloister of nuns dedicated to St. Agatha. It happened to be this Saint's day, and the nuns had been, together with the monks of a neighboring convent dedicated to St. Anthony, upon a procession, from which they were returning when overtaken by the storm. They had just got back, all together in the yard of the convent, and the gates being open, Cherasmin, who thought there would be perfect safety against the pursuit of the Spirit, upon holy ground, rushes in among them.

Huon soon follows him and instantly the dwarf appears in the midst of them, leaning upon the stalk of a lily, and with an ivory horn hung over his shoulders, which before they have recovered from their astonishment, he puts to his lips and

blows.——The sound immediately makes the monks, nuns and
Cherasmin all fall to dancing, but produces no effect upon
Huon.——Oberon, the dwarf, then accosts Huon, tells him he
has always been his friend, and adds that his power to punish
extended only to persons whose souls were stained with some
vice,——as for instance the monks and nuns were hypocrites;
and Cherasmin, though honest, was too free with his tongue;
but had they been perfectly virtuous, the horn would not
have affected them. At Huon's entreaty Oberon now waves
his lily wand, and the dancing ceases, but Cherasmin, being
exhausted by its violence, Oberon, after dismissing the monks
and nuns, gives him a golden cup, and bids him drink it off at
a draught—— Cherasmin hesitates, perceiving the cup to be
empty; but Oberon, reproving him for his incredulity, again
bids him drink. Cherasmin thereupon puts the cup to his
mouth, which immediately fills itself with a delicious and refreshing wine. He drinks and is instantly restored to strength
and spirits.

Oberon then turns to Huon and tells him that he shall accomplish the orders of Charlemagne——gives him the ivory
horn, and the cup——tells him, that if menaced by ever so many
thousand swords and lances, he has only to blow softly the
horn, and it will set them all to dancing till they can no longer
stand upon their feet—— But if he blows a loud blast (which
he must, however, reserve for occasions of the greatest extremity) it would serve as a call to Oberon himself, who would
instantly appear to assist him. The cup, he adds, will always
fill itself with the delicious wine whenever an honest man puts
it to his lips. But if held by a knave, will remain empty and
burn his hand. Oberon after admonishing Huon, never to fall
from virtue, disappears, and the knight with his old attendant
pursues his journey.

Book 3

On the fifth day of their journey, after their last adventure, the travelers meet the Prince of Lebanon, with more than twenty knights his attendants. The Prince accosts Huon: informs him that the Giant Angulaffer lives in a castle near at hand, and has had Angela, the Prince's beloved Lady more than half a year in his possession; that he is invulnerable by the virtue of a ring which he had taken away from Oberon, and that the Prince, determined to deliver his Lady, had for several months stopped every knight who traveled that way, and by unhorsing him in single combat, compelled him to engage himself to assist him in his purpose of delivering the Lady. He gives Huon therefore the choice, either of breaking a lance with him, or of joining with him and his other knights to rescue the Lady, or of undertaking to deliver her himself. Huon chooses the first alternative, unhorses the Prince of Lebanon, and all his knights successively, and then after partaking of a banquet with them, undertakes to go and rescue the Lady. He enters the castle of the Giant, and meets the Lady, who implores his assistance, tells him the story, how the Giant had carried her off, and how by the miraculous favor of the Holy Virgin she had hitherto been preserved from his violence. She adds that the Giant is now asleep, and that Huon may take the magic ring from his finger and then kill him. Huon takes the ring, but scorning to murder a sleeping enemy, wakes the Giant and slays him in single combat. Prince Alexis, the Lady's lover immediately after arrives, to whom Huon delivers her, though she appears half inclined to prefer her deliverer himself. Fifty other ladies whom the Giant had in like manner shut up, are now set at liberty, and Huon, without waiting to partake of the banquets served by invisible hands which the virtue of the ring produces, continues with Cherasmin his journey until night.

A tent now suddenly rises by magic, with a well-served table, and soft beds to refresh the travelers with food and sleep. Here they pass the night and are lulled to sleep by soft aerial music. Towards morning Huon has two dreams successively, in which a lady of wonderful beauty appears to him, with whom he instantly becomes deeply enamored and in which a mysterious anticipation of his future adventures is represented. Cherasmin wakes him and even after being awake he remains strongly agitated by the impressions of his dream, until he recruits his spirits by a draught from the magical cup.

Book 4

Huon relates his dream to Cherasmin, who advises him to believe the pleasing part of it and discredit altogether the rest. In the morning the tent disappears and they pursue their journey along the course of the Euphrates. They save the life of a Saracen attacked by a raging lion, and slay the animal himself. But upon Huon's offering the Saracen the magical cup to drink from, it remains empty and burns his hand. The Saracen runs away and carries Huon's horse off with him. Cherasmin purchases in the next village an old wretched mule to carry him the remainder of the journey. They arrive at length at Bagdad, and upon inquiring of an old woman whom they meet in the street, for an inn, are invited by her to take their lodging in her own hut, which Huon accepts. The old woman tells them, that she is the mother of the nurse to the Sultan's daughter, who was to be married the next day to her cousin Babecan, prince of the Druses, but that she did not love him, and had an unutterable aversion against the marriage, owing to a dream, in which, a few weeks before, she had seen a dwarf and an unknown young knight, very handsome, with blue eyes and yel-

low hair, and had fallen instantly in love with him. That
Babecan in order to gain her affections, had undertaken to kill
a dreadful monster who for some time past had desolated the
country, devouring men and cattle. That he had gone out that
morning upon his expedition, but returned apparently without
succeeding in his purpose to kill the monster. That the nuptials were however to be solemnized the next day with great
magnificence. Huon involuntarily exclaims that this shall not
take place, for that the dwarf and the knight will show themselves at the feast too. The old woman's curiosity being excited
by this declaration, she listens at the door after Huon and
Cherasmin have retired to their bedchamber and hears the conversation between them, but cannot understand it. Only she
observes that they often repeat the name of Rezia. Cherasmin
advises Huon to content himself with obtaining the Lady, and
not attempt the other part of Charlemagne's commands. But
Huon reminds him that having promised to accomplish the
rest, he will perform it, be the consequence what it will. Cherasmin soon falls asleep. But the anxiety of Huon, upon being thus
at the verge of his great adventure, keeps him awake all night.

Book 5

Rezia, the Sultan's daughter, having been kept awake all
night by her anxiety for the event of the ensuing day, falls
asleep towards morning, and in a dream sees again her unknown
knight. When her nurse Fatme comes to call her, she tells her
dream, and declares that she hopes to be delivered from the
odious Prince of the Druses in some way or other; but if nothing
else can avail she is determined to deliver herself by stabbing
herself with a dagger which she keeps in her bosom. Fatme is
very much terrified at this, but is soon called away by her
mother who comes to tell her of the strange knight who had

passed the night at her hut; whom by her description and account they all conclude to be the unknown knight whose image
had made such an impression upon Rezia's heart in her dreams.
As the time destined for the nuptial solemnities approaches, the
Caliph, with the Prince of the Druses, the Emirs and Vizirs
repair to the Hall, where the banquet is prepared. Rezia does
the same— They take their seats, the Caliph's daughter at his
right hand and Babecan her destined bridegroom at the left.—
Huon had fallen asleep likewise towards morning and slept
till noon. Upon waking he finds lying upon a chair by his bedside, a complete suit of magnificent clothes suiting an Emir
of the highest rank, which Oberon had conveyed there for him
to wear, that he might obtain admission without obstacle to
the Hall. He likewise finds at the door a horse richly capari-
soned, and two beautiful pages to serve him as guides. Huon
proceeds and upon entering the Hall sees that Babecan, who
sits at the Sultan's left hand, is the same man whose life he had
saved the day before from the lion, and who had made so ill
a return for the benefit. Huon with one stroke of the sword
smites off his head. This bold deed throws the whole company
into astonishment and the Sultan for some moments sinks
bereft of speech back upon his chair. Huon and Rezia recognize
each other as the persons they had reciprocally seen in dreams,
and Huon with a kiss three times repeated, puts upon her
finger the ring which he had taken from the Giant, and claims
her for his bride. The Sultan now breaks out in fury and with
all his attendants is ready to fall upon Huon, who prepares to
defend himself. Rezia, however, interposes, and he concludes
to blow gently through the ivory horn. Immediately the Sultan
and all his Court, with the single exception of Rezia, fall to
dancing. Cherasmin thereupon comes forward with Fatme,
and urges the knight immediately to depart with his bride, and
adds that everything is ready for the journey. Huon answers

that the worst is yet to be performed and as the effects of the music begin to abate, leaves Rezia and the ivory horn in custody of Cherasmin, advances toward the Caliph who has thrown himself upon a sopha; drops upon one knee and asks him in the name of Charles the Great for four of his jaw teeth and a handful of his beard. The Sultan flies again into a rage; Huon then offers him a compromise, and tells him that if he will turn Christian and make the people of Babylon do the same, no more shall be required of him. Upon this they all attack Huon with the utmost rage. He defends himself as well as he can until Cherasmin, seeing his knight's danger, blows in the horn with extreme violence. A dreadful storm of thunder and lightning, with darkness and earthquake ensues. The Sultan and his attendants lose all sense and motion. Oberon appears, approves the conduct of Huon and gives him Rezia for his reward, at the same time leaving her the choice to remain with her father or to follow her lover. She chooses the last. Oberon tells them that his coach is ready, and will carry them before morning to Askalon. He then disappears. Huon and Rezia together with Cherasmin and Fatme ascend the coach, which carries them through the air drawn by four swans and driven by a child.

Book 6

At dawn of day the coach lands on the coast of Askalon, where Huon and Rezia, with Cherasmin and Fatme, sit down together under the palm trees. Oberon appears in the midst of them; delivers to Huon a casket, containing the Sultan's teeth and beard, which he tells him to present to Charlemagne as the proof that he had literally executed his commands. He then tells them to hasten on before the Sultan can have time to pursue them. That close to the strand they will find a vessel ready to carry them in six or seven days to Lepanto, where

they will upon arriving find another ready to convey them to
Salerno, and that from this last place they must proceed as
speedily as possible to Rome, and receive the nuptial blessing
from Pope Sylvester. Above all until this shall take place they
must consider each other as brother and sister; for that at the
instant when they taste the fruit of forbidden love, Oberon
must be separated from them forever. After kissing them both
upon the forehead, he then disappears, with several tokens of
concern and apprehension.

The lovers though somewhat dejected at this, soon recover
their spirits and embark on board the vessel provided for them
by Oberon, which immediately sails very rapidly, though in a
perfect calm. Huon finding his love for Rezia growing constantly more ardent and impatient, undertakes by way of occupation to instruct Rezia as well as he can in the Christian
religion,—and she is at length by a monk of the order of St.
Basil, who happens to be on board the vessel, baptized by the
name of Amanda. After this, however, their mutual passion
waxes importunate to such a degree, that Cherasmin is alarmed
and concerts with Fatme various things to prop the decaying
virtue of the knight, and among the rest he concludes to tell
them a tale, appropriate to the occasion, which had formerly
been related to him by a Calender at Bassora.

It is the tale of January and May. Gangolfo, an old reformed
rake of sixty-five, marries a beautiful young girl named Rosetta. At seventy the husband is stricken blind. He soon after
grows jealous and torments his wife so much with every sort
of privation, that she at length concerts with Walter, the old
knight's young squire, means for her comfort and relief. One
summer's day when the ill-sorted couple were walking in the
garden, after the old man had been discoursing to his wife
upon their happiness in marriage and the falsehood of other
women, she points to a pear-tree in the garden and tells him she

longs for some of its fruit. Walter was by concert with her, already up in the tree; having obtained access to the garden by a stolen impression of the old man's key. The husband unable in any other manner to gratify his wife's longing, at length consents to stoop, while she uses his back and shoulders as steps to climb the tree and gather the fruit for which she longed. At this moment Oberon and Titania, king and queen of the fairies, happen to be sitting upon a moss bank, opposite the spot, and witness the whole transaction. Oberon's indignation is raised at the imposition practiced upon the poor old man, he exclaims against the treachery of women, and declares that to punish Rosetta, he will instantly restore to the old husband his sight. Titania on her part takes the part of her sex; lays the fault upon the old fool for marrying a young girl, and declares that whatever may happen, Rosetta shall be provided with such a justification as shall extricate her from all difficulty. Oberon restores sight to Gangolfo, who perceiving the situation of his wife, falls into a great rage. But Titania soon surrounds Walter with a cloud which conceals him from the husband, and Rosetta, inspired by the necessity of the moment, assures Gangolfo that she was only struggling with an evil spirit in the shape of a man, for the sake of restoring him to sight. Gangolfo easily believes her and is immediately reconciled to her. Oberon, yet more exasperated at this issue, now declares to Titania, that from that instant he separates himself from her, and never must they come together again, until a couple of faithful lovers shall bid defiance to death, rather than be false to each other, for all the glory of a throne.——He then disappeared in spite of all Titania's entreaties; and from that time, adds Cherasmin, has dwelt in some mountain, wood or valley, and made it all his delight to torment lovers,——Huon and Amanda being a single and extraordinary exception.——

Huon observes, that if a faithful couple is all that Oberon

wants, to be reconciled to his Queen, they are that couple; and as to the proofs, the sooner they are called for, the better. This gives rise to a tender scene between the lovers, which makes Cherasmin fear lest the whole effect of his moral tale should be lost.

Book 7

At the end of seven days the travelers arrive at Lepanto, where they find two vessels, one bound to Marseilles and the other to Naples. Huon, who begins to find the presence of his old mentor Cherasmin burdensome, orders him to embark in that for Marseilles,—and taking with him the casket containing the Sultan's teeth and beard, to proceed and deliver them in his name to Charlemagne, with the assurance that he himself will soon come and present the Sultan's daughter; after which he directs the Squire to return and meet him at Rome. Cherasmin obeys with reluctance. The favored couple, with Fatme, embark in the vessel for Naples. Huon soon repents having sent away his old faithful friend, and, distrusting his own resolution to keep the injunction of continence, for some time treats Amanda with reserve and coolness, which much distresses her. One night, when almost everybody on board the ship was asleep, the two lovers being in their respective cabins, and both kept awake by their passion, Huon at length sighs so bitterly, that Amanda goes into his chamber, which was separated from hers only by a thin partition, to inquire what occasions his distress. This leads to a violent struggle between the impetuous passions of the lovers, and their adherence to the charge of their protecting Genius, until all power of longer resistance fails, and instead of Hymen, Cupid crowns their union.

Immediately a dreadful storm arises, which soon brings the vessel into such imminent danger of perishing, that the Cap-

tain at length calls the company together and tells them that
the only resource left is to draw lots, as perhaps the vengeance
of Heaven pursues only the guilt of one individual, and if he
can be ascertained and perish, the rest may perhaps be saved.
They all consent to draw, and the lot falls upon Huon. He
acquiesces but delays executing the sentence of his fate until the
Captain urges him not to postpone it any longer. Amanda
throws her arms round him, and they plunge into the sea together. The tempest is instantly calmed, and two days later
the vessel arrives at its destined port.

At the moment when the vow of chastity had been broken
by the lovers, the ivory horn and golden cup, given by Oberon
to Huon, had vanished, but the ring taken from the Giant was
still on Amanda's finger and prevented them by its inherent
virtue from sinking. They soon land upon a desert island. Here
the only shelter is a rocky cave, and they suffer much from
hunger and thirst. Huon goes out to seek some sort of food
for their sustenance. After a long search he finds a fruit resembling melons of great beauty and fragrant smell. He carries
it with transport to Amanda, but upon cutting it open with
his sword, the beauteous fruit proves rotten throughout and
bitter as gall. They are now reduced to the utmost despair, and
Amanda is upon the point of perishing with hunger. Huon at
length finds a stream of fresh water, a draft of which relieves
her; and the next day he finds several palm trees loaded with
dates, upon which they subsist for some time until the approach
of winter. They then find themselves in great need both of
covering and food, and the situation of Amanda bearing already
the fruit of their love, aggravates their hardships. She notwith-
standing keeps up her own spirits and cheers those of Huon.
But as their absolute want of food grows urgent to the utmost,
Huon undertakes to explore a part of the island so extremely
difficult of access, that he had never before attempted it. He

succeeds in his endeavor, after escaping narrowly the most imminent dangers, not without some hurts.

Book 8

Huon continues his search and comes to a delightful spot resembling a Paradise, where he meets an old venerable hermit named Alfonso, who had been induced by misfortunes in early life to retire from the world, and had now resided thirty years in this delightful place. The spot itself had been formed by Titania, queen of the fairies, who soon after her quarrel with Oberon, had taken up her abode in this island, waiting with the warmest wishes but with very faint hopes for the accomplishment of the condition upon which the reconciliation with her beloved husband depended. The hermit and Huon are very much astonished at the sight of each other, but upon Huon's telling him the motive of his coming, the hermit welcomes him, and shows him another shorter and easier path, by which Amanda can come up the hill, which she does. After some days Huon tells his whole story to the hermit, who comforts him and advises him to take a voluntary resolution of continency for the future, in order to recover the favor of Oberon. This he accordingly does. Huon builds a little hut for Amanda, and they spend the winter together with the old hermit in such occupations as their situation requires, and such amusements as it admits. Upon the return of spring, as Rezia's time approaches, she feels much concerned how she shall be able without the assistance of a female attendant to go through it,—but for this Titania had provided. She had remarked the two lovers from the first day of their landing upon the island and conceived hopes that they were the faithful couple so necessary to the restoration of her happiness. She determines therefore to favor Amanda with special protection and kindness. There was

a grotto where Titania's throne was erected, into which neither
Huon nor Alfonso had ever been able to obtain access. But
Amanda one day succeeds in entering it, and there sinks entranced upon a seat of moss and roses, while by the assistance of
Titania, and three fairies her attendants, she is delivered of a
lovely boy, which Titania presents to her, and then disappears.
Huon after searching anxiously two hours for Amanda through
the whole grove, at length goes up to the inaccessible grotto,
finds it open, and upon entering into it, finds, with feelings
which are left to the imagination of pure minds and feeling
hearts, his Amanda with the boy at her breast.

Book 9

The ship from on board of which Huon and Amanda had
thrown themselves into the sea, is overtaken the second night
after by a violent storm, and at the end of seven days is wrecked
upon the coast of Tunis, where the Captain sells Fatme as a
slave to the King's gardener. (But see Book 7. St: 31.) [61] Cherasmin after arriving safely at Marseilles, proceeds to Paris, but
just as he comes in sight of that city, he begins to scruple
whether his delivery of the casket to the Emperor, instead of
Huon, will answer the purpose, and immediately concludes to
turn back, and go to Rome, where he expects to meet his knight.
Upon his arrival there he is disappointed, and after a fruitless
search for him all over the city and waiting for him six weeks,
he determines to set out as a pilgrim and seek for Huon all
over the world. In this pursuit he arrives after a length of time
at Tunis, where he finds Fatme. She informs him of what had
happened until the lovers had cast themselves into the sea.

---

[61] Adams here correctly calls attention to a slight contradiction in the narrative between Book IX, *stanza 3,* and Book VII, *stanza 31.* In the earlier account
of the ship's progress to Tunis there was no storm that wrecked the ship.

Cherasmin, still retaining a faint hope that Oberon had not totally abandoned his favorites, now resolves to wait at Tunis for the issue of events, and hires himself as a day laborer in the royal garden. In the meantime Huon and Amanda after spending three years upon the island, are anxiously desirous of returning again to the world. One evening their old friend Alfonso, before retiring to rest, has a pathetic conversation with them, upon his near prospect of immortality, and their future fortunes; in which he gives them comfort and advice. In the same night Titania, perceiving by the course of the stars, that some dreadful misfortune is about to befall Amanda, goes, and while she sleeps, steals away the child from her side, and delivers him into the custody of her three fairies with injunctions to keep him in her fairest bower. At the same time she plucks from the garland round her head three rose-buds, one of which she gives to each of the fairies, telling them that when they shall see these rose-buds turn to lilies, they may conclude that she and Oberon are reconciled, and must immediately hasten to her.

In the morning Huon and Amanda find Alfonso dead in his bed. Upon coming out of his cell they find the garden has totally disappeared, leaving nothing but rocks and precipices in its place. Amanda upon going to her own cell, now first observes that her child has disappeared. After a long and fruitless search after the child, in which the parents have strayed some distance from each other, Amanda is seized near the strand by the sailors of a Tunisian vessel, who had landed just then at the spot, to take in fresh water. Upon hearing her shrieks Huon flies to relieve her, but is overpowered by the number of the sailors, who carry him deep into the forest and tie him, bound hand and foot, to a tree, while others carry off Amanda to the ship; the captain of which proposes to sell her for a very high price to the king of Tunis.

Book 10

Titania hears the groans of Huon, while he remains bound to the tree, but being unable to relieve him, turns away from him, and finds upon the sand the magic ring, which Amanda in struggling with the rovers had lost from her finger. Titania with joy recognizes it as the nuptial ring which she had once given to Oberon and now considers it as a pledge of her speedy reconciliation with him.

The captain of the ship endeavors to comfort Amanda, promises her the most respectful treatment, which he enjoins upon his crew, and assures her that she shall soon be the happy queen of Tunis. In her extreme distress Amanda wishes for death.—Titania appears in a vision, assures her that her son and Huon are both living, and when she shall appear to her for the third time, the destinies will be accomplished, Oberon appeased, and both the fairy and the mortal couple happy by the means of each other. Meanwhile Oberon, sitting upon the point of a rock at the source of the Nile, looks toward the island where Huon is now, and is touched with pity at his condition. He calls one of his attendant Spirits, and charges him to go and invisibly loosen Huon from the tree, take him up and transport him before the door of Ibrahim, the gardener of the Seraglio at Tunis. The sylph performs his commission, and immediately after Huon is landed, Cherasmin comes out from the gardener's house, and the knight and squire with great joy recognize each other. Cherasmin relates his own adventures since they parted and informs the knight that Fatme is at Tunis and serves as a slave in the Seraglio. Huon immediately expresses great impatience to purchase, with some of the jewels in the casket still preserved by Cherasmin, a knightly armor with which he may set out to recover his Amanda. But on the same night he is seized with a violent fever, from which he recovers on the fourth day by the help of Cherasmin's knowledge of salutary herbs. Fatme now comes and tells him that Amanda must be near at hand, for that the night before a vessel had miraculously perished on the coast, from which only one very beautiful woman had been alike miraculously saved. She had been received with great kindness by the king and queen, who had seen the misfortune of the ship from the terrace, and was now lodged in the queen's summer palace. Huon now concludes that it would be impossible to recover Amanda from the king by force, and by the advice of Cherasmin determines to remain disguised, and work as a gardener under old Ibrahim, who is easily induced by an adequate reward to give out that Huon is a son of his own sister belonging to Damascus.

Book II

Huon urged by his impatience to discover his Amanda, passes three nights successively in the gardens of the Seraglio, where it was usual for the ladies to spend their evenings, but which by the laws of the country were inaccessible to every man, after sunset. On the fourth evening he is discovered by the queen Almansaris, a woman of exquisite beauty, who immediately falls in love with him, and instead of having him punished for his temerity, kindly dismisses him. His image pursues her so strongly, that she forms at length the project of introducing him by night into that part of the Harem over which she had the control,—a plan the execution of which was facilitated by the Sultan's having given himself up entirely to his passion for the beautiful new-comer, who was really Amanda, but had assumed the name of Zoradine. Titania had struck the vessel of the pirates with lightning, and had brought her safely to

the land. She returns the Sultan's love with great coldness. The
Queen perceives her husband's new passion, and is induced by
her own for the handsome gardener, to give it aid, and by her
proposal Amanda is lodged in a distant part of the Harem,
where the Sultan may without disturbance pay her every attention, and where she may not be troublesome by her presence
to the Queen herself. Fatme advises the knight, in order to discover Amanda, to send her a *Mahneh,* or emblematical bunch
of flowers, a customary mode of secret correspondence among
the Turks. Fatme undertakes to deliver this symbolical epistle,
in which Huon among other things had braided the initials
A and H. But by a mistake it comes to the hands of the Queen,
who mistakes the initials for those of Hassan (the name assumed by Huon) and Almansaris. She therefore sends word
to Huon to be ready at midnight, and he shall be introduced
into the Harem. This message, by the mistake of Fatme, Huon
supposes to come from his Amanda.

The design of Almansaris is favored by a great entertainment
which the King gives on the same night in honor of Zoradine,
—from attending which the Queen might excuse herself without suspicion and which would employ all the attendants by
whom she could fear to be detected. Huon is introduced at
midnight into the Harem, and sees with astonishment instead
of his Amanda, the Queen upon a throne in the greatest magnificence, surrounded by twelve beautiful nymphs. She uses
every art and displays every charm to enchant his senses and
captivate his affection; but all without success: he calls upon
the image of Amanda to protect him from the fascination, and
at length gives the Queen to understand that his love is irrev-
ocably fixed upon another woman. She then coldly orders him
to withdraw. Enraged at his disappointment he is with difficulty prevailed upon by the entreaties of Cherasmin and Fatme,
not to make his way by open force into the palace and rescue

his Amanda from the Sultan, but to wait three days longer, within which time they promise to devise some means of discovering the Lady.

Book 12

Almansaris contrives to draw Huon into the garden, one morning, while she is bathing, and there renews all her artifices of seduction upon him. He resists them all and attempts to fly. She stops him, by throwing her arms around him, with such a storm of tenderness, that he is again obliged to call upon the image of Amanda, and upon Oberon to protect his virtue and fidelity. In this situation they are discovered by Almanzor, and instantly the Queen accuses Huon of an attempt upon her honor. The Sultan orders Huon to be thrown chained into a dungeon and to be burned alive the next day. In the midst of the night Almansaris goes to Huon in his dungeon, apologizes from the necessity of the case for having accused him, and offers not only to deliver him from his prison, but by the means of her absolute control in the Harem, to set Huon himself upon the Sultan's throne, if he will return her love. Huon refuses her proposals, and all her threats and entreaties in support of them. She swears then that he shall perish, and leaves him with all the fury of disappointed passion.

Cherasmin and Fatme being informed of Huon's situation, strain every nerve for his relief. Fatme succeeds at length in finding out Amanda, and tells her of her lover's danger. Amanda flies instantly to the Sultan, and upon her knees implores of him a favor.—He swears to grant it. She tells him, it is to spare the life of the gardener Hassan, and this leads to the discovery that he was her beloved husband. The Sultan then offers, if she will consent to become his queen, not only to spare Hassan's life, but to heap him with royal presents and send him home to his own country. Amanda rejects the proposal with disdain. He entreats and conjures her on his knees to comply; but being still refused, swears that unless she yields, she shall perish in the flames with her lover. She prefers this alternative.

The next morning both lovers are tied to the stake, but at the instant when the pile is kindled, a clap of thunder is heard, the earth seems to quake, the flame expires, the cords which bound the lovers fall from them, and Huon perceives the ivory horn hanging round his neck. At the same instant Cherasmin, followed by Fatme, appears clad in black armor, with which he had resolved to attempt at all hazards the deliverance of his lord. Huon blows the horn gently and sets all Tunis to dancing. The coach drawn by swans, now appears hovering in the air, and descends at their feet. They ascend it and are transported to the Palace of Oberon, where they are magnificently received by him, no longer in the shape of a dwarf, but as a youth, blooming in immortal beauty. Together with Titania he gives the lovers a garland of myrtle, as the prize of their constancy, with the promise that as long as they keep it, they shall enjoy the happiness of the heart. The three fairy nymphs appear and upon their knees deliver the little Huonnet to Titania, who restores him to his mother. The lovers spend the night in the Palace, and in the morning find themselves transported, with their attendants, upon the banks of the Seine, in sight of Paris. They arrive on the third day of a Tournament given by Charlemagne, the prize of which was Huon's own lands. Huon appears without discovering himself, as a competitor, vanquishes the knight who had been victorious the former days, and then presents himself to the Emperor, with the proofs that he had accomplished his commands. Charles is now completely reconciled and only wishes that his Empire may never be without a prince so valiant as Huon.

OBERON

A POETICAL ROMANCE

IN TWELVE BOOKS

TRANSLATED FROM THE GERMAN OF WIELAND

BY

JOHN QUINCY ADAMS

(1799–1801)

JOHN QUINCY ADAMS

This portrait by John Singleton Copley, painted in London in
1795, is now in the Museum of Fine Arts, Boston, by whose
courtesy it is here reproduced.

OBERON

Book the first

1

Again the Hippogriff, ye Muses, bring
For one more journey to romantic land!
Round my unfettered breast, how sweetly cling
These lovely follies! whence this magic band
Around my temples? Who dissolves the dew
Which wraps the wonders of past time in shade?
Victorious, vanquished meet by turns my view
The goodly Christian sword, the glittering heathen blade.

2

In vain with rage the Sultan's eye-balls glare:
A grove of pointed lances threats in vain,
The horn of ivory breathes a tuneful air
And dancing fury seizes all the train.
See! round and round they reel, and gasp, and fall.
Huzza! Sir knight! thine is the lovely prize!
The streamer waves. Away to Rome! and call
The Holy Father's voice to bless your nuptial ties.

3

But oh beware! nor pluck before its time
The sweet, forbidden fruit of love's delight.
But two days patience, and the golden clime
Of fair Hesperia shall enchant your sight.
Save, save them, O thou faithful squire!—in vain—
Their madness hears not e'en the thunder roll!
Ah! luckless wights! what woes must you sustain
For one short joy! alas! can love so blind the soul?

4

To what a depth of sorrows are ye brought?
Who shall the little demi-god appease?
Lo! arm in arm upon the waves they float
Still blest at heart, that, swallowed by the seas
They sink embraced—alas! these hopes abuse!
On you the Fay still deeper woes will try.
His keen resentments all relief refuse;
E'en the last sad relief of misery, to die.

5

Lo! naked, helpless, on the desert shore
I see them roam, a cavern, strewed with sedge,
Dry, withered weed! upon the flinty floor
Their only bed, and from the leafless hedge
Their food, wild berries—in this dreadful plight
Their souls no distant chimney's smoke will cheer,
No friendly boat to aid them heave in sight.
Chance, Nature, Fortune, all combined their ruin swear.

6

And still th' avenger's wrath insatiate glows,
Unhallowed ardors yet the lovers bind
And while together they endure their woes,
The sharpest pangs of Fate remain behind.
But oh! while thunders roar, and lightnings glare,
Like brother vessels, from each other blown,
Hope's latest gleam expiring in despair,
Their miseries to crown, this, this remained alone.

7

Oh! thou, so late their Genius and their friend!
Must boundless vengeance love's offense pursue?
I see the tear adown his cheek descend;
When Oberon weeps, the worst must needs ensue.
But Muse, thy frantic visions, who inspires?
Where art thou soaring, upon eagle wings?
Thy hearer stares, what aileth thee, inquires,
And all thy sights to him are strange mysterious things.

8

Come, on this sopha, take a seat by me.
Say not, I see, what no one sees beside;
But plainly tell us how it came to be;
Behold thy hearers open mouthed and eyed
Prepared to take the fond deception well,
If thou, on thy part canst deceive with grace—
Well then! be silent all, and hear me tell
From first to last in course how every thing took place.

9

The knight with whose adventures our intent
Is, those who can be pleased to entertain,
Bound by his promise, long his course had bent
To Bagdad, by command of Charlemagne.
What he had promised to accomplish there
Was e'en in Charles's days a desperate game;
And what the bravest now would scarcely dare
For all the laurel wreaths that deck the fields of Fame.

10

"Son"—said the Holy Sire at Rome, whose feet
The knight, his nephew, deeply contrite, pressed
While with full tears, for soft repentance meet
Like a good Christian, he his sins confessed;
"Son, go in peace: Thy purpose shall succeed"
(Blessing and absolution as he gave)
"But, when to Joppe thou shalt come, take heed,
And visit, first of all, the Saviour's hallowed grave."

11

The knight now, reverend, kissed the holy shoe;
Obedience vowed, and humbly took his leave;
His work he hopes, however hard at view
He shall, by God's aid, and St. Kitt's achieve.
He lands at Joppe, takes a pilgrim's weeds,
Before the hallowed tomb adoring falls:
Then with fresh hope, and faith renewed, proceeds
Impatient to arrive before proud Bagdad's walls.

12

Still, as his rapid courser scours the plains
His inward thoughts are, shall I soon be there?
But many a rugged hill, to pass remains
And many a forest wild, and desert drear.
And still to aggravate his toilsome way,
His tongue of Oc, was Greek to all the land;
"Is this the road to Bagdad?" would he say
At every door he passed—but none could understand.

13

Once, through a wood, he rode, the live-long day
Amidst a storm of rain, compelled to take
Now at the right hand, now the left, his way
And often with his sword a pass to break.
At length a broader prospect to command
A hill that lay before him, he ascends,
And sees a boundless forest round him stand:
Alas! the more he looks, the wider it extends.

14

This natural view, was magic to his mind.
But, in this wild, how dismal was his plight,
Where at midday, he scarce his way could find
To be o'ertaken by the shades of night.
Sure, his distress no higher pitch can gain;
Through the thick boughs, no star-light can he see;
He leads his steed at random by the rein
And stumbles as he goes each step against a tree.

15

The raven-black, thick mantle of the sky,
An unknown wood, the new, tremendous sound
Of roaring lions from the mountains nigh,
Re-echoed by the rocks, whilst all around
A death-like silence reigns, the gloom to raise
And all at once, all terrors to assemble—
The man who never trembled in his days,
In such a state as this, would for the first time tremble.

16

Our knight himself, though never human eye
Yet saw him quake, now feels his sinews slack,
His arms and knees their wonted aid deny
And ice-cold shiverings thrill along his back.
But nothing can the dauntless mind withstand
Which first impelled him to his bold emprise.
Still with drawn sword, his courser by the hand
He goes until a path between the rocks he spies.

17

Anon, there seems to flash before his view
A small and glimmering ray of distant fire.
Into his cheeks the sight brings blood anew.
And now, between the doubt and strong desire
Here in these wilds a fellow man to find,
He follows on, attracted by the light,
Which as the path ascends or sinks inclined,
Now vanishes in gloom, now flashes to the sight.

18

Deep in the rocks at once there yawns a cave
Before whose jaws the crackling flames aspire;
From sable clefts, wild bushes o'er it wave
While its dark sides are colored with the fire,
Which from the foliage, takes a tinge of green.
In strangest forms, it flits before his sight.
And now, to contemplate the magic scene
He stops, with mingled sense of horror and delight.

19

Halt! from the cavern bursts a thundering sound,
And straight a man, of aspect wild appears:
His limbs in skins of mountain cats are bound,
Which coarsely stitched, about his loins he wears.
Down to his waist, in wavy ringlets hung
A beard of mingled colors, black and gray;
A cedar club across his shoulder swung,
Fit at a single blow the stoutest ox to slay.

20

Alike without a fear, beholds our knight
Man, club and beard all issue from the rock,
And straight begins his hardships to recite
In the sole tongue he knows, his speech of Oc.
"What hear I?" cries the tenant of the cell . . .
"Oh! lovely music of my native land!
Since on my ears thy charming accents fell
The sun full sixteen times his yearly course hath spanned.

21

"Welcome! brave Sir, and double welcome too
To Lebanon! though easily I see
That when this dragon's nest you travel through,
It is not truly for the love of me.
Come, take your ease, and of my humble food,
Deign to partake, its seasoning is good-will.
My wine ('tis from this rock) will thin your blood
And give your sparkling eyes a brighter lustre still."

22

The knight, with such an honest greeting charmed,
The hermit follows to his dark abode;
Lays helm and mail aside, and stands unarmed
Before his host, a seeming youthful God.
And as he now unclasps the helmet's band,
Down fall his ample curls of yellow hair.
The inmate of the woods can only stare,
And looks as were he touched by Alquif's magic wand.

23

"In every feature, forehead, mouth and eyes,
How like!" (cries he)— "Like whom?" returns the knight—
"Forgive! young man! one moment of surprise,
A sweet, yet bitter dream of past delight.
It cannot be! and yet these ringlets flow
Your shoulders down, with just his shape and air—
Fore God! I see himself, from top to toe
But for his broader breast, and your more yellow hair.

24

"My countryman, I judge you by your tongue.
Perhaps your likeness may be more than chance,
To my dear Lord, whom sixteen winters long
I mourned, thus distant from my native France.
Him to survive it was alas! my doom,
I closed his eyelids with this very hand,
With faithful tears, these eyes bedewed his tomb;
How strange to see him then, in you before me stand."

25

"Such are the sports of chance," returns the youth . . .
"It may be so," the fur-clad man proceeds,
"But brave young man, for you, in honest truth,
'Tis no vain whim, my sympathy that breeds.
Oh! grant Cherasmin's ardent wishes then,
And to him kindly deign your name declare."
"My name, good friend, is Huon of Guyenne,
The valiant Siegwin's son, and of his dukedom heir."

26

"Oh!" cries the old man, falling at his feet—
"My heart spoke true— Oh! welcome to these climes;
A thousand welcomes to this lone retreat!
Oh! Son of him with whom in better times
I weathered many a hard adventure out.
The brave, wise, pious lord, I so lament.
In childhood's earliest garb you skipped about,
When to the hallowed grave our votive course we bent.

27

"Who had then fancied we should meet again
Here in this cavern, after eighteen years.
Henceforth let no one give despair the rein,
When hope's last star in darkness disappears.
But oh! forgive me, Sir, this thoughtless prate!
The joy to see you spurs my tongue too fast—
But let me rather now hear you relate
By what strange storm you here on Lebanon were cast."

28

Sir Huon sits, the hermit at his side
Upon a bank of moss, before the fire;
While honey, with a draught the spring supplied
His weary limbs with strength renewed inspire.
He now begins his story to his host
Who ceases not upon him still to gaze
And some new likeness to the lord he lost
Delighted still perceives, the longer he surveys.

29

The knight relates in youth's diffusive vein,
How by his mother he to Court was brought;
(The proper place a Prince's youth to train)
And there in pious lore and knighthood taught.
How swift the lovely dream of childhood flew,
And when his chin the down of manhood took,
How, at Bordeaux with pomp and splendor due,
He from the palace stairs had been proclaimed as duke.

30

How thereupon with idle sports and plays,
With hunting, jousting, reveling and show,
Two years had passed away like single days,
Till Amory, his house's deadly foe,
Had blackened him to Charles with malice base,
Whose wrath before, 'gainst Huon's sire was warm—
And how the Emperor, with seeming grace
Had summoned him to court, due homage to perform.

31

How his said foe, of Hautefeuille, knavish lord,
Conspired with Charlot (Charles's second boy),
The vilest Prince all Europe could afford,
Who Huon's dukedom hankered to enjoy,
For him a pit to dig upon the road,
As he to court was traveling in state,
And how one morning ambushed in a wood
Near Montlery they lay to murder him in wait.

32

"My younger brother Gerard"—he proceeds,
"His hawk in hand, the journey with me made;
And none of us mistrusting evil deeds,
Far from our troop the sportive stripling strayed,
And loosed his falcon after him to race;
The rest of us meanwhile our way pursue,
Nor heed it much when in the frolic chase
The falcon and the lad both vanish from our view.

33

"At once our ears are shocked with piercing cries,
And as we hasten to the piteous sound,
Thrown from his horse, behold my brother lies
Weltring in blood and filth upon the ground.
Above him stood a man in steel complete—
'Twas Charlot, though unknown to all our band,
With lifted heel to tread him under feet—
The hawk, a dwarf the while, held fluttering on his hand.

34

" 'How could that boy, unarmed,' (with wrath inflamed
I called) 'give thee offense, uncourteous wretch!
That thus to treat him thou art not ashamed?
Stand off—nor at him more a finger stretch,
Else twixt thy ribs my sword shall find a sheath' . . .
'Ha! is it thou?' he cried . . . 'the man I seek,
On whom I long my glowing heart to breathe,
And in thy dastard blood my just revenge to wreak.

35

" 'Knowst thou not me? Then tremble when I tell
That Diederic, Duke of Ardennes was my sire;
Thy father Siegwin once contrived so well
By fraud (so burn his soul in endless fire!)
The tourney's prize from mine to bear away,
And then, due punishment to shun, he fled.
But I have sworn it; thou for him shalt pay—
Take that from me! and look, O villain! to thy head.'

36

"And speaking thus he rushed with pointed spear
At me, all unprepared for such a dance;
Yet, though aware of no such greeting here,
By great good fortune I repelled his lance.
Involving round the weaker arm my cloak,
I raised it quick, and warded off the blow;
Then, with the pommel of my sword, a stroke
On his right temple struck, which laid the traitor low.

37

"He fell, in one word, never more to stand;
Now numerous horsemen midst the woods appear;
Yet to avenge their dead, the coward band
Towards' us held it useless to draw near.
Distant, while Gerard's wounds we bound, they stayed
And quiet till we vanished from their sight;
Upon a steed the bleeding corpse then laid
And at the palace doors they hastened to alight.

38

"Unweeting how this scene would Charles provoke
Our journey we resumed—to Paris came.
A hoary sage, my uncle, for me spoke,
As abbot of St. Denys known to fame.
The emperor Charles received us, full of grace;
All seemed in train my warmest wish to sate,
When at the banquet as we just took place
Stopped Hautefeuille with the corpse before the palace gate.

39

"Twelve pages bring it muffled in black crape
Up the high steps—all who behold are dumb
With wonder. . . . To the hall their course they shape:
The doors fly open, and twelve spectres come,
Into the middle of the hall who bear
A bier, o'er which a bloody pall is spread.
Old Charles turns pale; up stands on end our hair,
And I, methought a bolt of thunder struck me dead.

40

"Now Amory comes, lifts up the bloody fold,
And cries to Charles: 'Behold thy darling slain!—
And here the butcher of our peace behold,
By whom this wound both thou and France sustain.
To aid thy son, I came alas! too late—
He fell the victim of an ambushed fight,
From base assassin hands he met his fate;
Not by a knightly sword, as fits a valiant knight.'

41

"The boy was still the father's flesh and blood,
Though long his plague by daily mischiefs done.
With horror motionless at first he stood
Then cried in agony: 'My son! my son!'
And fell upon the body in despair.
The father's anguish stabbed me to the heart.
I then had shed my dearest blood, I swear,
The breath of life again to Charlot to impart.

42

" 'Hear! Sir,' I cried—'my will was not to blame:
He said the Duke of Ardennes was his sire,
And what he did, my anger to inflame,
By Heaven! the meekness of a Saint would fire.
He struck that youth, who never did him harm,
My father's honor with foul slander stained;
Me unawares attacked with murderous arm—
I fain would see the man, who could have cool remained.'

43

" 'Ha! villain!'—glaring with a lion's rage
Cried Charles, as from the corpse he sprung aside
And snatched a shining weapon from a page,
Which in my blood his fury would have dyed,
Had not the princes held him, standing by.
The knights are roused, an hundred falchions start,
And while they flash their lightnings from on high,
The thirst for murder seem to kindle in each heart.

44

"The palace thunders with tumultuous sounds;
The pavement trembles, the old windows clatter;
With Murder! Treason! every tongue resounds:
Amidst us a new Babel seems to chatter;
We pant, we clash, in act to strike we stand:
The abbot whom his holy garb defends
Alone from outrage, with uplifted hand
Against our swords at last his scapular extends.

45

" 'Revere in me the Holy Sire,' he cries;
'Whose son I am— In God's name Peace! desist!'
He spoke the words with such a voice and eyes
As not the fiercest heathen could resist.
The waves of uproar instantly subside;
Each heart no longer blood and slaughter breathes,
Each warrior's angry face grows calm, while slide
Dagger and falchion back in silence to their sheathes.

46

"The abbot now to Charles the whole affair
Relates, and from his lips persuasion falls;
But what to me could that avail? while there
Lies the son's corse, and vengeance loudly calls.
'See!' cries the Sire—'pronounce for me, and say,
On my son's murderer what should be decreed.
Yes! ghost incensed, his blood thy thirst shall lay!
Yes! let the traitor die, and hungry ravens feed.'

47

"With swelling breast, I here exclaimed aloud,
'I am no murderer—in his proper case
No judge is just—but my accuser proud,
Is, mighty Prince, himself a traitor base.
My life I stake, his perjured heart to bare,
And prove that he a liar was and is,
And will be, while his breath infects the air:
This mischief he contrived: this fatal work is his.

48

" 'No less than he, of princely birth am I,
A peer of France, and here my right demand;
'Tis what the Emperor cannot deny.
There on the ground my gauntlet braves his hand,
Let him dare raise it, and the voice of God
Shall doom, of us two, which from guilt is free,
And which in hell shall burn for Charlot's blood:
Right makes my bosom bold; his thunder frights not me.'

49

"Th' assembled princes of the empire held
My sentence as a wrong, alike to all;
Like waves before the distant tempest swelled,
They murmur, they entreat, for right they call.
In vain—for fixing on the corse his eyes
No prayers can move the hapless father's breast;
Though Amory a foe like me despise,
And his entreaties joins, in concert with the rest.

50

" 'Let me chastise the culprit,' he exclaimed.
'What risk I, Sire, with right and duty's shield.'
'Ha!' loud I cried, with shame and wrath inflamed,
'Vain scorner, tremble! for howe'er concealed,
Not always slumbers Heaven's avenging fire.'—
'My sword shall heap it, murderer, on thy crest'—
Quoth he. My warmth but kindles Charles's ire
Till to his guards he gives to seize me the behest.

51

"At the rash charge, of all the maddening knights
Once more the falchions glitter, to maintain
In my defense their violated rights—
'Guards seize him!' cries imperial Charles again,
But round me sees of knights a rampart strong
With outward pointed swords; the holy man
Meanwhile half smothered in the thickening throng
Now menaces in vain, with interdict and ban.

52

"Lo! on a hair hangs France's fortune now.
Of Charles, his sages on their knees implore
The right I claim, of knighthood to allow,
But move him less, as they entreat the more.
At length, Duke Nayms, who often in his life,
His wits to Charles in time of need had lent,
First whispers him, then turns, to end the strife,
And for the combat gives the king's consent."

53

Sir Huon's narrative proceeds to show
How, instant at this word, the uproar fell;
How all the knights who circled him withdrew,
And Charles, with rancor though his heart still swell,
With rage half-stifled and with brows in shade,
Fixed for the fight, the eighth succeeding day;
How both the knights high preparation made,
And how securely proud, his foe expects the fray.

54

Though in his breast a fierce accuser smite
At which he felt his haughty courage quiver,
Yet, conscious of an iron arm in fight
Wont many a grove of spears before to shiver,
In a foe's presence knew not he dismay,
And deadly fight his dearest joys supplied.
Yet naught availed him in this bloody fray,
All his gigantic strength or all his towering pride.

55

"The day came on— In crowds the people pressed;
With all whose love, I freely say it, cheered
My shield of silver gleaming on my breast
Within the lists of battle I appeared.
Already there my bold accuser stood—
Charles from a balcony the fight surveyed,
And seemed to thirst with Hautefeuille for my blood,
As with his peers around in royal state he laid.

56

"The sun is shared— The judges take their seat—
To hear the clarion Hautefeuille seems on fire—
Now, now, it calls, and with impetuous heat
We rush together with a shock so dire
That both our coursers sink beneath the crash
Upon the knee: we scarce the saddle keep.
And from our stirrups, in a lightning's flash,   [leap.
We spring, while from their sheaths our glittering falchions

57

"No picture of the fight from me demand—
As in experience, so in rage and might,
Superior plainly was my rival's hand—
But my protection was my conscious right,
Which strung my sinews equal to my will.
Long, long in doubt the victory remained."
Th' accuser's blood gushed out, in many a rill,
While Huon still unhurt, fresh cheer and heart retained.

58

When Amory beholds the purple tide
His corselet stain, with rage renewed he glows;
And like a storm which ruins far and wide
On Huon thunders down his deadly blows.
Stroke flashes upon stroke until at length
My youthful knight himself can scarce defend.
Before an arm, the match of Roland's strength,
He after combat long begins at last to bend.

59

Of triumph sure, already Hautefeuille stands,
And with one blow to end the mortal fray,
Now grasps his mighty sword with both his hands,
But from the stroke Sir Huon slips away.
Then, ere the foe restores his balance, brings
Just where the helmet buckles to its band,
A gash, in Hautefeuille's tingling ears that rings,
While loosened from the sword, down drops his nerveless hand.

60

The scorner sinks at his opponent's feet;
Upon him Huon springs, with pointed steel;
"If yet the thought of life," he cries, "be sweet,
Discharge thy conscience, and thy guilt reveal.
Confess upon the spot my cause was right"—
"Bandit!" cries Amory with accent fell;
(For one last blow collecting all his might)
"Bandit! take this," he cries, "and follow me to hell."

61

But happily, aimed upwards from the ground,
The thrust weak, trembling hands alone impel.
Sir Huon, quickly turning shunned the wound.
The weapon barely grazed his arm and fell.
Our youthful knight forgets while vengeance fires,
That to make known while Amory survives,
To Charles, the truth, he still some breath requires,
And raging down his throat the thirsty falchion drives.

62

The felon pours in waves of crimson flood
His hideous soul. The conqueror stands clear;
Cleansed to all eyes in his accuser's blood—
The herald sounds it forth to every ear.
A general shout of joy the welkin rends—
Now all the knights haste up the blood to stay,
Which down the edge of Huon's mail descends,
Then to the Emperor attend the victor's way.

63

"Yet Charles" (the youthful hero thus goes on
His story to the hermit to relate)
"His rancor holding cried: 'And can my son
By this new murder be redeemed from fate?
What proof of innocence from this can flow?
The charge of Hautefeuille unretracted stands:
In endless banishment then let him go
And forfeit to the crown his chattels and his lands.'

64

"Harsh was the doom; the dooming voice severe,
But to resist it, what alas! could we?
Entreaties were our only resource here;
At Charles's feet the knights and peers, with me
All kneeling round his throne but bruise our knees
And finally to move his heart despair;
Till silence long he breaks with words like these:
'Well, be it, peers and knights, according to your prayer.'

65

"Towards' the footsteps of the throne he bends
And says: 'My gracious pardon thus I seal,'
(While down to me, the sceptre he extends)
'But, this condition nothing can repeal.
Far from our realms thy banished foot must roam:
Our high behest in every part fulfill;
Death, certain death awaits thee here at home
While unperformed remains one tittle of our will.

66

" 'Go hence to Babylon, and at the hour
When at a feast the Caliph thou shalt find
With all his emirs, backed by all his power,
Strike off the man's head at his left reclined;
Then, while his blood the table o'er shall flow,
Up to the heiress at the Sultan's side
In sight of all with chaste assurance go,
And with a threefold kiss, salute her as thy bride.

67

" 'And should the Caliph no such scene expect
And thy presumption with surprise behold,
Then as the customs of the East direct
Before the footstool to his chair of gold,
With lowly reverence falling prostrate down:
Four teeth request him from his jaws to spare,
A gift for me, our amity to crown,
And from his hoary beard, one handful of the hair.

68

" 'Go, I repeat it, and the word is fate;
Before thou shalt our whole command fulfill,
Undoubted death on thy return shall wait—
Meanwhile towards' thee, gracious is our will.'
He spoke and ceased—but all attempt were vain
To paint the deep surprise in every eye,
A will thus gracious could (the thing was plain)
To me no better mean, than sentence me to die.

69

"Through the vast hall, low hollow murmurs run;
'Now, by St. George,' (exclaims one valiant peer,
Who many a deed of glory bold had done
In Lancelot's and Tristan's rough career)
'I speak for one—my trembling fits are few;
My head, as soon as any man I'll stake;
But, what the Emperor bids Huon do,
Not brave Sir Gawin's self had dared to undertake.'

70

"Why waste more words? . . . too clearly this displayed
That Charles intended for my life a snare;
But, be it, that fool-hardy I was made
By stubborn pride, foreboding or despair,
Advancing up, I said upon the spot:
'Sir! your commands cannot my heart appal;
I am a Frank; impossible or not
I undertake the charge, be witness for me, all.'

71

"Hence, good Cherasmin, I here meet thy view;
Resolved for Babylon to speed my way;
Wilt thou the shortest passage thither show
Out of these mountains?— Be my thanks thy pay.
Else I myself shall trace it as I can"—
"My dearest Lord!" the tenant of the cave
Cried, (down his cheeks while tears of kindness ran),
"To life you call me back once more as from the grave.

72

"Here . . . take a sacred pledge of what I swear. . . .
An old, indeed, yet not a nerveless hand:
That I with you, the dearest son and heir
Of my good lord, in life and death will stand.
The work which to accomplish you are sent
Is hard, yet by it glory you may gain.
Your guide am I, whatever the event,
And dauntless my last drop of blood with you will drain."

73

Touched by this pattern of unrivaled truth,
Upon his neck the grateful hero falls,
Then on the straw lay down— The princely youth
Sleeps as on down, till morning twilight calls.
At the first dawn, with cheerful looks he wakes,
And soon, to buckle on his armor rose;
Cherasmin on his back the wallet takes,
And with his club in hand full cheerly onward goes.

OBERON

Book the second

1

Thus our brave pair, fresh, frolicsome and gay,
As sun-shine or as star-light comes, by turns,
Three days down Lebanon pursue their way,
And, o'er their heads, when noon-tide radiance burns
Amid high grass, which aged cedars shade
They rest. . . . Meanwhile the gentle tribes of air
Their throats attune, in varied plumes arrayed,
And of the dinner snatch, with confidence a share.

2

On the fourth morn, of horsemen a small group
At no great distance, on a hill appear.
"That," says Cherasmin, "is an Arab troop,
And if my judgment I may venture here,
'Twere best, if possible their way to shun;
Too well the ruffian race is known to me"—
"Heyday! what thinkest thou?" said Siegwin's son.
"Where didst thou ever hear of Franks, my friend, that flee?"

3

The sun-beams which the hero's helm refracts
Carbuncles in their eyes, and rubies flash,
And magnet-like the desert's sons attracts.
Down, down they storm; their bows and arrows clash,
And naked falchions in their hands they shake.
One man on foot, one mounted on a steed,
An object scarcely for attack could make,
They deemed, but found anon, their error great indeed.

4

Now sheltered by his shield, among them springs
The knight, and him who seems the troop to lead
Strikes with his spear, and from his courser flings—
His nose and mouth in copious torrents bleed.
Straight all rush on, to venge their captain's fall
Upon his conqueror, with cut and thrust;
The squire defends his back against them all
And at a blow one more lays sprawling in the dust.

5

The hero labors with an hand so stout,
The dust a second and a third soon kissed;
Here flies a head, at each returning bout
And there an arm, the falchion yet in fist.
With no less warmth Cherasmin deals his blows,
And brandishes his weighty club on high.
To Mahound, cursing, howl their heathen foes,
And all who yet have strength, in all directions fly.

6

The field a heap of limbs and corses strews
Of man and horse in ghastly mixture tossed;
Sir Huon waits but till his friend can choose
The fairest steed which had his rider lost,
And from the spoils, a sword, as lawful prize;
Then spurs his courser with an eagle's flight,
Tŏwards′ the valleys, which before their eyes
Spread at the mountain's foot, and stretch beyond their sight.

7

A land, it seemed, by culture highly tilled,
With streamlets intersected through and through.
Flowers clad the meadows, sheep the pastures filled
And peaceful huts, mid palm-trees rose to view,
Where dwelt a race, who at their daily task
Cheerful, though poor, with riches deem them blest;
And to their rustic meal the pilgrim ask
When in the cooling shade from hungry toil they rest.

8

Here, when the sun too fiercely pours his rays,
Fresh milk and bread supplies a shepherd lass;
Half terrified, askance the good folks gaze
At the strange iron man upon the grass.
But soon his tone to win their hearts began,
And children venturing, sported with his hairs.
Charmed with their trustful play, the valiant man
With them become a child, their lovely pastime shares.

9

How happy! thinks he, in these huts to dwell!
Vain wish! . . . his fortune calls him far away.
Parting at eve, he feels his bosom swell
And for the good folks' friendly meal to pay
Throws in the woman's lap a purse of gold. . . .
E'en what it was, knew not those happy men,
Their hospitable fare who gave, not sold,
And so the gentlefolks must take it back again.

10

Now on they fare, till dawning day returns,
When lo! before them stands a tangled wood.
"Friend!" says the knight, "like fire my bosom burns,
Till I to Charles shall make my promise good.
Four years it seems since I began the ride;
Yet was thy vow, the nearest way to show!"—
"'Tis through this forest," the old man replied.
"But that way by no means should I advise to go.

11

"Its fame is bad; at least, no man, they say,
Who ventured in there, ever yet came out.
Ay! smile Sir! but a spiteful little fay
Keeps house, believe me, somewhere hereabout.
It teems in there with foxes, deer and roes
Who formerly were men as much as we;
And ere tomorrow comes, Heaven only knows
What ugly beast of prey, both you and I may be."

12

"If through this forest leads, direct, the way
To Babylon, I fear not," Huon said.
"Sir! dearest Sir! upon my knees I pray,
God knows, for your sake more than mine I dread.
Believe my words securely, from this ghost
'Tis vain to fly, against him vain to strive,
But five or six days later at the most,
Alas! e'en then too soon, at Bagdad you'll arrive."

13

"Fearst thou?" said Huon; "then remain thou here;
But nothing my resolve to go can shake."
"No!" cried Cherasmin—"death is bitter cheer,
Yet none but villains can their lords forsake.
Are you resolved? without delay I go—
God and the Holy Virgin lend us aid!"
"Come then!" said Huon riding, pale as snow
Into the wood. The squire pursues him all dismayed.

14

Scarce through the glimmering twilight had the knight
Proceeded on two hundred paces more,
When racing at the left hand and the right,
A flock of deer and roes tŏwards' him bore.
With warning looks they seemed, and eyes in tears
(In the dim light, so thinks the squire to see),
Bent, in compassion to alarm their fears,
As would they say: "Oh! flee! O hapless mortals, flee!"

15

"Observe," he whispers, "how it stands, I pray:
Another time, Sir, will you credit me?
Befalls it not exactly as I say?
These pitying beasts who snuff at us you see
Are men, Sir, men, and if you further go
You'll have the goblin at your heels anon:
Be not so stubborn then, and to your woe,
In friendly counsel's spite, thus rashly headlong run."

16

"What? when my course direct to Bagdad lies
To ask the Caliph for his teeth and beard,"
Returns the hero, "thou canst still surmise
That I by doubtful dangers may be feared?
Where, where are all thy senses flown, old lad?
Who knows? perhaps the goblin means me well.
At least these creatures threaten nothing bad;
See! in a moment I the herd entire dispel."

17

Thus speaking, up to them he spurs his steed;
Dispersing straight they all gave way like air.
And now, Sir Huon and his guide proceed
Long undisturbed, and silent onward fare.
The day was sunk and night to all around,
In sable stole, her dose of poppies gave.
In slumber's ponderous fetters all was bound,
And through the forest reigned the stillness of the grave.

18

At last the squire no longer can forbear:
"Sir! you my weakness will forgive, I trust,
Should I disturb your castles in the air—
For, in the dark, I own it, talk I must,
Such is my way from childhood's earliest prime.
'Tis stillness here, as if great Pan were dead;
But for our horses' hoofs from time to time
A man I think might hear a mole-warp scrape its bed.

19

"Afraid, you think me—yet without a boast
(Mere gifts, our talents are, Sir, after all)—
Where clatter swords, in battle or at joust,
Yes, many a living witness I might call,
Man against man, nay, only two or three
To five or six, whether for cut or thrust,
In case of need, Cherasmin there would be,
There, in his proper bones, a man may put some trust.

20

"If made, in short, of flesh and blood my foe,
I am his man—but freely I allow—
In a church-yard, at dead of night to go
Starts up my hat a little from my brow.
Suppose some ghost who comes across of me
Should find my face not wholly to his taste;
What can my sword and arm do, *Ventregris!*
While blows invisible rain down upon my waist.

21

"Suppose (and such examples are at hand)
Smooth from the body, I shave off the head;
While on the ground it rolls, already stand
Upon the stump two new ones in its stead.
Nay, oft the trunk itself is known to race
After the head, and put it on anew
Just like a hat, which stormy winds displace,
Now, what is mortal man with such a thing to do?

22

"Indeed no sooner crows the cock, you know,
Than every midnight phantom, ghost or fay,
Who in the darkness flits, dispersed must go,
As if a tempest swept them all away.
But he who dwells within the forest here,
Is truly, Sir, another sort of sprite;
Like one of us eats, drinks, makes merry cheer,
Holds open court and walks in day's meridian light."

23

"My ardent curiosity to swell,
Friend," said the hero, "thou hast done thy best;
Of ghosts they talk so much, such lies they tell,
We laymen know not where our faith to rest.
Once came a man deep studied to our court
Who loudly swore 'twas idle fancy all;
Of phantom-seers he made his constant sport:
A Manichean him, our chaplain wont to call.

24

"Oft o'er a flask of wine would they debate,
But when their liquor mounted to the head,
They mingled so much Latin with their prate
I scarce could understand a word they said.
Methought then—learned as your talk may be,
Nothing but what ourselves have tried we know;
Would that some ghost were kind enough to me,
To tell me in good truth how matters stand below."

25

Conversing thus, our wandering couple found
Themselves enclosed within a park ere long,
Through which so many crossing by-paths wound
'Twas scarcely possible to shun the wrong.
The broad-faced moon, now risen over head,
While for an issue they both strained their sight
A darkling glimmer all around them shed
Their vision to confuse with false, delusive light.

26

"Sir!" said the squire, "they have it here in view,
Us in a mazy labyrinth to wind—
Our noses, at all hazards to pursue
Is our sole chance a passage hence to find."
This plain and simple counsel (wiser far
Than seems to many a deep, sagacious wight),
Soon brings our pious ramblers to a star,
Where all the forest roads in central point unite.

27

And distant, in the hedge before them seems
A palace, as of evening twilight wove,
To rise in air, and shed around its beams.
In Huon's bosom joy and horror strove:
Doubtful if dreaming or with wakeful eye,
Rooted he stands and stares with speechless awe;
When lo! the golden gates wide open fly,
And issuing from them rolls a car which leopards draw.

28

And fair as on the lap of beauty's queen
The god of love, a boy exalted high,
Who held the silver chariot's reins was seen.
"See there!" aghast, the squire began to cry
And by the bridle seized Sir Huon's horse.
"Fly! we are lost! see there the dwarf! oh! see!"
"How fair!" exclaimed the knight— "So much the worse.
Fly, dearest Sir! away! though ten times fairer he.

29

"Away! or else of us there is an end!"—
Fruitless are all the struggles of the knight;
Behind him still Cherasmin drags his friend,
Still urging onward his most rapid flight.
Nor ceases over forest, wild, and brake,
O'er stock and stone, o'er hedge and ditch to drive,
Until their way they from the thicket make
And down upon the plain both safe at last arrive.

30

A storm ensues, rain pours and lightnings flash,
A fearful total night the moon conceals,
Winds howl around; the rattling thunder's crash
Seems the whole wood to shiver as it peals.
The elements in short have burst their chains,
Their fierce contending fury spurns all bounds.
Yet from amidst the storm, in gentle strains
The Spirit's lovely voice from time to time resounds.

31

"Why dost thou fly me? come, in me confide—
Thou fly'st thy bliss!—turn back—stay, Huon—stay"—
"You're lost, Sir, if you do," Cherasmin cried;
"Away! the fingers in your ears!—away!
Nor speak a word! He means you nothing good."
And now, through thick and thin they rush again.
Drenched by the beating rain's impetuous flood,
Until a cloister's walls their rapid race restrain.

32

A new adventure here the travelers found:
St. Agatha's high festival it proved,
The blest protectress of this virgin-pound.
Now, scarcely at a musket shot removed
Of plump, high-pampered youths a convent stood,
Who to St. Antony their vows had paid,
And both the troops in friendly neighborhood
To celebrate that eve a joint procession made.

33

Just to the gate returned, whence issuing first
They waddled two by two in fair array;
A remnant of the storm upon them burst,
The mad-cap winds with cross and banners play,
Through the veils' folds the streaming rains pervade.
Vain all attempt decorum to maintain.
A strange, tumultuous, comic scene displayed
All running to and fro, the motley mingled train.

34

Here wades, with coats above her knees, a nun
Amid the mire; there, down a friar slips;
And as a virgin group before him run,
Upon them staggering, catches by the hips
The lady-abbess, from the fall to guard.
Yet when the storm had blown its fury o'er,
Wet, breathless, spattered, in the convent yard,
The sisters and the monks, assembled all once more.

35

All was confusion here, and tumult loud:
When lo! Cherasmin dashes through the gate,
And rushes full amid the cloistered crowd,
Safe as in Heaven itself he deems his state,
Once in the pale of consecrated ground.
Him Huon follows, and anon prepares
Excuse to make, when lightning flashes round,
And straight amid them all, the beauteous dwarf appears.

36

Instant, the clouds are from the sky withdrawn
And all again is dry, serene and bland.
Fair as a new-born cherub in the dawn
He stands and leans upon a lily wand,
While from his neck an ivory horn descends.
Yet in each breast, mysterious horrors thrill:
Fair as he is—for o'er his brows impends
A cloud of wrath severe, collecting stern and still.

37

The horn applying to his lips, he blows
Melodious tones, and straight the giddy squire
With strange, resistless lust for dancing glows—
He grasps a toothless nun, with keen desire
Alike expiring, rigadoons to make.
Like two young goats they caper, prance and bound
So swift, that all who see, with laughter shake,
While petticoat and veil wave wide in air around.

38

Soon a like frenzy spreads among them all—
See! by the hand each monk a sister strain,
And now begins between the troops a ball;
Not soon will such a ball be seen again.
No modesty restrains the cloistered bands,
No dance of fauns could whirl about more light.
Alone, upon his feet, Sir Huon stands,
Their capers wild beholds, and laughs with all his might.

39

The lovely dwarf draws near, with earnest ken,
And in the language of the knight complains:
"Why dost thou fly me, Huon of Guyenne?
What?—Silent still?—by God in Heaven who reigns,
Speak! Answer me!"— At once in Huon's mind
Calm confidence returned— "Declare," said he,
"With me, thy will"— "Fear naught," the boy rejoined,
"The man who dreads not light, a brother finds in me.

40

"From thy first childhood I have loved thee still,
Nor to a son of Adam e'er did show
Such favors as to thee intends my will:
Thy heart is pure, thy paths no windings know,
Thy sense of duty, flesh nor blood can shake.
Thyself thou trustest; proof thy valor stands.
No, never can my kindness thee forsake—
Polluted souls alone my power to punish brands.

41

"Were they not hypocrites, these cloistered drones,
Did not the guilty souls of all the band
Belie their looks demure and canting tones,
Spite of the horn they firm like thee would stand;
Cherasmin too, whose honest eye pleads strong,
Yet for his hasty tongue's offense must prance.
No will of theirs impels them thus along:
Poor things! they cannot choose; their sentence is, to dance."

42

Again is seen the whirlwind to begin,
The dancing fauns more rapidly revolve;
So high they caper, and so swiftly spin
They in their heat, like snow in wind dissolve.
Each panting heart beats up into the throat—
The knight could bear the painful scene no more;
All this young blood compassion claimed, he thought,
And for them straight began forgiveness to implore.

43

The lovely dwarf extending forth his hand,
To break the spell his lily sceptre waves;
St. Antony's fat wards astonished stand
And, pale, as were they rising from their graves,
Each nun her petticoat and veil redressed,
And what was else disordered by the shake;
The squire alone, too old for such a jest
Sinks forceless on the ground, and thinks his heart will break.

44

"Ah! gracious Sir!" with gasping voice he said,
"Did I not tell . . ." "Cherasmin!" quoth the fay,
"I know thy spirit, but sometimes thy head
Runs with thy valiant heart, my friend, away.
Why didst thou rashly rail at me on trust?
Fie! child in judgment, with a beard so gray!
With patience take this slight rebuke, as just.
You—for your sisters' sins and for your own, go pay."

45

At this, the cloistered troop, ashamed, withdrew,
And thus the dwarf pursued, with accents kind:
"What?—on thy brow still dark suspicion's hue?
—Yet shall thy honest heart forgiveness find.
Come nearer, good old toper, trust in me,
Thy spirits are exhausted—take this cup,
With soul from fear of all deception free,
And at a single draught, drink all its contents up."

46

The fairy king thus speaking, to his hand
A goblet, turned of finest gold supplies.
Cherasmin, on his legs who scarce can stand
Beholds it empty, with no small surprise.
"What!" cries the dwarf; "old lad, distrustful still?
Fresh! to the mouth; discard all doubt, and drink!"
The good old man obeys with half a will,
And sees the goblet blush with Langon to the brink.

47

And having drained the liquor, as he quaffed
There seemed through all his veins to shoot along
New life and spirits from the genial draught.
He feels his sinews unimpaired and strong
As in his choicest days of youthful heat
With Siegwin when he sought the holy lands.
Awe-struck he falls before the fairy's feet:
"Now like a mountain firm my faith," exclaims he, "stands!"

48

Then to the knight thus speaks with looks intent
The fairy king: "Full well is known to me,
The charge on which to Bagdad thou art sent.
Thou seest the tempest Charles prepared for thee.
His rancor, sure, intends thy blood to shed,
But count on my assistance to achieve
The deed thy Faith to promise did not dread.
Here, Huon, from my hand, this ivory horn receive.

49

"Pour down its spiral throat with gentle breath
A soft sweet note, and though with sword and lance
Ten thousand men should menace instant death,
Straight as they hear, shall they begin to dance,
And dancing spin with ceaseless whirl around,
As here thou seest, till on the ground they fall—
But fill its coiling womb with deeper sound
And I the blast will hear, and answer to the call.

50

"Though many thousand miles remote I were,
Thou should'st behold me fly to aid thee still;
But this, for times of urgent pressure spare.—
This goblet take too, which with wine will fill
When to a virtuous mortal's lips applied—
Its nectar flows from springs that never drain:
But should its power by knavish hands be tried,
Those hands it straight will scorch, and empty still remain."

51

With thanks Sir Huon takes the wondrous pledge
Of his new patron's favor from his hands;
And seeing now the purple orient edge
Of heaven all burnished o'er with gold, demands
Anxious, to Babylon the shortest way.
"Go"—said the fairy, pointing to the place,
"And never, never may I see the day
When Huon's noble heart a weakness shall disgrace.

52

"Not that I aught distrust thy strength of mind;
But oh! a child of Adam's race thou art,
Frail-tempered clay, and to the future blind!
Short joys too oft are sources of long smart.
My warning let not thy remembrance lose;
Here, touch this lily sceptre I extend."—
Thus as the Spirit speaks, Sir Huon views
From his blue beaming eyes, two crystal pearls descend.

53

And as he truth and fealty would swear,
The forest fairy vanished from his sight,
And lilies, where he stood perfume the air—
Astonished, speechless, stands the youthful knight
And rubs his eyes and brows like one who wakes
From a fair dream, intent to ascertain
If that in which such deep delight he takes
Be true, substantial bliss, or nightly vision vain.

54

Doubts had he formed, to clear his scruples up,
Hung o'er his shoulders by a golden chain
The horn sufficed. But most of all the cup
Cherasmin, now restored to youth again,
Deems the first gem of all the fairy wealth.
"Come, Sir!" the stirrup holding,—"come," he cries,
"Once more the honest little goblin's health!
His wine, upon my faith, is liquor for the skies."

55

Now for the future journey fresh and light,
O'er hill and dale the live-long day they went,
As knights were wont, while of the scanty night
A small part sheltered under trees they spent.
Four days without event of note they ride,
Our knight at Bagdad all the while, in mind,
His trusty friend still happy at his side
That Siegwin's son it is, with whom his fates are joined.

Book the third

1

The fifth, as through the mountain stole their way,
Pitched in a narrow vale, at once they found
A number of rich tents, in fair array
And more than twenty knights upon the ground,
Who under cooling shade of palms appear
In groups reposing after long carouse,
While on low branches hung each helm and spear
And in the lofty grass their steeds at freedom browze.

2

Scarce did the knightly company perceive
Our pair of travelers yet upon the hill,
When starting up, their noon-tide rest they leave,
And gathering, full of speed, the valley fill,
As had they heard the blast for battle blow.
At once confusion reigns o'er all the vale,
They fly to arms, they hurry to and fro;
The squires prepare the steeds, themselves the knights enmail.

3

"Come," said our knight, "Cherasmin, let us see
What all these warriors in disquiet throws,
Who but this moment calmly seemed to be
Enjoying full-fed afternoon repose."
"Ourselves must be the cause," Cherasmin cried;
"Be guarded, in half-moon they come displayed."
"See here *my* guard from harm," the knight replied,
And coolly from its sheath drew forth his trusty blade.

4

Now from the circle steps in armor bright
A handsome youth, salutes them both with grace,
And hearing craves— "With your good leave, Sir knight,
Whoe'er hath shown his person in this place,
Of knightly rank, within this half a year
Hath found himself arrested on his way:
Take then your choice, with me to break a spear,
Or instantly perform whatever we shall say."

5

"What's that?" said Huon with a modest air.
"Near this," quoth he, "the Giant Angulaffer
Of a strong castle makes his wonted lair,
Worse for fair women raging than a Caffer;
A fiend-like foe to every Christian soul,
And what is worse, from hack or thrust secure;
Safe by a ring which from a dwarf he stole,
The same, Sirs, through whose park you traveled on this tour.

6

"Sir, of Mount Lebanon I am a prince,
And vowed to serve the fairest of the fair,
Whom ere to crown my truth I could convince,
Three years did I the meed of love forbear.
And as her girdle to unbind I sought
At last, when I had gained a bridegroom's right,
In popped the wolf, her arm in fury caught
And with my tender lamb, packed off before my sight.

7

"Near seven long months, my zeal, for her relief
With ceaseless vigilance its utmost tries;
And still that tower, her prison and my grief,
At once *my* entrance, *her* retreat denies.
Through all this interval, of love's delight
This single fruit hath been enjoyed by me:
Perched on a tree, whole days to stretch my sight
And from afar the walls, the hated walls to see.

8

"I sometimes fancied I beheld her stand
Before the window with disheveled hair,
And lifting up tŏwards' the skies her hand
As if their pity to implore in prayer.
It stabbed me to the heart, and deep despair
Compelled me from that day, by utmost need
To do, what you and all these warriors share;
No knightly guest, in short, unfought can hence proceed.

9

"Me to disseat and from my saddle throw
Should you succeed, as none succeeded yet,
Where you shall list thenceforward you may go,
Without resistance. Else must you submit
Like all these Gentlemen, to my commands,
Nor from this spot a single step must ride,
Till we have rescued from the Giant's hands
(The great event achieved) my dear lamented bride.

10

"Yet should you rather swear into the tower
Alone your way to force, my fair to free
And bring her back, the choice is in your power
And will deserve besides warm thanks from me."
"Prince," quoth the knight; "what needs a choice to make?
Enough, that you this grace to me have done—
To talk of that another time we'll take
And now one tilt with you and all your knights I'll run."

11

The handsome knight consents, in deep amaze—
The trumpets sound—they start—a single blow
The prince of Lebanon quite harshly lays
Upon our good old mother's bosom low.
Then, as in turn the noble knights succeed,
Just like their lord Sir Huon treats them all;
First lays them prostrate, each beside his steed,
Then kind and courteous helps to raise him from the fall.

12

"Fore God! Sir knight!" (tŏwards' him limping up
The prince of Cedars cries) "How sharp, your spear!
Come, share with us a peace restoring cup
And brotherly repast, as eve draws near"——
Grateful, our knight indulges this request,
Three rapid hours the joke, the bottle roll.
The knights, delighted with their charming guest
Their bruises in the ribs forgave him from the soul.

13

"Now, having gained, my gentle Sirs, and friends,"
Quoth he, "my honorable right of you,
Straight to the Giant know my purpose tends,
Which e'en before, I was resolved to do
And to perform still more intensely burn,
With this good man to act a friendly part."
Then for their pains he thanks them all in turn,
And folds them one by one in kindness to his heart.

14

And when the nearest passage they had shown
Through a fir-grove towards the monster's hold
Sir Huon takes his leave and vows that soon
They shall hear tidings of their lady told.
Farewell!—Good luck!—And, smack! his courser flies.
The morning sun scarce tipped the trees with red,
When at an open plain arrived, he spies
A vast, enormous tower, rear to the clouds its head.

15

The work seemed all composed of iron cast
And was so firmly closed on every side
That one small gate alone tŏwards' it passed
And at the passage, scarcely two feet wide
Two brazen giants, armed with each a flail
Incessant thrashed, with magic life endured;
Stroke after stroke between them flew like hail,
That not a ray of light, unshattered could intrude.

16

And while revolving how he should begin
The knight in short deliberation stands,
A damsel at the window from within
Quite modestly to call him waves her hands.
"Well may that Lady at a nod be deft!"
Exclaims the squire; "but no such madman you!
Look at those Switzers to the right and left:
No single bone of yours would pass unbroken through."

17

Yet to the rule of knighthood ever true,
Not to the devil himself the back to show,
Sir Huon judges he has naught to do
But at the gate, right through the flails to go.
He rushes on, eyes closed, and falchion high,
And, fair betide him! finds his faith not vain.
The brazen monsters slack as he draws nigh
And stiffen at his touch, and motionless remain.

18

Scarce had the knight obtained his passage through,
Leaving his squire upon the steeds to tend,
When to receive him the fair damsel flew,
Whose coal black tresses to her waist descend.
Her robe, white satin, trailed along the ground,
And at her breast (a lightly shaded place)
Was by a golden zone together bound;
The loveliest model she, to carve a Muse or Grace.

19

"What angel," sweetly diffident, said she,
And touched his hand, and blushes sweet displayed,
"What angel, Sir, directed you to me?
Just to the Holy Virgin as I prayed,
Before the window— You from her were sent,
In you mine eyes her messenger behold;
She, who so oft her shielding hand hath lent.
Oh! welcome to my aid, a thousand, thousand fold!

20

"But above all, avoid we time to waste,
I hate each moment, in this prison passed!"
"Nay," quoth the knight, "I come not so to haste;
Where is the Giant?"—"Bound in slumber fast,"
Replies the dame—"a chance for you most kind,
For were he once aroused from sleep again,
His finger, while his magic ring should bind,
To vanquish him, your hopes, alas! would all be vain.

21

"Yet now this jewel from him to convey
You just have time."—"How so?"—"No common sleep
Is that which thrice or four times in a day
Is wont his senses in a spell to steep.
He two hours longer will remain thus lamed,
And I can tell my story in a word.
My father, Balazin of Phrygia named,
In fruitful Palestine, of Jericho is Lord.

22

"The fairest Prince of Lebanon's high hill
Near four years past began my love to woo,
And if my cold reserve distressed him still,
My heart, believe me, nothing of it knew.
'Twas hard— But I when first his suit begun
To Saint Alexia vowed in maiden pride,
Should his chaste passion three full winters run
Then and not else would I become the prince's bride.

23

"My love in secret daily gathered strength.
Long was the time of trial; yet it passed.
Our troth we pledged, and found ourselves at length
Shut in the nuptial room together, fast.
When open flew the door, with thundering sound
In shot the Giant, seized me, fled away.
And seven long dreary months have now gone round
Since captive I remain beneath his cruel sway.

24

"To judge, Sir, whether I have found it light
Against him storms unnumbered to withstand,
Look at the man— In still renewing fight
'Tis hard I ween, to keep the upper hand.
One moon-shine-night, (I shudder as I tell)
Me to the last extreme when he had brought,
Upon my knees, with wringing hands I fell,
And for relief in prayer, God's holy mother sought.

25

"Heaven's blessed Queen, the virgin full of grace,
With ears of soft compassion heard me pray,
Down sunk the tempter breathless on the place
And six hours impotent to hurt me lay.
From that day forward this mysterious spell
Whene'er he tries the odious strife again,
Is still renewed, his arrogance to quell;
Against the wondrous trance, his very ring is vain.

26

"Such has precisely been this day the case,
Of six hours slumber, four are passed away.
His sinews then new life and vigor brace,
As had they suffered nothing of decay.
Such the ring's virtues—from all fatal harms
His life, while that protects him, is secure.
You scarce would credit all its mighty charms!
But what forbids your eyes themselves to make it sure?"

27

It happened just to Huon as to you:
He had expected, from the Giant's name
A monster of Titanian birth to view
Like one of Earth's wild children, damned to fame,
Who once to storm the palace of the sky,
Up from the earth tore Pelion, roots and all,
And heaped the mass on Ossa's shoulders high—
Instead of that, behold! a man of seven foot tall.

28

Did Glycon's work fall ever in your way?
The mighty son of that long lingering night—
Th' original?—or copied but in clay—
Then think you have the very man in sight
Who to the last extremity had brought
Upon the moon-shine night the lovely dame.
The shrewdest modern ancient would have thought
As thus he lay, to see of Hercules the frame.

29

I mean, Sir, of a Hercules at rest,
As from the cleansed Augean filth he came;
Broad-shouldered thus, and with as high a breast
Lay Angulaffer stretched—his dress, the same—
Our hero started—knowledge of antiques
Was not his forte— In the chaste eye of day
This costume of the old, heroic Greeks
Was nakedness to him, was heathenish display.

30

"No more delay, Sir!—While asleep he lies,
The ring!" (she whispers) "and one final blow!"
"Nay! my own fame too much for that I prize,"
Quoth he—"a sleeping and stark naked foe
Is safe with me—I first will rouse him up."
"Then of the ring at least possession gain."—
The knight draws near, secures the golden hoop
And unaware acquires o'er Spirits full domain.

31

This curious property the ring attends,
With many a virtue yet unknown, beside
Its size: to every finger instant bends
And still at need contracts or waxes wide.
Our hero at the magic jewel's sight
With horror shudders, while delight he takes.
Then seizing on the Giant's arm with might,
Shakes with unwearied hand, till he at length awakes.

32

Scarce had the Giant roused, when took to flight
The child of Balazin with piercing cries.
True to his courage and his rank, the knight
Stood calm and met the heathen's furious eyes.
"Who art thou, paltry little wretch?" quoth he,
"Who dar'st disturb me thus, in slumber sweet.
Thy head and neck at strangest odds must be
Since of thy own accord thou lay'st them at my feet."

39

Sir Huon raised her with respectful hand,
Returning all her thanks with courteous phrase,
The good old age of knighthood's manners bland,
Which spun less fine than those of modern days
Were firmer stuff, and color better held.
The knight's first law was virgins to defend
And though no single spur his heart impelled,
At every damsel's call alike his blood to spend.

40

The youth with close inspection to survey
With time nor ease the fair had yet been blessed;
She moved him now, his arms aside to lay
And straight had fain more numerous eyes possessed
Than ever Juno's royal bird displayed;
So much appeared our hero to her ken
From head to foot, in form and gesture made
For greatness and for charms the first of mortal men.

41

Not that with any one between her heart
And him, precisely she compared the knight;
She pleased her eyes without restraint or art
And sure there lurks no sin in simple sight.
This pleasure to disturb no scruple came,
Sweet, round her breast the dear illusion caught,
For what made thus secure the beauteous dame
Was that her gentle spouse not once engaged her thought.

42

Oh! blameless Angela! what bliss for thee,
That in his breast thy looks no tinder stirred;
Nor let us wonder that it so should be,
For, if as now and then by chance occurred
To meet her looks the hero's halfway came,
'Twas but the vacant gaze of lifeless clay;
And o'er a flower pot, or a picture's frame
With more indifference, more coldness could not stray.

43

A secret impulse like the magnet's sway
Seems the sharp edges of his looks to turn
Straight on for Bagdad to impel his way
And every charm of Angela to spurn.
In vain her shape is like a beauteous vase
Where Love's own hand its utmost skill has tried.
In vain her nose, soft rising on her face
Joins to the polished brow, in majesty of pride.

44

In vain her bosom like a double hill
Snow-clad, in mist involved, heaves up its lace;
In vain her skin is like the glossy rill
Where bright Aurora views her rosy face.
In vain has beauty's hand on every part
So evidently stamped her royal seal
That far exalted o'er the reach of art
Her charms no dress can grace, and no attire conceal.

45

With all her charms in short, however bright,
For him, the maid is fair and young in vain.
And far from anxious wishes, the delight
Of her sweet presence longer to detain
His breast each moment more intensely glows
Back to her bridegroom's arms to yield the fair;
And as the damsel no impatience shows,
To mention it himself at last cannot forbear.

46

Scarce had he vowed to be her guide and guard,
She scarce poured forth her gratitude sincere
When sudden, hark! within the castle-yard
A trampling noise of men and steeds they hear.
Up the long spiral stairs the sounds revolve—
The damsel starts— "Who can it be?" she cries.
But soon her terrors into joys dissolve.
For lo! her darling spouse, Alexis greets her eyes.

47

The thought had struck him, somewhat late indeed,
That his own share of glory would be small,
Should Huon to redeem the fair succeed
While he, her husband, with his horsemen all,
In idle ease extended in the shade
Thinning his blood with wine of palms should lay.
Nay— Who could answer but the lusty blade
With his angelic spouse, himself might run away.

48

And having heard this singing in his ear
He had resolved to mount his steed at last,
And now smart trotting with his train drew near,
That should the danger haply all be past,
From the strange knight he might receive his dame,
Wish Heaven to speed him for the service done,
And to himself take, think ye? somewhat shame—
But then he was indeed a Prince—of Lebanon.

49

Sir Huon thus, by kindly chance relieved
The fair from guiding to the palmy vale,
Of all the handsome lords the praise received,
Pleased nothing less than had he heard them rail.
And now, his favors to complete, the knight
But eyes the ring, and straight by viewless hands
With all that serves the palate to delight
In high profusion decked a large round table stands.

50

"Ah! how could I so long the thought forbear?
The banquet ere we taste, go valiant knight,
And with your proper hands," exclaimed the fair,
"Reveal the Giant's harem to the light.
Here fifty maids besides myself, enclosed,
The sweetest tulip-bed, of virgin bloom
That odious monster kept, and still proposed
In offerings to devote to Mahound, I presume."

51

The harem, opening now unfolds to view,
In rich attire a group of damsels fair,
Of Mahound's paradise an image true.
Sir Huon straight commends them to the care
Of all the knights, and far had rode away
While still behind him jumbled jabberings roared;
All his kind friends entreating him to stay
At least with them to share the banquet on the board.

52

Now evening's purple tints in gray decayed,
And calm in majesty, the moon arose;
When the brave knight, whose steed fatigue delayed,
Resolved to seek a spot for soft repose.
He looks the grass-plots o'er to find a bed,
While on the steeds Cherasmin's cares attend;
When sudden, close at hand before him spread
Our wondering hero sees a splendid tent ascend.

53

A costly carpet, stretched along the ground
Holds just proportion to the tent in size,
And cushions bolster all its sides around
Which at each pressure softly breathing rise,
Instinct with life— A jasper table stands
Full in the midst; upheld by golden feet:
To craving hunger, work of godlike hands,
For on it ready served the banquet calls to eat.

54

The knight in deep amaze at all he sees
Cherasmin calling, cries: "What have we here?"
"That, we can tell" (replies the squire) "with ease—
Friend Oberon must certainly be near.
Instead of finding here a couch so light—
We but for these soft swan-down beds he sends,
On mother earth's hard lap had passed the night;
That now is what I call remembering one's friends.

55

"Come! lay we dearest lord, our arms aside,
Repose will after this long fare be sweet;
Though but a transient supper to provide
The dwarf has spared no pains his friends to treat"—
The knight complies—half-seated at the board,
With stomachs keen they shared the rich repast—
Sung merry Gascoon ditties, and encored—
The goblet, draining oft, which filled again as fast.

56

Insensibly the gentle hand of sleep
Soon loosens of their nerves the slackening tie,
While music swells on aether's tranquil deep
Sweet as the tuneful strains of spheres on high.
On all the trees around, how soft it floats!
As in each leaf a warbling throat had sung;
And Mara's angel, soul-entrancing notes
In each melodious throat a thousand fold had rung.

57

At length subsides this harmony divine,
Full as at first, yet weakening by degrees,
Till to soft whispers the sweet strains decline
Like leaves scarce fluttering to the summer breeze,
When round the knees of bathing virgins gay
The silver streamlet's rippling water flows;
The dozing hero hears the sounds decay
Till his unconscious sense dissolves in deep repose.

58

He slept at once till bright Aurora came
And the cock crowed, to see her rosy steeds,
When a strange dream convulsed his inmost frame;
Through paths unknown his fancied step proceeds
O'er shadowy fields, beside a limpid stream
When lo! before him stood a godlike maid
Whose eye glowed mild, with Heaven's serenest beam,
And all the charms of love around her person played.

59

What then he felt, no language can express;
Then conscious first of love's supreme control,
Breathless, transported with delight's excess
And pouring out with every look his soul
He stands and to the ground seems rooted fast;
Her form when vanished still in fancy spies;
And when the dear illusion melts at last,
At seeing her no more, expiring shuts his eyes.

60

In conscious death upon the shore he lies
Entranced, when sudden, a warm, gentle hand
To his stiff breast its seeming touch applies.
Roused, as from death, he sees beside him stand
The damsel beauteous beyond all compare,
The sweet enchantress of his heart, once more;
Thrice lovelier now, thrice more divinely fair
Than to his ravished eyes, she had appeared before.

61

Each, in deep silence at the other stares,
With looks which say— Oh! how much stronger say
What neither yet in words to utter dares:
To him, her eyes a Heaven of bliss display,
Where in a sea of love the soul may dive;
Soon joys excessive sharpen into pains;
The spurs of strong, resistless impulse drive
Till sinking in her arms her panting breast he strains.

62

He feels her heart against his bosom play,
Enraptured bliss! how quick! how strong! how warm!
When sudden, vanishes the beam of day—
Black, rolls on thunder's blazing car the storm,
Loud howling tremble tempests' moody swarms;
And rapt in whirlwinds by a viewless might
The nymph is torn in fury from his arms
And dashed amidst the stream that flows before his sight.

63

Her shrieks he hears— And, oh! the hellish doom!
In vain, would follow her!—aghast he stands;
Stiff as a marble statue on a tomb
And struggles, pants and fights with legs and hands.
In ice wedged up he seems, the throat above,
Sees her expanded arms implore, to save;
Yet cannot speak, nor as impelled by love
Plunge headlong down the steep, and tear her from the wave.

64

"Sir!" calls the squire, "awake! awake! I say—
Sure an ill dream that dismal snorting made!"
"Away! ye Ghosts!" cries Huon—"make me way!
What! would you even rob me of her shade?"—
And starts up, furious, from his fearful dream,
His heart with mortal anguish trembling still—
Wild staring he beholds the morning gleam,
And down his pallid cheek, cold clammy dews distill.

65

"That was a grievous dream!" Cherasmin cries;
"Upon your back, too long you must have lain."
"A dream?"—With calmer looks, Sir Huon sighs—
"Ay!—but that dream my bosom's peace hath slain."—
"Nay!" quoth the squire—"dear Sir! may Heaven forefend!"
—"Tell me"—returned the knight with looks intent—
"Dost thou not think that sometimes dreams portend
Events of after time, as warning heralds sent?"

66

"There are examples, Sir"—replied the squire,
"And since with you, I nothing dare deny—
Yet— Is the naked truth what you require?
I am not one, who much on dreams rely.
At least in all my dreaming I must own,
That flesh and blood their part will always play—
This to our good forefathers was well known,
As in their honest rimes they still were wont to say.

67

"Yet—I perchance might something better say,
Would you confide the substance of your dream."
—"That will I" (said the knight) "without delay.
—Yon tree scarce reddens with the morning beam.
Time will not fail—but reach the goblet here
Ere I begin the story to relate;
My drooping spirits with a draught to cheer—
Here at my breast it lies, like many hundred weight."

68

While now the magic bowl refreshment gave,
Cherasmin, silent kept his lord in view;
Disturbed to see the son of Siegwin brave,
More than a man beseems, of weakness show.
What! (with himself he muses—) broad awake!
About a dream!—(and pensive shakes his brow)
An empty dream!—such vast ado to make!
Well! since it so must be, go we to breakfast now.

Book the fourth

1

Now thus begins the knight to tell his dream:—
"Whatever you, at heart, Cherasmin dear,
Of what I purpose to disclose may deem,
It is no fiction, but the truth sincere;
That I, thank God! in body and in soul
Such as you see me here, am chaste and pure—
Nor through my life's whole progress, Love's control
Did in my spotless heart before this hour endure.

2

"There was at my dear mother's court in truth
Large store of damsels, young and passing fair;
And good occasions to mislead a youth—
Chief, when at forfeits playing, were not rare.
There, oftentimes were garters to untie
But I unmoved the neatest foot could see—
Had queen Genevra's foot then met my eye,
'Twas after all a foot—'twas nothing more to me.

70

3

"The many naked necks, and bosoms bare
I saw, among the causes might be one;
For custom treats us like Medusa's hair
And for the fairest turns us into stone.
But what avails that to my twentieth year
My freedom I preserved with care extreme?
My hour is come! alas! my lot severe,
Was the first woes of love to suffer—in a dream.

4

"Yes, dear Cherasmin, I have seen her now,
Her, for my victress whom the stars design;
Have seen her, yes, and unresisting bow
From the first glance my heart before her shrine.
A dream, man?—Never so profound a trace
Was yet impressed by phantom of the brain.
Call me a thousand madmen, to my face;
She lives, I had her once, and have her must again.

5

"Oh! hadst thou seen that Angel-form, like me!
Cherasmin! had I but the painter's art,
That glowing form I still in fancy see,
Should straight to cinders burn thy aged heart.
Oh! that some trifling remnant I possessed,
Her soul-inspiring beauties taught to live,
Merely the nosegay blooming at her breast—
What, on the spacious earth, would I not for it give?

6

"Form to thy fancy, with youth's purest glow
A woman molded from the forms above;
The rose's blushes and the lily's snow;
Give all her limbs the finest shape of love.
Around her face a smile of seraphs draw
And with majestic grace each beauty raise.
At once desire to irritate and awe;
Yet of her charms all this the shadow scarce conveys.

7

"And when attracted by her looks divine
I strained this lovely woman to my breast
And felt the tender heart o'erflow in mine
Of this bright cherub in a mortal vest—
How could I not expire, with joy like this!
Now tell me 'twas a dream; now coldly chide.
How flat! how blank! how dead to every bliss
Compared with such a dream, is all my life beside!

8

"Once more, my friend, this was no phantom vain
Formed in the Fancy's seat, from fumes of wine;
A strong, unerring feeling cries too plain
She lives and from her birth was destined mine.
Is it a whim? Oh! Spare the error sweet
To think, 'twas Oberon brought her to my eye,
Yet, tell not me of whims! Is this a cheat?
Oh! then is all a cheat! then Truth herself can lie."

9

Cherasmin shakes his head, with doubts full-fraught
As when you hear a marvel-teeming tale;
A tale of which at heart you credit naught,
Though to disprove it cogent reasons fail.
"What art thou thinking?"——to his loveless friend
Quoth Huon——"Sir, that's puzzling, I confess.
Some scruples to suggest I did intend;
And yet——of what avail, to sharpen your distress?

10

"Just for the present, as your word indeed
Has pledged your princely faith to Charlemagne,
Suppose for Bagdad we should straight proceed?
And on the way this charm may cease again.
Nay——Oberon himself may do his best,
And the dream-princess on a sudden show.
Meantime! dear Sir, if Hope can soothe your breast,
Hope on! 'twill make your blood at least more briskly flow."

11

While thus Cherasmin speaks, with downcast eyes
Sir Huon stands, for in his love-sick brain
The scene was now reversed, and straight he cries:
"Ah! friend! deceive me not with comfort vain.
Unfriendly planets over me bear sway,
What hope can glimmer in this cruel state?
The storm which tore her from my breast away,
Alas! too plainly told the harshness of my fate!

12

"Torn from me, still she stretches from the wave
Her arms to me— It freezes still my blood—
And I, in helpless impotence to save,
As fettered to the ground, unhappy stood."
—"Ay! in the dream—but not all dreams are true.
Why for yourself this needless torture make?
Trust me, dear Sir, the wisest plan for you
Is from it only what just pleases you to take.

13

"Thus in a dream your bosom's queen to show,
Was in the ghost a kind and friendly act;
On this our faith we safely can bestow
And e'en receive it for undoubted fact—
The stream, the whirlwind, and the chains forsooth,
Are mere additions by the dream impressed,
And I myself have suffered in my youth
Full often much the same, from night-mare at my breast.

14

"I take a walk, for instance—when a bear
All black and shaggy, coming God knows whence,
Stops me—I gripe my hanger in my fear
And tug—and tug—with fruitless impotence.
Within me every nerve and sinew dies
Meanwhile the bear still swells before my face
With jaws that yawn like hell, to seven-fold size.
I struggle—I would fly—I cannot quit the place.

15

"Another time, as from a drinking-bout
You dream returning, by a wall to go;
A little window-shutter creaks, and lo!
Long as your arm a nose comes poking out.
Half dead with fear, when you attempt to fly,
You see a crowd of spectres standing by;
Who stare you in the face, on every side,
And from long necks loll fiery tongues out wide.

16

"Trembling, you sidewards squeeze yourself, to stand
Against the wall, and feel a withered hand
Through a round hole, pass o'er your back like ice
And passing try to pinch you here and there.
On-end upon your head starts every hair;
The issues all are choked up in a trice,
While visibly the street still narrower grows,
Still frostier the hand, and longer still the nose.

17

"The like full often happens, as I said,
Which after all, is but a merrymake,
A farce, within your brain by spectres played,
For nose and fear both vanish when you wake.
I, Sir, the thing in no sort would regard,
But hold to what the dwarf has promised plain.
Be brisk! my mind forebodes it must go hard
But we shall find the dame at Babylon again."

18

The knight springs up; new life his heart expands
As had he nothing like a vision had;
While neighing to the morning air, his pad
Saddled and bridled, ready for him stands.
He mounts, and looking backwards from the plain,
Sees that the tent has disappeared again.
A single breath had raised it from the clay,
A single breath now blew it all away.

19

Now on the banks of deep Euphrates' tide
By shrubs and palm-trees hid from scorching day,
Across the loveliest land on earth they ride,
Silent, though not for want of what to say;
For each was plunged in other cares beside;
The balmy breeze, the morning soft and gay,
The birds' sweet carol, the still-rolling stream,
Both fancies to awake from soothing slumber seem.

20

Her magic mirror to the knight displays
Naught worthy seeing but the much-loved face.
Upon his shield the goddess he portrays
And climbs the steeps of Taurus her to trace.
E'en Merlin's grave, to find her, dares ascend.
His hands the giants and the dragons quell—
Placed, where she pines the castle to defend,
And wrest her by main force from all the powers of hell.

21

While with imaginary joy the knight
Clasps to his bosom his hard rescued bride,
Cherasmin's fancy steals with fond delight
Far from Euphrates to his Garonne's side,
Where first his childhood culled the flowret gay;
"No," thinks he; "nowhere God's good Sun is seen
So mild as where I first beheld its ray,
So lovely smiles no mead, so fresh no other green.

22

"Thou little spot, where light first on me shone,
Where first I suffered pain, first pleasures knew,
Be ever thou unnoticed and unknown,
Still shall my heart to thee forever true,
In Paradise itself an exile find,
Still drawn tŏwards' thee by a secret tie.
Oh! may I trust secure my boding mind
And on thy lap one day beside my fathers lie."

23

In dreams like these melts gradual the space
To Bagdad till the fierce meridian ray
Drives them within the woods to seek a place
Of rest and shelter from too fervent day.
On moss-grown seats, beneath an aged tree
The magic draught their fainting spirits cheers.
A third time full the fairy bowl they see,
When hark! a thundering shriek of horror rends their ears.

24

Up they both spring— The hero grasps his blade,
Hies to the spot from which the cries proceed,
And, with a lion struggling, all dismayed
A Saracen beholds upon a steed,
Still fighting from despair; but drenched in blood,
Exhausted, faint, while fallen on the plain
His courser wallowing in the sanguine flood
Had bit his bridle through in agony of pain.

25

The lion, snorting rushes on his foe,
And shoots from either eye a stream of fire—
Sir Huon sideways aims a fruitless blow,
At which the king of beasts, inflamed with ire,
Returns the greeting, with a long deep gash
Which Huon's blood from thousand streamlets drew.
But for the magic ring that single dash
Beyond all doubt had cleft the valiant knight in two.

26

The remnant gathering of his strength, the knight
Who sees his death in flaming eye-balls flash,
Thrusts through the lion's throat his sword, with might.
In vain swings round the tail a second lash
Which, had not Huon featly sprung away,
His lifeless limbs upon the ground had spread;
In vain the fearful fangs their points display,
Stabbed by Cherasmin's hand, there lies the monster dead.

27

The Saracen (who from the gems that gleamed
Upon his turban high, appeared to be
A man of rank) to sweat with pain yet seemed.
And now they led him gently to the tree
Where they were sheltered from the sultry day.
Reached him the cup, fresh vigor to inspire,
While in Arabian to him said the squire,
"Your thanks Sir! to the God of Christians you might pay."

28

He looks askance, and takes from Huon's hand
The goblet full, and to his lips applies,
When instantly the liquor from it dries,
And inward guilt avenging, like a brand
It burns his palm. He hurls it to the ground,
And stamps and raves and curses without bound.
At hearing him blaspheme, our hero hurt
Draws forth his hallowed sword, the heathen to—convert.

29

But conscious he was overmatched in might,
That varlet thinks it proper not to fight,
But to the field runs like a hunted hare,
Where feeding in the grass both coursers were.
Sir Huon's steed straight seizing by the mane,
In haste he mounts him, and with loosened rein,
Quaking, away with such a speed he springs,
As if he sat between a tempest's wings.

30

Unpleasant this adventure was, 'tis true,
But what availed the villain to pursue?
They find by good luck in a hamlet nigh,
A creature like a mule, and cheaply buy.
Transparenter than glass, the poor thing seemed
Life, e'en to reach the journey's end, to want;
Yet, on his chine to ride Cherasmin deemed
Better than still on foot behind his lord to pant.

31

And now tŏwards' the wished for port again
As briskly as they could their course they steered;
The Sun descending, on Heaven's skirts appeared
When distant, in a wide extended plain,
With towers unnumbered crowned, arose the queen
Of cities, glittering in the twilight's gleam;
While through a garden of unfading green
The rapid Tigris rolled his copious stream.

32

A mixture strange of horror and delight,
Of secret bodings and new fears oppress
The hero's heart when first unfolds to sight
The scene, where rather his own hardiness
And word, than Charles's orders urge a deed
From which no better issue he could see
Than death— The danger, always sure indeed,
So great, as when thus near, had never seemed to be.

33

In awful pride, with pinnacles of gold
The court, the throne which Asia shakes with fear,
Like an abode of Gods his eyes behold;
And thou, (thinks he) for what art thou come here?
And shudders; but the faith and valor bold
Which yet had led him, soon his spirits cheer,
And to his ears a voice in whispers calls
That he his lovely fair shall see within those walls.

34

"Be brisk!" he cries, "and spread all sail, my friend,
Thou seest my long and weary journey's end.
With Bagdad yet ere dark we must come up."
And now they trot, that horse and horseman pant;
The squire, in pity, from his fairy cup,
On his beast's tongue pours of the wine aslant.
"There—drink, thou good and honest lad!" says he;
"The goblet never drains for such as thee."

35

He spoke the truth— The creature's tongue scarce drew,
Panting and hungry as a glowing coal,
From the enchanted gold the cordial dew,
When, with all vivifying impulse stole
A stream of fire his limbs and members through.
Braced with new strength, in lungs and heart made whole,
Fleet as a greyhound now he trots away,
And Babylon they reach before the close of day.

36

While through the suburbs wandering they go
At random in the twilight to and fro,
Like strangers led by accident alone
They chance a little goody in the street,
Leaning upon a tottering staff, to meet,
Gray haired and long since shrunk to skin and bone.
"Ho! mother, be so good and if you can,
Direct us," cries Cherasmin, "to a Han."

37

The good old wife, upon her crutch yet bent,
Shakes up her head, the strangers to survey;
"Sir, to the nearest Han is a long way,"
(Says she) "but if you can yourselves content
With little, come into my hut, I pray,
Where at your service milk and bread you'll find,
And good fresh straw, and for your cattle hay;
There rest, and with the dawn go further, if inclined."

38

With thanks the knight her friendly offer takes,
And follows her. To him no bed seems hard,
The open door where truth and kindness guard;
The bed of straw the second Baucis shakes,
Strews from her garden orange-flowers and thyme,
Before them creamy, foaming milk presents,
Figs from the tree and peaches in their prime;
And that this year her almonds failed, laments.

39

Our hero thinks that never in his life
A meal with so much pleasure he enjoyed;
What in the fare was wanting, the old wife
With confidential gossiping supplied.
"The gentlemen just come in time," she said,
"For a great feast"—"How so?"—"Why, don't you know?
'Tis now the only talk of Bagdad, though.
The daughter of our lord, tomorrow is to wed."—

40

"To wed? the Sultan's daughter? and to whom?"—
"The bridegroom is a nephew of his own,
Prince of the Druses, rich, in beauty's bloom,
And, as they say, surpassed at chess by none.
A prince, in short, whom all the world suppose
Worthy the lovely Rezia to wed;
Yet in strict confidence I can disclose
That she would sooner take a dragon to her bed."

41

"That's wonderful indeed!" said Huon here;
"And more than we can easily believe"—
"I tell you, in her arms she would receive
A dragon sooner than let him come near.
Be sure of that— Long known have been to me,
The why and wherefore of the thing withal—
They made me promise hard, quite close to be—
But give me now your hand, and you shall hear it all.

42

"Perhaps you wonder how things come to be
To such a woman as myself revealed,
To others, and the palace, all concealed;
Know then: the mother to the nurse you see
Of lovely Rezia! and though sixteen years
Are past since Fatme held her to the breast,
Of her whole confidence she is possessed,
And now, you guess with ease how matters reach my ears.

43

"For some years past, the Caliph it is known,
Proud of his daughter, often at his feasts
Has made her come, where to her have been shown
Full many a handsome man among the guests.
But town and country likewise always knew,
That none her special favor could obtain.
Indeed she seemed them not so much to view
With maiden bashfulness as with disdain.

44

"Prince Babekan however it was guessed
(Him whom to marry her the Sultan meant)
She better could endure than all the rest;
Not that her heart beat when he came or went,
For, not to shun him purposely, at best
Was all he ever gained of her consent.
But then, no other pleased her more, they knew;
And after marriage, soon love, thought they, will ensue.

45

"But now forsooth, within a few weeks past,
A total change in Rezia has occurred;
On the poor Prince her eyes she scarce will cast
And all her heart revolts to hear a word
About the wedding said . . . and what may seem
Incredible, the change has by a simple dream
Been caused"—"A dream?" cries Huon all on fire—
"A dream! how very strange!" exclaims the squire.

46

"She dreamt" (the old wife thus her tale renewed)
"That like a roe, hunted by Babekan
In a wild wood she down a mountain ran
In deadly fear, by twenty hounds pursued.
All hopes of making her escape were vain,
When all at once a dwarf most wondrous fair,
Came in a phaëton by lions drawn,
Flying to her relief at full speed through the air.

47

"The dwarf, extended in his little hand,
Held out a blossom-loaded lily wand
And at his side in knightly garb arrayed
Sat a young stranger, as an angel fair.
His azure eyes, his long and yellow hair,
That Asia could not boast his birth betrayed.
Yet, from what land soever he was brought,
At the first glance her little heart he caught.

48

"The carriage stopped. The dwarf his wand extended
And touched her. Off the roe's skin fell apace.
At his request she now the car ascended
And with a blush beside him took her place
And next the youth to whom her heart was staked,
Though love and shame still in her bosom strove.
The phaëton up hill now smartly drove
And struck against a stone and she thereat awaked.

49

"Her dream was gone, but not expelled her heart
The stripling with the long and yellow hair;
His image still, the source of pleasing smart
Before her plays, and since that hour the fair
No longer could endure her former lover,
Or without wrath so much as hear or see.
Vain all attempts her motives to discover,
Still secret, dumb, immovable was she.

50

"Her nurse alone, of whom as I have said
I am the mother, knew the way to find
How the strange mystery which on her preyed,
Out of her breast insensibly to wind.
But you know whether simple reason's aid
Can cure a hurt which charms our secret mind.
Vexed with herself, poor Lady! She would fain
Have Fatme soothe and flatter up her pain.

51

"Meanwhile the day she so abhors drew nigh;
The Prince, to recommend himself indeed,
To better credit with the fair so shy
Left naught untried, but nothing would succeed.
She to the brave was partial it was known,
A light in which he never yet had shone.
Let us, thinks he, perform a deed of fame,
And thus extort applause from the relentless dame.

52

"Now, for a long time past a beast of prey
The country all around with terror fills;
Attacks the villages in open day,
And in his fury men and cattle kills;
Just like a dragon he has wings they say,
Claws like a griffin, like a hedge-hog quills.
He far exceeds an elephant in size,
And when he snorts, a storm o'er all the country flies.

53

"Time out of mind no such a beast was known,
Hence a great price upon his head was set;
But as each one still valued more his own,
None felt inclined the recompense to get.
The Prince alone, held it a worthy task
Fair Rezia's pride by boldness to abate,
And went in pomp the Sultan's leave to ask,
That he against the beast might try his fate.

54

"The Sultan gave unwillingly consent,—
And mounted on his fleetest horse he went
This morning before day— What further passed
Remains unknown, but he came home at last
On a strange horse, without parade, quite still,
Nor of the monster brought a single quill.
They say, no sooner had he reached his door,
Than straight he went to bed and took Bezoar.

55

"Yet with unheard of splendor they go on
For the approaching nuptials to prepare;
Tomorrow without fail it will be done,
And the next night, herself the charming fair
In Babekan's detested arms shall view."
"Before this happens" (broke Sir Huon out)
"Creation's wheel shall stop; for do not doubt,
The knight and dwarf are of the banquet too."

56

Hearing this word, the matron with surprise
Of what she scarce had marked now notice took,
The stranger's yellow hair, and azure eyes,
And that he only broken Arab spoke;
His knightly garb; and that she ne'er had seen
So fair a man, long as her life had been;
This likeness, with the hasty speech combined,
All struck as something singular her mind.

57

Whence came he? Why? Who is he? twenty more
Such questions ready from her lips to drop
Found in Sir Huon's earnest looks a stop.
As needing rest he lies down on the floor.
The goody wishes him delightful dreams
And trips away, and shuts the door behind her;
But it was gnawed in worm-holes, and had seams
Through which her itching ears to listen soon inclined her.

58

On tiptoe slipping back, close as she could
Before a cleft she pressed her listening ear;
Holding her breath, with open mouth she stood
And every word the strangers said could hear.
They spoke aloud, and seemingly in heat,
But from the words no sense could she obtain.
Yet could she now and then with comfort sweet
Discern the name of Rezia very plain.

59

"How strangely," Huon cries, "my Fates unwind!
By Oberon how truly was it spoken!
Weak is earth's race, and to the future blind.
Charles thinks he certainly my neck has broken
And so intended by his dire command;
Yet he but did the will of Fate supreme.
The lovely dwarf extends his lily wand,
And to my source of bliss conducts me in a dream."

60

"And that the very lady" (says the squire)
"Who in a dream has set your heart on fire,
The same infanta should turn out to be.
Charles named your bride; that in a dream too she
With you, as you with her should fall in love;
One scarcely for all this can trust one's eyes."
"Yet, did this wife not forge it," Huon cries,
"The knot was plainly wound by Fate above.

61

"How to untie it only is the art!"
"That," says Cherasmin, "should not trouble me;
And if in this case I can make so free
As my poor judgment fully to impart,
I would be short, and cut it straight in two;
The left-hand man, with windpipe safe should go.
His teeth the Caliph in his jaws retain
And I would be content to get my Dulcimain.

62

"Think but yourself—the service to begin
With slicing off a head, before her face,
Then her old Sultan-father's jaws and chin
So largely of his teeth and beard to thin;
And in his sight his only child embrace;
Fore God! 'tis not a practicable case.
Fate cannot of us possibly require
Thus grossly to defeat the end of our desire.

63

"The dwarf will doubtless for the best provide;
The great point after all, we have in view
Is, from the hare-foot prince to filch his bride,
Which Rezia sure herself will help us do
As soon as goody shall have signified
That yellow hair no other is than you.
While two fresh racers all prepared to fly
My care shall be to keep, the palace garden nigh."

64

"Squire!" (says the knight) "you seem to have forgot
That Charles my word of honor did receive,
His orders literally to achieve,
Nor of them shall there fail, my friend, a jot.
Come of it what there may. It suits not me
With anxious thought such matters to foresee."
"Why then," (replies the squire) "beyond a doubt
The dwarf in case of need, himself must help us out."

65

Mid such discourse the old man by degrees
Sinks into slumber, while to Huon's eyes
The boon, all night, his anxious mind denies.
Tossed like a boat upon the stormy seas
His boding heart, of swelling thoughts the sport
Is driven about, as passion's billows rage—
So near to, yet so distant from the port,
One instant seems to him an endless age.

Book the fifth

1

Thee too, O Rezia! on thy downy bed
The cordial balm of soothing slumber fled.
Lost amidst rocks whence thou no path couldst see,
With hatred thou beheldest and with dread
The twilight tinge the sky with festal red,
And odious Hymen's call, this day to thee.
She tossed and sighed, until the soul oppressed
With inward strife her head sunk down upon her breast.

2

She slept, and Oberon her spirits cheered
By visions new, before her eyes which flit.
She dreams by moonlight in a bower to sit
Within the garden of the Harem reared,
Sunk in the phantasies which love inspires.
A pleasing pain, and timid soft desires
Heave in her breast—her eye with moisture swells,
While still upon *the youth* her hopeless fancy dwells.

3

Roused by disquiet thoughts with haste she flies;
Through every flowery field and thicket roves;
With searching look in every arbor pries,
And breathless traverses the verdant groves.
Her wild, yet tender beaming tearful eyes
Of every being ask the form she loves.
Oft anxious she stands still, with listening ear,
If but a shadow move, or falling leaf she hear.

4

At last, as where amidst the thicket's night
A lucid moon-shine breaks, she turns to gaze—
Oh! ecstasy! if no delusive light
Her willingly mistaken vision daze,
The object of her search appears in sight.
Her timid look, his looks meet all in flame:
Impatient, yet with shuddering delight,
In doubt she stands, as if twixt love and shame.

5

To her with open arms in haste he strides;
She would escape, but cannot move a knee.
At length with pain behind a tree she hides
And in the sweet distress the visions flee;
To call them back how happy would she be!
Herself and the detested tree she chides,
And strives to sink once more to sleep—in vain!
Her only joy is now to think it o'er again.

6

A third part of his race, the God of day
Had run while it was yet with Rezia, night;
So great, though now awake, was her delight
Of her sweet dream to lengthen out the stay.
Long without giving sign of life she lies
Till to the golden bed her nurse advances,
The curtain draws and finds with great surprise
The lady broad awake, and in the best of fancies.

7

"Again I've seen him, Fatme! wish me joy!"
Cries Rezia—"yes! again I have him seen"—
"Indeed!" returns the nurse, with look so sly,
Searching the room, as if the bird to spy;
The damsel laughs—"How is thy wit so green?
Thou canst not, sure, misconstrue what I mean.
'Twas but in dream that he appeared to me;
Yet in the neighborhood he certainly must be.

8

"My mind forebodes he is not far away,
Nor, if thou lovest me, do thou say nay."
—"Then I am silent"—"Why? what in the hope
Is there so bold, but I may give it scope?"
Still dumb remains the nurse, and heaves a sigh.
—"Nay, who shall Love's almighty power defy?
The lion-tamer, and my patron now,
He will deliver me, albeit I know not how.

9

"Silent, thou sighst! Too plainly I perceive
What thou by silence, Fatme, fain wouldst veil.
Thou hast no hope my passion to relieve,
And *I* but hope, as better comforts fail—
My ruin is decreed beyond a doubt—
The hour draws near—already clank my chains—
A miracle alone can help me out—
A miracle alone! if not—then *this* remains."

10

While thus she spoke, fire flashing from her eye,
She from her bosom forth a dagger drew.
"See, Fatme, this exalts my hopes thus high,
This pledges Fate, all things for me to do."
"Ha!" cries the nurse, and staggers to a chair,
Pale as a corpse, and trembling as a reed,
And weeps, and wrings her hands in deep despair,
"Ha! is that all?—then God be merciful indeed!"

11

The damsel stops her mouth— "Hush! hush!" she cries,
And puts the dagger back— "On earth's wide round
Thou knowst that naught so hateful to mine eyes
As this same prince of Druses can be found.
Sooner than wed him, Fatme, shall this breast
A sharp-toothed adder's deadliest venom feel:
Comes not my love to aid me, thus distressed,
On what can I rely, but on this faithful steel?"

12

Scarce had she spoke, when at the door that led
To Fatme's chamber they a knocking hear;
The nurse goes out, but to the lady's bed
Soon hastens back with tidings, oh! how dear!
Wild with her joy, and breathless with her haste,
She scarce finds utterance for the charming sound.
"At length" . . . she stammers . . . "all our woes are past;
Joy! lovely princess, joy! . . . the knight at last is found."

13

In a loose night-gown, like a vapor hung
Scarce round her beauties, from the sheets she flew;
Herself, on Fatme's neck, in transport flung—
"Found? where? where is he? Dream! then spok'st thou true!"
The nurse herself in joy's tumultuous haste
Can her own senses scarce enough command
Round the half-naked lovely dreamer's waist
A little dress to throw, with heedless, hurried hand.

14

And now the matron is herself called in,
From her own lips to hear at once the tale;
She, from the egg her story to begin
Lets the minutest circumstance not fail.
No feature, not a word that slipped her guest
Does the good mother's narrative omit.
" 'Tis he! 'tis he!" cries Fatme,—"I protest
Things cannot better suit.—Upon our man we've hit."

15

Again the old wife is with questions pressed
And for the third and fourth time must repeat
Whatever did, said, did not say her guest,
Again describe him o'er from head to feet.
How yellow, and how long his hair, again,
How large and blue his sparkling eyes, relate;
And still, inquiries numberless remain
Of things she in her haste forgot to state.

16

While thus by twenty years at least more young
The nurse's tattling good old mother grew,
Beneath *her* hand the lofty fabric sprung
Of Rezia's locks with pearls more bright than dew
In spiral curls through all her long black hair.
Her ears, neck, waist, such glittering jewels grace,
That by the sun reflected in the face
The dazzled eyes their lustre scarce can bear.

17

Now by her nymphs in bridal trim arrayed,
Adorned complete, and to the feast proceeding,
Bright as a Sun appeared the royal maid,
And lovely as a roe, mid roses feeding.
Her charms undazzled not an eye can see,
Though now by female eyes alone espied.
She only, seemed quite ignorant to be
How all the stars must vanish by her side.

18

The splendor flashing in her beauteous eyes,
The restless look, the lurking soft desire
Which swells her lips, the vivid glowing fire
Which her smooth cheeks with unused purple dyes,
Make all her maidens with amazement stare.
Is this the obstinate, reluctant fair
(Thus to each other whispering they say)
Who looked but over night with horror to this day?

19

Meanwhile the Emirs, and the Vizirs all
Pranked for the feast, met in the nuptial hall.
The royal banquet stands served up in state,
And at the sacred mansion's golden gate
Mid trumpets' clang, and numerous slaves, appeared
In pomp the Sultan with his hoary beard;
The Drusian prince yet somewhat pale of face
Behind him proudly marched, and held the bridegroom's place.

20

The Harem's ivory door on th' other side
Opens, and fairer than the damsels bright
Of Mahomet's Heaven, comes the intended bride;
A veil her angel face withdraws from sight
And like a silvery cloud appears to hide
Th' excessive rays of her all-dazzling light.
Yet sudden, more than earthly splendors, seem
Through the whole hall, at her approach to beam.

21

The Drusian's heart alternate sinks and swells
While still his eye upon her beauties dwells.
He seeks in hers what he would fain behold
But meets a look, than Alpine ice more cold.
Yet Vanity with self-deceiving strains
To his infatuated bosom say
That Rezia the prudish look but feigns.
Oh! thinks he, all that snow shall melt ere dawn away.

22

Whether he hoped too much, will soon be found;
Nor shall we now describe with needless care,
How thereupon, after the Iman's prayer
While noisy kettle-drums and horns resound
They take their seats—the Sultan first in place,
At his right Rezia, at his left her lover,
With things of course which must themselves discover;
For now tŏwards' our knight, 'tis time to turn our face.

23

He, as you recollect, the night had passed
Impatient, flushed, of hopes and fears the sport,
Upon his straw, in not more easy sort
Than one amidst a storm, rocked on a mast.
But scarcely had Aurora's rosy hand
Opened the golden portals of the skies,
When like a night sinks down a vapor bland
Of poppies, lilies, elders, on his eyes.

24

He slept; and still in slumber's ties was bound,
When the Sun's chariot half its daily round
Had run. Meanwhile the good Cherasmin hied
The castle's situation to explore
And for the flight the needful to provide,
While to her hearth the hostess brought her store,
For dinner preparation due to make,
Half peevish that her guest delayed so long to wake.

25

At last she slips away, and at the door
Stoops and peeps through the crevices once more;
And hits the moment with a lucky chance
When Huon's eyes first open to the day.
Fresh as amid the maze the son of May,
When with the nymphs the Graces hold a dance,
She saw half upwards the fair hero rise,
And, guess what object first salutes his eyes.

26

A caftan, such as on great days alone
By Emirs of the highest rank is worn,
On a gold ground which richest pearls adorn,
Before his eyes, across a chair lies thrown.
On it a turban that seems wove of snow;
And to complete the Emir, round it swung
A diamond belt, whereby a falchion hung,
Whose sheath and hilt his eyes half blinded with their glow.

27

Of the whole dress, in short, from head to foot,
From the morocco, gilded edg'd half-boot,
Up to the diamond on the turban high
That held the ostrich plume, naught failed. The knight
Thinks he still dreams—who could this pomp supply?
The matron cries: " 'Tis witchery downright,
Else I had surely something of it known."
"The dwarf," exclaims the squire, "has done the work alone."

28

The knight assents. . . . This, thinks he, to the hall
Will through the train of heathens ope my way;
Then straight puts on the caftan, belt, and all
While his good hostess helps him to array.
"But of this turban what are we to make?
Cut the fine hair off, for its sake?
Not for the world!—But stay—beneath 'twill go:
The thing appears on purpose rounded so."

29

Except his lily smooth and beardless face,
Like a true Sultan now Sir Huon stood.
His person round the good old woman viewed,
Still finding room to add another grace.
His faithful squire now whispers in his ear,
And thereupon he kindly takes his leave.
"Farewell, until we meet again—and, here!
This purse of gold," says he, "good mother, pray receive."

30

In doing naught by halves, brave spirits pride;
A gorgeous courser stands before the door,
And two fair boys, with silver dizened o'er,
Holding the golden stirrup at his side.
Sir Huon mounts; the boys start fresh before
And by a side way path the hero guide,
Through flowery hedges on the river's strand,
Till opposite they saw the lofty castle stand.

31

Huon the first court has already passed,
Lights in the next, and enters now the last,
And seems a guest of highest rank to be;
Deceived by this appearance, every where
The guards make way. He marches proud and free,
And to the door of ebony draws near.
Twelve moors, like giants stand with falchions bare,
And to intruders bar all entrance there.

32

But when the knight before the lofty gate
Appeared, his royal air and splendid state
The points of all these swords at once avert,
Towards' him from a distance all inclined.
The doors rush open— His heroic heart
Beats high, when waving round, they close behind.
Two rows of pillars next a garden pass,
And to another door conduct, of gilded brass.

33

It was a front hall, with a slavish herd,
Of every color and of neutral kind,
Who at the source of joys forever pined,
And now, when as an Emir clad, appeared
A man, in pomp, before their hollow eyes,
Each servile heart within its bosom dies.
Crosswise, their arms upon the breast they fold,
And scarcely from behind the hero dare behold.

34

Now, from the hall, of cymbals, fifes and drums,
Of voices and of chords the clangor comes.
The Sultan's head with wine begins to doze,
More loud and free the festive banquet grows.
The lovely maid alone, shares not at all
The ardor in her lover's eye that glows.
As on her plate her looks intently fall,
Enters with noble air, Sir Huon in the hall.

35

As he draws near the table, with surprise
Turns on the stranger every brow to stare;
While thinking of her dream, the lovely fair
Still on her plate keeps fixed her pensive eyes.
The Caliph too, a bumper just had crowned,
And naught his notice from the rite could call;
While Babekan, of his approaching fall
By no good Spirit warned, his lengthy neck turns round.

36

The hero sees of yesterday the wretch
Who dared with scorn the Christian's God to treat.
Next the gold chair, he holds the left-hand seat,
And seems for punishment the neck to stretch.
Swift as the angry flame of Heaven, starts out
The gleaming sword, off flies the heathen's head.
Large streams of blood in foaming torrents spout,
Spatter his neighbor's garb, and o'er the table spread.

37

As when in Perseus' hand the dreadful face
Of Gorgon, by a look at once deprives
The wildly raging rebels of their lives;
Still smokes the dome, still uproar fills the place,
Still murder boils in every savage breast.
But scarce he shakes the snake-entangled crest,
When in each hand the dagger stiff has grown,
And every murderer hardens into stone.

38

Thus, at the sight of such bold treason here,
The blood forgets in every breast to flow;
All from their seats start up in deadly fear
As if they saw a spectre from below,
And grasp their swords— Each arm denies its aid,
By terror lamed—undrawn remains each blade;
While impotent in rage, with stiffened stare,
Back sinks the Sultan speechless in his chair.

39

The raging uproar through the hall that storms
Amidst her revery, the fair alarms;
Astonished she looks round, the cause to learn
And as her brows towards' Sir Huon turn,
What were his feelings when he met her eyes?
" 'Tis she! 'tis she!" with ravishment he cries,
Lets fall the turban and the bloody blade,
And by his flowing curls, to Rezia stands displayed.

40

" 'Tis he!" she too begins to call, but shame
Arrested in her rosy mouth the sound.
How did her heart within her bosom bound
When in the sight of all, he flying came!
By love emboldened caught her to his breast,
And while she reddens now, and now grows pale,
As love, and virgin fear by turns prevail,
A burning kiss upon her lips impressed.

41

His lips had now the second kiss bestowed,
But for a wedding ring, where could he look?
The ring by good luck on his finger glowed,
Which from the Giant in the tower he took.
Its worth as yet he little understood,
The meanest ring to him had seemed as good.
Yet this, from need he to her hand applied
And said: "Thus take I thee, for my beloved bride."

42

Thus speaking to the soft reluctant fair,
The third kiss to her lips he now applied.
"Ha!" while he gnashed his teeth the Sultan cried,
And stamped his feet— "Ha!" cried he, "can you bear
The Christian dog to scorn me in this way?
Seize him! 'tis deadly treason to delay;
And let his filthy blood by drops expressed
My vengeance on the monstrous deed attest."

43

In Huon's eyes a hundred falchions shone;
Down in a storm they rush from every side;
Scarce giving him the time to snatch his own
Which now with threatening look he brandished wide.
At once with love and fear, the fair, distressed
Throws one arm round him, shields him with her breast,
And one extends, his deadly steel to stay.
And wildly cries: "Away! rash, cruel men, away!

44

"Begone! There is no passage to this heart,
Unless through mine!" with loudest voice she cries.
But now as mild as Cupid's bride, her eyes
Now from despair Medusa's terrors dart.
"Bold men," she to the Emirs calls, "forbear!
Stand off! oh! spare him! dearest father, spare!
And thou to whom Fate gives me as thy wife,
Spare, in each other's blood, oh! spare my life!"

45

In vain! The Sultan's rage can naught restrain,
At his command the heathens forward press,
The hero waves his flashing sword in vain.
Still Rezia holds his arm— Her deep distress
Pierces his heart— Yet what resource remains
Except his ivory horn, to guard the fair?
He puts it to his mouth, breathes gentle air,
And from its winding throat draws most melodious strains.

46

Behold from every fist its weapon fall!
The Emirs' hands in hasty tumult cling
Each to its neighbor's in a dancing ring,
A loud bacchantic Huzza! rends the hall
And young and old, whate'er has feet must spring,
The potent horn allows no choice at all.
The fair alone, at Huon's side amazed,
Amazed at once and joy'd, upon the wonder gazed.

47

The whole divan in giddy maze whirl round,
The old bashaws snap time in cadence nice
And now the Iman, as on smoothest ice,
Is with a swarthy gelding seen to bound.
No age, no rank from capering is spared,
Nor can the Sultan's self forbear to skip,
But seizing his grand Vizir by the beard
The old man would instruct one goat's leap more to trip.

48

Anon this unexampled frenzy passed
Into the antechambers, and soon drew
Tŏwards' the hall the mutilated crew,
The train of females next, the guards at last.
Among them all the jovial madness flew:
The tumult soon the Harem open threw,
The very gardeners came in aprons green
And reeling round in rows, with youthful nymphs were seen.

49

As one who scarcely can believe her eyes
Stands Rezia there, of breath well-nigh bereft.
"What wonder at the moment comes," she cries,
"When nothing else to save us both was left?"
"A friendly genius is with us, my queen,"
Returns the hero— Meanwhile, through the trains
Of dancers, hastening on with anxious mien
His way the faithful squire with Fatme strains.

50

"Come! Sir," he panting calls; "we cannot stay
To see them dance; the horses are at hand;
The palace is stark mad—wide open stand
The doors without a guard; why the delay?
On Mistress Fatme too I chanced to light
Packed like a beast of burden for the flight."
"Stay!" says the knight—" 'tis not yet time to go;
The hardest of the work, is yet, my friend, to do."

51

The damsel now turns paler than a sheet,
Her eye appears to ask and to entreat,
"Why stay? why on the verge of ruin stay?
Oh! let us hasten on the wings of winds,
Before the tumult shall dissolve away
Which all the senses of our foes now binds?"
The knight with looks which ardent love express
Contents himself her hand upon his heart to press.

52

The horn's effect subsiding by degrees,
The heads turned giddy, weak became the knees;
On all the dancers not a thread was dry
And in the breathless bosom swelling high
The curdled blood in lazier currents flows.
Th' unwilling joy becomes distracting pain.
Wet through, as if he from a bath arose
The Caliph staggering back, sinks in his chair again.

53

At every moment stiff and senseless falls
Where heave the swelling bolsters round the walls
One weary dancer by another's side.
Pell-mell the gasping slaves and Emirs slide
Down by some Harem nymph as chance disposes
And seem as by a whirlwind scattered there.
Thus, panting on the selfsame couch reposes
The kitchen scullion with the favorite fair.

54

Sir Huon of the moments makes the best,
While all are sunk throughout the hall to rest,
And leaving near the door his fair in ward
Of his good squire, bids him be on his guard;
Gives him, in case necessity should call
The horn, and then draws near the spot, alone,
Where feeble yet, and breathless from the ball
Stretched out the Sultan lay upon his bolstered throne.

55

With wings expanded in dull silence lies
Soft breathing expectation all around.
In giddy sleep, their senses almost drowned,
The dancers strive to open still their eyes
To see the stranger who from such a deed
With hand unarmed and gestures that entreat
Draws slowly near th' astonished Sultan's seat.
What, think they, from all this, will finally proceed?

56

Before the monarch on one knee he bends
And mildly thus, with cool heroic brow:
"Imperial Charles, to whom I homage owe,
To greet the lord of eastern nations sends,
And—pardon what I speak reluctant strong—
To him my lips as well as arm belong—
Four teeth requests thee from thy jaws to spare
And from thy silver beard, one handful of the hair."

57

He spoke and ceased—then stood with placid look
The answer of the Sultan to await.
But where shall I find breath, in words to state
The fury into which the old lord broke?
How wild his features in an instant are!
How snort his nostrils! with what fierceness fell
As from his throne he starts, his eye-balls glare
And with impatience how his veins all swell.

58

Rage, as he strives to curse with frantic stare
On his blue foaming lips breaks every word.
"Up, slaves! his heart out of his bosom tear!
Hack him up piece-meal! drain his blood abhorred
With needles! let him in the flames be cast!
And to the winds of Heaven his ashes strew!
His emperor Charles may God forever blast!
What? such a thing to me? and in my own house too?

59

"Who is this Charles, that dares me thus defy?
If he thus longs to have my teeth and beard,
I should be glad to know the reason why
Himself comes not to pluck them out to try."
"The fellow's intellect must be impaired,"
Says an old Chan— "To ask for such a thing
A man at any rate to be prepared
Three hundred thousand men should with him bring."

60

"Caliph of Bagdad!" (now the hero said
With noble pride) "let all be silent here
And hear me! Heavy at my breast have laid
Long, my own word, and Charles's charge severe.
The ties of Destiny are cruel bands;
Yet her control what power on earth can shun?
Still, what to do and suffer she commands,
This must be suffered and that must be done.

61

"In me a mortal, like yourself behold
Standing alone, prepared my life to stake,
Spite of your guards, my promise good to make;
And let me now one offer more unfold.
Be all the errors of your faith retracted;
Your Mahomet's false tenets here abjure;
Take up the cross, the Christian's symbol pure,
And you will thus do more than ever Charles exacted.

62

"Then, to discharge you, on myself I take
Without exception, from all other claim;
And he my neck must in the first place break
Who more shall ask! Young, single as I am,
What has already happened here to you
Loudly enough, that One is with me, cries,
Who more than all your thousands, Sir, can do:
And now, the best part choose as you are wise."

63

While, like a herald from the skies, in might
And beauty's grace appears the youthful knight;
The threatening lances round him while he braves,
Thus boldly speaks, thus valiantly behaves;
With cheeks where love and rosy pleasure glow
Tŏwards' him bends the fair, with neck inclined,
Yet shuddering with anxious fear to know
How all these wonders would at last unwind.

64

Sir Huon scarce the last word had expressed
When the old Shaw began, like one stark mad,
To cry, to rave, to stamp, and beat his breast
And altogether lost what wits he had.
All starting from their seats by fury pushed
The heathens snorting came with threatening stride;
And all at once spears, falchions, daggers rushed
Against the prophet's foe, from every side.

65

Unhurt, the knight his foes impending sees,
And wrenches from an hostile hand a lance;
Around him like a club he makes it dance,
And to the wall draws backwards by degrees.
A large gold dish upon the side-board found,
Of shield and breast-plate serves at once his end;
Already many gasp upon the ground,
Who, in his fury, with him dared contend.

66

The good Cherasmin, distant, at the door
To guard the ladies, mid the storm of fight
Thinks he beholds his former lord once more,
And stands a moment and enjoys the sight.
But soon dispelled, the pleasing fancy flies,
At Rezia's shrieks— He sees the heathens rave;
Sees his lord's danger, straight the horn applies
And blows as if the dead to summon from the grave.

67

The palace cracks beneath its echoing sound,
A dreadful night straight swallows up the day;
Like rapid lightnings spectres flit around
And constant thunders rock the solid ground;
The heathens' hearts all sicken with dismay,
They reel as drunk, no longer see or hear;
Out of their slackened hands, slip sword and spear
And all about in stiffened groups they lay.

68

The Sultan, strained with all these wonders o'er
Appears to struggle with the pangs of death.
His arm is nerveless, hardly heaves his breath,
His pulse beats feebly, and at length no more.
At once, the storm is calmed, the sky serene,
A lily fragrance gentle zephyrs wave,
And like an angel's form upon a grave,
The king of Fairies on a cloud is seen.

69

A cry of joy and fear escapes the dame;
Involuntary shudderings contest
With timid confidence to rack her frame;
She stands with folded arms across the breast
And sweetest virgin consciousness of blame
Beside the youth of all her heart possessed.
And while her cheek a rosy blush displays,
Her eyes she scarcely dares on her deliverer raise.

70

"Huon, 'tis well; thy promise thou hast freed,"
Said now the elf; "thy conduct I approve;
Be this fair maid thy knightly valor's meed:
Yet, from this place before you shall remove,
On her resolve, let Rezia's thoughts advise;
Before she haply with repentance vain
Rue the rash choice of fascinated eyes;
Fate leaves her free to go or to remain.

71

"From royal grandeur's splendid state to flee,
The court and throne, her birthright to forsake;
And with a man upon the world's wide sea,
A dubious pilgrimage to undertake:
To live for him alone, the ebb and flow
Of luck with him to bear, the blows of fate;
(From a dear hand, comes oft, alas! the blow),
First with her heart 'twere well the question to debate.

72

"Still, Rezia, shouldst thou view the risk with dread,
'Tis still with thee to balk the wish of love:
These only sleep, who seemingly lie dead,
And will revive when I my staff shall move.
In spite of what the Sultan by it lost
He freely will forgive thee what has passed,
And Rezia see, as she beheld before,
Again the whole world her bright charms adore."

73

Here ceased the dwarf, and while with strong dismay
Sir Huon stands to hear the damsel speak
The sentence threatened by the cruel fay,
To ashes sinks the fire upon his cheek.
Too noble or too proud a doubting heart
With bribes of love's soft eloquence to gain,
Upon the ground he stares with deep felt pain
Nor suffers e'en a look in his behalf to dart.

74

But Rezia burning with his earliest kiss
No tinder more the flame to kindle needs:
How little all she must resign she heeds,
In him to hold her sum of earthly bliss.
Up to the eyes with love and shame she glows,
And hides her visage and the tears that stream,
In his fond arms, while with delight extreme
Her beating heart springs up, with his to close.

75

And Oberon tŏwards' them waving slow
The lily wand, his blessing thus imparts
Upon the tender union of their hearts
And drops a tear on either lover's brow.
"Oh! hasten then upon the wings of love
Thou charming pair! my chariot is at hand,
Ere the next dawn the tribes of shade remove,
Safe with you on the shore of Askalon to land."

76

Thus speaking, ere the last word reached their ears
The Spirit vanished from before their eyes.
As from a dream awaked the bride appears
Eager to scent the fragrance sweet that flies
Yet floating in the air——her timid sight
Upon her sire, as dead he seems to lie,
She sinks; her bosom heaves a sorrowing sigh
And mingles bitterness with all her heart's delight.

77

She veils her face—— No sooner Huon spies
(Love keens his sense) the sorrows of her eyes
And marks the anguish on her heart that preys,
Than throwing his right arm about her waist
With soft constraint he draws the fair in haste
Out of the hall—— "Come! come away!" he says,
"Ere night surprise us, and each arm awake
By Oberon bound in slumber for our sake.

78

"Come! let us haste ere some new foe appear
And seek perhaps our passage to impede;
And be assured that when we once are freed,
Our guardian of these sleepers will take care."
Then down the steps, with youthful vigor light
He brings her to the car before the door,
By Oberon provided for the flight,
And never mortal man a sweeter burden bore.

79

The palace through a grave-like silence reigns,
While with their senses in deep slumber bound
The guards like corpses lie dispersed around
And naught to stay the flight of love remains.
Yet with the knight is Rezia not alone,
With them the squire and nurse the car ascend,
And Fatme, who the like had never known,
Poor woman! scarce can guess where all these wonders tend.

80

How strange! Instead of horses to behold
On looking back, four swans the chariot bear
Drove by a child! how all her blood runs cold
When, lifted up and swimming through the air
She feels herself! nor can her wits devise
As scarce she breathes, how, without turning o'er
With such an heavy load the chariot flies
And steadier than a boat, on slender clouds can soar.

81

When finally the shades of darkness came,
What wonder, fear at last should vanquish shame?
And Fatme to the squire as close should creep
As to her pillow for the sweets of sleep?
Belike in him she small reluctance found,
The heart is seldom shy for such a game;
Yet to the old man's praise it must redound
That like pure gold he stood the trial of this flame.

82

Quite otherwise were tuned the youthful pair,
Whom with his mother's swans the God of love
Now seems to drive—for whether through the air
Or in the common paths their journey move;
Whether they roll or swim, drive swift or slow,
Easy or hard, by swan conveyed or steed—
Whether with danger or without they go;
Of all this took they not the smallest heed.

83

A new delicious dream with Heaven replete
They deem their present state, and naught can do
But speechless with a never sated view
Gaze on each other, while with ardor sweet
To the full heart they press the glowing hand;
And when both Heaven and earth have vanished far,
And they alone remain, by turns demand,
"Is it, or dream we still? and are we in one car?"

84

" 'Twas then no dream, when dreaming I saw thee!
'Twas Huon"— "It was Rezia met my view."
"It was a God, who brought thee now to me!"
"Thou mine? I thine? who could have hoped it, who?
Thus wondrously to meet! no more to part—
Say, can the heart such bliss ecstatic bear?"—
And then anew they on each other stare,
Again each other's hand press close to lips and heart.

85

In vain with vapor-loaded wings the night
Veils all the sky— Love's ken it cannot stay.
Their eyes beam forth a more than earthly light
In which each other their warm souls survey.
Night is no night for them. Elysian shores
And Heaven, in all around them they behold;
Their sunshine from within its radiance pours,
And every moment senses new unfold.

86

Th' ecstatic joys insensibly proceed
The swelling heart in magic sleep to lull:
The eye-lids close, the senses all grow dull;
The soul in fancy from the body freed,
By one exclusive feeling all surrounded,
Inspired, and filled, and penetrated through,
By that alone its own existence knew;
But oh! that single feeling!—how unbounded!

OBERON

Book the sixth

1

Scarce had Aurora chased the shades away,
And oped with rosy hand the gates of day,
When from the strand of Askalon not far,
By swans transported thither through the air
Beneath the shade of palm-trees stopped the car,
And by a shock awaked our double pair.
One from the pleasing lap of slumber drove,
The other from the wakeful dreams of love.

2

The damsel trembles, in a sweet dismay,
When for the first time to her eyes ascends
Th' unbounded ocean in the morning ray;
Ranging in unimpeded course extends
O'er all the watery mass her wondering sight;
Before her, boundless space appears to be;
Yet shudderings mingle with her new delight,
In boundless space herself so small to see.

3

"Where am I?" she exclaims with clouded mien;
But soon the knight, who from the chariot springs,
With open arms, to bear her to the green,
Back to itself the fluttering spirit brings.
"Be without fear, my dearest life," he cries
(While his fond lips, which ardent passion warms,
He presses to her breast, that silent sighs),
"Be without fear! thou art in Huon's arms."

4

Once more with keen delight she feels to be
Encircled by her lover's arms again,
And ivy clings not closer to its tree
Than Rezia's arms round Huon's body strain.
Now with his load he to the palm-trees hies,
Seats her in shade upon a mossy spot;
Sits down himself beside his charming prize
And would not change his place for any Sultan's lot.

5

To them the squire and Fatme soon repair
Both he and she, firmly resolved in mind
To the last gasp to serve the lovely pair.
Scarce was Cherasmin on the green reclined
Next to his lord, a place while Fatme sought
Beside the knee of her young lady fair,
When, as if sped upon the wings of thought
The handsome dwarf came swimming through the air.

THE FRONTISPIECE OF THE 1789
EDITION OF *OBERON*

This engraving by Geyser, after a drawing by J. M. Kraus, shows
the arrival at Askalon (Canto VI, stanza 3, 2–4).

6

As he drew near, the mildly radiant light
Of friendship from his eyes through sorrow beamed;
And studded thick, a casket met their sight
Which like a sun beneath his left arm gleamed.
"Take this," said he, "friend Huon, from my hand
Though not expressly asked by Charlemagne.
Be this thy proof on seeing him again,
That thou hast word for word accomplished his command."

7

Observe (albeit the thing to have declared
Had been unfit in presence of the fair),
That the old Sultan's four jaw-teeth and beard,
Packed up with cotton, in this casket were.
A viewless elf of Oberon's trusty band,
While in his chair yet stiff the Caliph lay,
With active zeal had plied a nimble hand
And taken without shears or pincers all away.

8

"Haste!" says the dwarf, "before the Sultan gain
Time for pursuit; there in the harbor lays
A vessel, which in six or seven days
Will to Lepanto bear you o'er the main.
Another ready there when you arrive
To bring you to Salerno you will meet;
Then, swift as love and your desires shall drive,
Straight in the shortest way to Rome direct your feet.

9

"And deep, oh! Huon, grave it on thy sense,
Till pious pope Sylvester shall dispense
Heaven's blessing on your ties,—behold each other
The time between, as sister and as brother.
Forbear! nor pluck before the nuptial rite
The sweet forbidden fruit of love's delight.
For know, the instant when you taste, forever
Must Oberon himself from you dissever."

10

He spoke and sighed and silent sorrow swelled
His eyes. At his command they near him drew.
He kissed their brows— Then, upwards they beheld
And like a cloud he vanished from their view.
The face is mantled of the golden day,
Along the palm-trees rustle mournful sighs;
O'er earth and main damp chilling vapors rise,
And in a shapeless mass they seem to melt away.

11

Still terrors and strange pangs the pair oppress—
Each other they behold with pallid cheek;
Upon their lips expires what they would speak.
Each to the bosom would the other press,
But secret horrors still their arms restrain.
Yet soon, at once the dreary vapors fall;
In sunshine smiles once more around them, all,
And joy and spirit come to fill their hearts again.

12

And hastening on, the ship with joy they find
Prepared to sail and gallantly arrayed
By their protector's kindness— A fresh wind
Blows from the shore— The anchor straight is weighed;
The sailors shout— Swift as a bird can fly
The ship with wings expanded cleaves the main;
Clear and serene above them is the sky
And smooth as glass below, the liquid plain.

13

Soft-floating o'er the waves, with swan-like pride,
The bark scarce left a trace upon the tide.
The sons of Ocean view it all amazed;
"No, never mortal such a passage made,"
They all exclaim— Hours long our couple stayed
Upon the deck, with arms entwined, and gazed;
While each successive scene upon the deep
Like opium lulled their passion's stings to sleep.

14

When o'er the boundless plains they bend their sight
To where the blue wave melts in skies away,
Of his dear native country talks the knight;
The land how lovely! and the folks, how gay!
And how, from East to West, the rolling sun
Can shine on nothing after all more fair,
Than on the blooming banks of his Garonne,
And to all this fails not his trusty squire to swear.

15

The heart within him never fails to bound
When his dear Gascogne's praises he can chant.
Though now and then the lovely Rezia found
The words they spoke to her a meaning want,
Untired she listens, for she loses naught
Of what, with joy ineffable her heart
New as it is, with ease the sense has caught
Of what—to her Sir Huon's eyes impart.

16

Of the warm trembling hand a gentle squeeze,
A sigh, the full heart of its load to ease,
Snatched from the rosy cheek, a whispered kiss,
And oh! a look fresh bathed in Cupid's dew;
What can persuade and win and move like this?
Spite of the fleetest dart, whatever flew
So swift from heart to heart, with aim so nice?
Or to so little weariness gave rise?

17

Mid such discourse of souls between our two
The mere discourse of words in silence died;
Oft, witnesses to shun, they both withdrew
And at the cabin-window side by side
Stood, or themselves upon their sopha seated.
Yet even then not quite alone they were;
At least the nurse was always with them there,
Not to be left alone, the knight himself entreated.

18

"Pluck not before the rite," in tone severe
A dreadful voice sounds ever in his ear;
"For know," said Oberon, "that we must sever
If otherwise the case should prove, forever."
What meant this threat? For o'er his looks was spread
Deep meaning; still his brows more earnest grew,
Still more o'ercast—his eyes were bathed in dew
And ah! his face no more its usual splendors shed.

19

The hero's heart some fearful ill forebodes,
Himself he trusts not— The least jest of love
Awakes the fear lest Oberon disapprove,
While still within the smothered flame corrodes.
The air in which he breathes is magic air,
Because he shares it with his charming fair;
Her breath floats in it; her sweet shadow flies
Round every object where he turns his eyes.

20

She shines herself alike in morning's ray,
Eve's twilight, or the moon's soft shady day.
In each position he descries some charm,
In every attitude admires her form.
The veil which hides her close from every eye
Now falling back, to leave her charms confessed,
Permits the timid vent'rous look to pry
And suck itself like bees into her neck and breast.

21

He felt the danger— "Fairest!" oft he cried:
"If possible,—to keep the stern resolve,
Within a seven-fold veil thyself involve
And under thousand folds each beauty hide;
Let o'er the living ivory of this arm,
Down to the fingers' ends the sleeves extend;
And above all, good Oberon! my friend,
To turn my heart to stone, oh! use thy strongest charm."

22

Though the knight often felt his strength to fail,
He warmly wished the victory to gain.
In virtue's hardest combat to prevail,
A triumph great and fair was to obtain.
Merely to undertake 'twas great and fair,
And ten-fold fair and great to carry through;
Yet, by what means an enemy subdue,
With whom the more you fight, his powers the stronger are.

23

Naught to this enemy resigns the day
So speedily, as with the cherished fair,
In silence to your feelings to give way.
Sir Huon chances in his mind to bear
His duty, as the knightly customs claim,
In Christian doctrines to instruct the dame.
Poor child! In heathenism he sees her lie,
And Mahomet believe, albeit she knows not why.

24

The damsel of this pestilence to heal
He makes what speed he can (love bids him speed)
His little Christian wisdom to reveal.
In zeal no martyr could the knight exceed.
His faith was strong; his knowledge weak indeed.
Nor was theology his shining side;
Unglossed, his pater-noster and his creed,
It must be owned, was all his learning him supplied.

25

Yet what perhaps of solid grounds or light
The doctrine wants, the teacher's fire supplies;
A foe to wordy strife, our valiant knight
Proceeds as in a common enterprise.
To what himself believes, makes bold to swear
And offers with his sword, on earth and main
'Gainst the whole world of heathens to maintain,
And make in personal encounter clear.

26

Great is truth's power, by lips beloved conveyed!
In league before-hand with them stands the heart.
And silent lists to learn what they impart;
For, what as love so easy to persuade?
A look, a kiss, its grounds of faith express;
The fair, in questioning small trouble takes;
Her Huon she believes, and shortly makes
Upon her brows and breast her cross with much address.

27

The holy Christian sprinkling to confer,
Our hero's simple heart, athwart the way
Sees nothing left—and 'twas enough for her
To make her ardently desire the day,
That Huon wished it, and delay abhorred.
By chance on board, of heathens a great foe,
A monk of Basil's rule, for due reward
Was easily induced his functions to bestow.

28

Amanda now by name, the lovely fair
Since she the holy Christian faith assumed,
Not only gained the right Heaven's joys to share,
But fairer to the youth than ever bloomed.
But from that hour, from our enraptured knight
His better genius fled— In keen delight
No end the heart and hands soft pressures find;
In vain Cherasmin winks himself half blind.

29

In vain the nurse sits down before his bride;
In his soul's fever the good knight forgets
At once the dwarf, the danger and the threats;
The old man might have winked until he died.
His ecstasies to such a pitch attain:
The fair, whose kiss now angels e'en allow,
To call Amanda, to his heart to strain,
They quite distract his sense and cloud his 'wildered brow.

30

And Rezia, since she bears another name,
No longer Rezia, thinks herself more free
From all the bands of harsh restraint to be;
So much the readier forgets the dame
Court, country, royal pride, and sooth to say
Whate'er is not Amanda— Though her breast
Remembrance heavily till then depressed,
With her baptismal name, it fell at once away.

31

For Huon, with new life she is indued,
All what she was, for him she has resigned,
For love, a mighty throne itself declined,
And feels within his arms her loss made good.
Herself she gave and is Amanda now,
For love alone, through love alone to live,
Henceforth has naught else in the world to do,
Can nothing else receive and has naught else to give.

32

The honest squire with consternation sees
Our amorous pair in transports such as these.
I know not what strange ardor in their eyes,
That longs to pluck forbidden fruit, he spies.
'Twas plain, a witness they no longer brooked;
If but his back he for a moment turned,
Rapid and thirsty, how their kisses burned!
And how they blushed if on them he but looked!

33

His own youth's mirror but too well discovers
To him, what now, no longer see the lovers;
Unpractised virtue like a moth he sees,
Thoughtless draw near the taper by degrees.
How soft the warmth and mild effulgence feels!
And, while her innocence itself betrays,
In narrowing circles round and round she wheels,
Till, ah! her wings at once are in a blaze.

34

In this extremity the faithful squire,
Leagued secretly with Fatme to that end,
Leaves naught untried, which he believes will tend,
The virtue of the knight to keep entire
Till Rome— Now this occurs to him, now that,
To interrupt, employ, or dissipate;
And when he finds all other means to fail,
One evening to gain time, concludes to tell a tale.

35

A tale he calls it, though in truth 'twas more;
Which from a Calender he had received,
At Bassora, when of his lord bereaved
He wandered through the east, and long before
He in Libanus' wilds had to his cave
Retreated, from the world's tempestuous wave—
And as 'tis lively in his mind renewed,
He thinks it as a word in season may do good.

36

And thus begins:— Some hundred years ago,
On the Tessino's banks there lived a knight,
In wisdom not a little green, although
His hair and beard had long since turned to white.
With rheumatism and gout, of past excess
The bitter fruit, nigh martyred day by day,
A courtier else of talents and address,
And skilled the warlike game of love to play.

37

He, having long indulged his sinful heart
In love's free chase, while single he remained,
Ranging o'er hill and dale the game to start,
And whereso'er admittance he obtained,
Shameless to lie beside his neighbor's wife.
This very man at last the fancy took,
His stubborn neck, just on the verge of life
To bend to holy wedlock's gentle yoke.

38

With taste refined and well cooled blood he sought
A damsel, pious, good and safe to wed,
Alike for earnestness and sport well taught,
And fitted equally for board or bed;
Unpractised, modest, innocent and fair,
Chaste as the moon and free from idle freaks;
Young furthermore, with coal-black eyes and hair,
Round arms and breast and rosy-colored cheeks.

39

Of all the three and thirty points entire
Which go a handsome woman to compose,
To find his bride want none was his desire,
And least of all an eye with fire that glows
Where swims a light moist cloud—a small, soft hand,
Lips that swell outwards the warm kiss to meet,
A rounded knee, hips that with grace expand,
And to soft pressure the resistance sweet.

40

One thing alone, the five and sixty years
Which sprinkled snow already o'er his head,
The knight forgot on buying such fine wares.
Prompted indeed by some foreboding dread,
He by the very contract bound the bride
On him to lavish all her tender flame,
And be ice-cold to all the world beside;
But who to such a clause would answer for the dame?

41

Rosetta did— Rosetta was a child,
Who like a tender violet in the shade,
Bloomed in retirement—gay of heart and wild,
And in her future husband naught surveyed
But one who her a lady was to make,
For her rich clothes and thousand fine things bought,
In which a child delight by day could take;
Her little heart as yet of nothing else had thought.

42

The nuptials now were solemnized in state;
The bridegroom, marching at Rosetta's side,
Though somewhat stiff treads with so firm a gait—
Sure, his church-books by twenty years have lied.
Whate'er has eyes, crowds wondering to behold,
As to'wards church proceeds the rich array.
"A stately couple!" whispers round them rolled;
"As much alike, as *January* and *May*."

43

Rosetta's innocence, as oft betides
In such case, was the pride of Gangolf's heart.
Next morn, with exultation how he strides!
And treads the carpet straighter than a dart!
It was the latest shoot of withering wood,
For soon the ills that with gray love reside,
Came with the knight to take up their abode,
And melted him the more, the warmer grew his bride.

44

Meanwhile he doubles in another way
His proofs of tenderness—jewels and lace,
New gowns and fashions gives her every day,
In short, whate'er to beauty adds a grace.
Whatever can contribute to her bliss,
Cost what it will, delights the husband's heart;
For it he asks in turn, at most a kiss,
And in one word performs—the old man's part.

45

Pleased with her lot, the young Rosetta still
Spares naught the old man in his way to please,
Sits on his lap as often as he will,
And suffers him to rock her on his knees.
In all his weakness fosters him with love,
With dandling such as he can give complies;
And if as oft befalls, he sleepy prove,
His heavy head upon her bosom lies.

46

While thus like turtle-doves in wedlock's bond
They live, their years in happy union fly;
The man so full of faith, the wife so fond,
That every one was edified thereby.
Amidst her jests the good old man forgets
His gout and in his back and loins the pains;
And for his sake alone, the fair regrets
When he his tenth climacteric attains.

47

It came alas! and to their heavy woe
An evil with it, on his hoary head,
Which robbed him of his dearest joys below,
And darkness o'er his aged eyeballs shed.
Her sunshine never more shall glad his sight,
No more that charming oval cheer his soul,
Of which, for angels and madonnas bright
So many a painter the soft features stole.

48

Poor, blind old man, were not Rosetta there
What solace would his tedious moments know?
What were his fate, did not her duteous care
Its consolations day and night bestow.
Incessantly she lends him eye and arm,
For him to read or write, with temper sweet;
Explores his wants, and oft his gout to charm,
With soft, warm hand rubs down his knees and feet.

49

Rosetta, gentle, complaisant and kind,
Without a murmur and without constraint,
This duty too fulfills with patient mind,
And though in secret his ill humors taint
At times her temper, she resolves, her care
Shall leave her spouse no reason to complain;
Till spite of her good will, in his armed chair
The worst of whims began to seize his brain.

50

The direst foe that ever slipped from hell,
To torture and make sport of mortals here,
Came in this hapless husband's breast to dwell;
Old, weak and blind, can he the thought forbear
That, much as his young wife an angel seems,
She is but woman?—tempters lurk about.
With open eyes the world about her teems,
And ah! the eye, which her should light, is out.

51

Thus young, thus fair, thus formed of tinder quite,
Who without glowing can behold her charms?
Where were cheeks ever seen to bloom so bright?
More sparkling eyes, and rounder lily arms—
Chaste is she truly and will fly the foe,
But will she not slip down in the endeavor?
'Tis polished steel o'er which her steps must go,
And she who once falls, falls alas! forever.

52

Her very virtues, her obliging ways,
Her lively temper's gay and kindly frame;
All that had tended most his love to raise,
E'en of her chaste embrace, the lovely shame;
Whatever else, of all her thousand charms,
Unveiled and beautified, remembrance brings;
With double venom now suspicion arms,
And in his wounded heart still deeper sinks her stings.

53

The slavery in which the good young dame
From that time languished, you can scarce conceive.
Forever buckled to his sickly frame,
His side she neither day nor night can leave.
His ears prick up at every whisper light
While at his fingers' ends he bears his eyes;
And lest she from his bed should slip by night
His bony hand, about, upon her lies.

54

Mild as she was, a treatment such as this
Weighed at her heart— He calls it love, forsooth;
But she, too well perceiving what it is,
Instead of wasting in complaint her youth,
Begins to think— As such a mortal's wife,
Whom gout and stone and seventy winters load,
With him to wade, as through a swamp, through life,
And plagued besides, she deems too much for flesh and blood.

55

Much that with patience she had overlooked
Seems as it now appears before her eyes,
Not by the sweetest temper to be brooked,
Her heaviest woes now from his fondling rise.
His jests are coarse—she sickens at his kiss—
If more he dare— Heaven bless her! she will die!
Yet—cruel fate! her youth and charms are his;
And what he cannot use, she must herself deny.

56

And, what reward?—forbidden fruit to her
Are all the city's joys—the play, the ball;
To visit her no human foot will stir;
The house seems as if haunted, shunned by all.
A garden which a lofty wall surrounds,
Where she can lean against a tree and muse,
Is all she has, to walk within its bounds,
And there her tyrant still her privacy pursues.

57

In Gangolf's castle bred, a noble page
Whom the old knight had lately made his squire,
Now first seemed worthy her regard t' engage.
He had indeed with languishing desire,
Long since presumed Rosetta to survey,
And oft his mouth had tried to own his flame,
But from occasion still she slipped away,
And he withdrew again with reverence for the dame.

58

But now amidst her troubles and vexation,
The tedious day and still more tedious night,
She feels the want of some such dissipation,
And sees the thing in quite another light.
She thought it hard in these her fairest days
From all life's comforts thus to be excluded,
And Walter now, whose look new heart displays,
Unwearied still, himself as comforter obtruded.

59

The more he speeds, the more his zeal is warmed,
And while he supplicates, and she denies,
A secret concert is between them formed,
Of which the only agents are their eyes.
For Gangolf's ears were truly far from blind,
And for an hundred eyes one ear oft serves;
The old man's straight to listen are inclined,
If in her clothes one fold to rustle he observes.

60

The forms of struggling are not long retained
In such constraint: the lady and her lover
Soon went so far that nothing more remained
Than how to draw still nearer to discover.
Watched by her jealous dragon day and night,
Whose cough no rest allows him to obtain,
On what expedient will Rosetta light
Some little time and space for Walter now to gain?

61

Want whets the wit. While she revolves in mind
This and that project, chooses and rejects,
E'en to the best her thoughts objections find,
Till she by chance a pear-tree recollects,
Which on the terrace in the garden rears
(Where, round a fountain, myrtle hedges grow),
Its high o'erhanging boughs, that rise like stairs,
And shelter from the sun the seat below.

62

The old man often to this cool retreat
Round which breathes always a soft balmy air,
When all was panting with the summer's heat,
Used with his darling consort to repair.
Along the fountain's banks to lie and rest
An hour or two, upon her lap reclined;
The garden key himself alone possessed,
And not a soul besides admittance there could find.

63

How shall the lovers now this key possess
Which Gandolf always in his pocket wears?
She slips it out, quite softly, with address,
At bed-time, while the old man hums his prayers.
Next day, the print in wax contriveth she
Unnoticed into Walter's hand to slide;
With a short note to indicate the tree;
Walter himself will for the rest provide.

64

Well—and what next?— It was a fine warm day
Tŏwards' the end of August, when our knight
Felt, as a shelter from the scorching ray
The myrtle bower to noontide rest invite.
"Come"—said he to his other self—"my dove!
Come! lead me, Rosy, to that quiet place,
Where since the God of wedlock crowned our love,
His eyes have seen so oft our chaste embrace."

65

Rosetta nods; before them Walter springs,
And opens without noise the garden gate;
Shuts it again and as if borne on wings,
Flies to the fountain; mounts the pear-tree straight;
Then where the broadest bough soft arching bent,
Mid thickest leaves the lady's throne he chose;
Meanwhile with tottering steps the old man went
Slow limping on and held fast by the arm his Rose.

66

The lips were nearly all he still retained
His great and various failings to redeem;
Oft therefore in discourse his lungs he strained,
His love, and wedlock's paradise his theme.
Thus, to divert his wife the old man aimed,
Then, on his side perhaps to bribe her soul,
About her charms much poetry declaimed,
And chiefly with a preachment closed the whole.

67

In this tone preaching he descants
Until she now has safely reached the spring
Where, you remember, the dear pear-tree flaunts;
There too he tells her many a tender thing;
And though his cough much tortures the poor man,
He strokes her blooming cheeks with wanton air;
And, to conclude, the preachment just began:
Dull pastime underneath the pear-tree to the fair!

68

"Is there," quoth he, thus sitting on the ground
Beneath the shade, his head upon her breast,
Stroking her satin arm so smooth and round
Backwards and forwards—"is there aught so blessed
As these pure joys, these comforts, this repose?
Thus loved; thus conscious to deserve the bliss:
All, that in short if thou dost love me, Rose,
Thyself must feel; can aught on earth compare with this?

69

"Say, my Rosetta"—here, to stroke her cheek
The old man still more tenderly begun,
"But freely, and without dissembling speak,
(One hears us, who can be deceived by none)
Are not thy poor blind husband's wishes vain,
With fondness like his own beloved to be?
And can his breast the dear hope entertain,
As thou art all to him, that he is all to thee?

70

"In truth if ancient sayings we believe,
A man cannot perform a sillier part,
Than pin his faith upon a woman's sleeve,
Trust in her looks or give her all his heart.
Diogenes the madman from his tun,
And Solomon the wise man from his throne,
All trust in women teach alike to shun.
Her fickleness, they say, her craft can match alone.

71

"To say no more of history profane,
Do we not e'en in holy scripture find
From the beginning, woman's faith but vain?
Brought not the first a curse upon mankind?
By his own daughters was good Lot beguiled;
The very sons of God, as Moses sings,
Before the flood, by wicked women spoiled,
Burnt in their punishable flames their wings.

72

"Of Jaels, Dalilahs and Jesabels,
Of Bathshebas and others howe'er named,
Whose histories the holy scripture tells,
I need not speak, albeit for truth not famed.
But when that Judith in her arms the brave
Old Marshal Holofern contrives to strain,
Makes drunk with love, then hurries to his grave,
Who that beholds it, can from tears refrain?

73

"But were of women e'en the greatest part
So rich in vice, so poor in virtue's page,
Yet thou, sole chosen darling of my heart,
Light of my eyes and comfort of my age,
Yet would I trust that thou wouldst faithful prove
And though the best should fail, wouldst firm remain.
For sure thy Gangolf's pure and tender love
Thou never wouldst reward with such a cruel pain."

74

"Wherefore"—with conscious cheeks replies in haste
The youthful dame, and draws her swan-like arm
(Which she had cast about the old man's waist)
Away in anger—"wherefore"—quick and warm
She cries—"this long discourse? declare what cause
I ever for it gave, in all my life?
How? must I think your heart could ever pause?
Or for a moment doubt the honor of your wife?

75

"Ah! woe is me! of all my love is this
The meed? to whom gave I my youthful prime?
To whom, of virgin innocence the kiss?
And oh! my fondness now is made my crime!
Me, he can doubt, who but for him have eyes.
My heart, which beats for him alone, distrust!
Proud man! will not this victory suffice?
Must you torment me too? how cruel! how unjust!"

76

Here ceased the fair, as if excess of smart
Choked up her voice's utterance in her breast—
He fell upon her neck, and to his heart
The faithful wife, with sobs repentant pressed.
"Weep not, my darling! oh! forgive the fault
Of love alone—I meant not thee to pain.
Forgive and kiss me— By this heavenly vault!
Of my Rosetta's truth, no doubt I entertain."

77

"So are you men"—thus saying, she recoils
Soft struggling from his kiss—"so are you all.
With flattery first you draw us in the toils,
And are we yours, possession stirs your gall
Instead of making your blood cheerly flow.
Woe to the woman then who must content you!
The very flame yourselves took pains to blow,
But kindles jealous rage, in secret to torment you."

78

The good man, whom at most unlucky time
His hip-gout seizes, knows not what to do;
But to his faithful wife again the chime
Of tender protestations to renew.
He swears that from his breast forever wide
All shadow of suspicion shall be drawn;
And then a loving kiss on either side
To ratify the bond of peace is given.

79

Into deep silence the fond couple fell,
From hearts too full or empty as you will—
She sighs— The old man begs her why? to tell;
"Nothing"—says she and sighs, in silence still.
He urges her— "Be not concerned, dear heart!
'Tis but a longing and will soon pass o'er"—
"A longing? So!—what bliss dost thou impart
To my declining age!"—Silent, she sighs once more.

80

"This"—cries he joyous, "thy cold baths have done;
But speak; shouldst thou suppress thy wish, I fear
It might both hurt thee and thy little one"—
"Oh!" quoth she, "if you saw this pear-tree here!
How fresh its leaves! and how its branches bend
Beneath the loads of golden fruit it bears!
I nothing said, for fear I might offend;
But I would give an eye for one of those same pears."

81

"I know the tree, and none throughout the land
Bears fruit so fine"—the good blind man replied.
"But what to do? nobody is at hand,
The servants in the field are scattered wide.
The tree is high and I am weak and blind;
Oh! were that rogue our Walter now but here!"
—"A sudden thought," quoth she, "just strikes my mind,
We need no soul besides ourselves, my dear.

82

"If for a single moment you would please
Leaning against the tree, your back to bend,
I from the terrace border here, with ease
Upon your shoulder could at once ascend.
Thence to the tree would only take a step,
To the first bough 'tis scarcely two spans high.
From childhood I was used to climb and leap;
I'm sure it will succeed—nay, do but try."

83

"With all my soul," the old man makes reply—
"And yet—if with misfortune thou shouldst meet?
Should a bough break—how then alas! could I
Assist thee?—What if thou shouldst wait, my sweet?"
—"I cannot wait, my love, once more I say;
You grudge me the small service, well I see.
Let me by no means give you trouble, pray;
Yet how could it be known? Here is but you and me."

84

What could be done?—The being of an heir
On that same longing might perhaps depend;
Half by constraint, half yielding to her prayer
At length the old man helps her to ascend.
He takes his stand, his back receives her feet,
And from the good old dotard's patient pate
Fresh she springs up into her airy seat
Where for her stolen joys beneath the foliage wait.

85

It happened now, to witness all this scene,
That opposite, upon a rosy steep
Sat Oberon, who with his fairy queen
Chanced on this spot their noon-tide rest to keep.
Meanwhile their zephyr-like, attendant elves
About the garden, from the heat of noon,
Had most of them in flower-stalks hid themselves,
In slumber there to wait the rising of the moon.

86

Unseen they sat, and of the words that passed
Between the man and wife had heard the whole,
And as upon the tree their eyes they cast,
It stung the fairy monarch to the soul.
"See there!" he to his consort cries—"see there!
How great the truth all wise adepts divulge!
What is too bad for woman's front to dare
Her sordid, filthy passions to indulge?

87

"Well did, friend Solomon, thy wisdom speak:
'A single honest man may yet be found;
But should you for one honest woman seek,
The search were fruitless all the world around.'
Seest thou, Titania, in that tree concealed,
How that vile wife her blind man has betrayed?
She thinks the night in which his eyes are veiled
Shrouds her as safe as Pluto's darkest shade.

88

"But, by my throne, by this my lily wand,
And by the awful power the fairy reign
Committed with this sceptre to my hand,
His blindness and her craft shall both prove vain
To help her— No! she shall not bear the prize
Of treason unavenged before my face;
I will remove the film from Gangolf's eyes
And in the flagrant act expose her to disgrace."

89

"Will you, indeed?" returns with hasty tone
And glowing cheeks the queen of fairy land;
"To match your oath then please to hear my own:
I swear, as sure as I your consort stand,
And of the fairy kingdom queen: the dame
To help her out shall not want ample powers.
Is not the husband too forsooth to blame?
Must freedom be your lot, and naught but patience ours?"

90

Yet Oberon her anger little heeds;
And as he swore, the old man's vision clears.
As, with the lily sceptre, he proceeds
To touch his eyes, the dimness disappears.
Amazed—delighted—he looks up, and straight
As if a swarm of wasps flew in his face,
Shakes his old head—he sees—oh! hellish fate!
His faithful consort—in a man's embrace!

91

Impossible! he did not rightly see!
His eyes were dazzled by unwonted light;
The *best of wives* thus guilty cannot be!
He looks once more—the same heart-piercing sight
Once more beholds—Like one possessed, he cries:
"Oh traitress! Siren! hell-born viper! Say,
Art thou not then ashamed before my eyes
So shamefully thy truth and honor to betray?"

92

As by a clap of thunder from the clouds
Rosetta roused springs up; an unseen arm
In magic mist the pallid lover shrouds.
The lady wonders what untimely charm
To make her blind old tyrant see again
Just on this luckless moment should have hit.
Yet had the elfin-queen not sworn in vain
That she to help her out should not at need want wit.

93

"What ails my dearest lord? and why this heat?"
She calls— "Oh! strumpet! Canst thou still inquire?"
—"And is suspicion the reward I meet?
Because to help you, such was my desire,
That, to restore your sight, I was contented
E'en to try magic? and oh! hapless wife!
Here with a sprite shaped like a man consented
To struggle, and have lamed my right arm in the strife.

94

"What merits thanks, you make a crime, my dear,
And with strange words of foul reproach pursue."
—"Ha!" cried he: "Job would lose all patience here;
Dost thou call struggling what I saw thee do?
So surely may the gracious hand of Heaven
Continue with its light these eyes to bless,
So surely, wretch! mayst thou to Hell be driven,
As that no decent word can such a deed express."

95

"How!" cries she, "can my Gangolf speak like this?
Ah me! too surely something there must be,
That in the magic process worked amiss;
Your eye from clouds is plainly not yet free.
How could you else, in terms of such despite
Dare thus to murder your most faithful spouse?
Your sight as yet can be no real sight
But the mere glimmer of uncertain shows."

96

"Oh! could I possibly deceived have been!
Happy the man whom only doubts torment!
But I," he cries, "unhappy I have seen!
Seen what I saw."—"Immortal powers relent!
Was ever a more wretched wife alive,"
(With floods of tears the cunning traitress whined)
"Oh! must I this misfortune too survive?
My poor, dear husband is beside his mind."

97

And say, what tender-hearted man, though wise,
In all his senses' spite, would not be so;
On seeing such a bosom heave with sighs
And such fine eyes with gushing tears o'erflow?
The old man cannot long resist such charms;
"Be pacified! I was too quick," says he.
"Forgive me, and come down into my arms;
'Tis plain as day, my love, I did not rightly see."

98

"Titania! hearst thou?" says the monarch now.
"What with his eyes he saw, a single tear
Has washed away! 'Tis thy work! triumph thou!
But of all oaths, the sacredest now hear!
I thought I was beloved—it made me proud—
It was a dream and thou hast waked my heart;
Hope not a tear my senses too can cloud,
From this time forward you and I must part.

99

"We never more, in water or in air,
Where flowery hedges dewy balsam rain,
Or in dark caverns the lank griffin's care
Enchanted treasures guards, must meet again.
The air in which you breathe, I loathe—begone!
On your whole faithless sex my curses fall!
And on the coward slaves by whom are drawn
Your odious chains! alike I hate you all.

100

"And where a man, whom woman's arts abuse,
A heedless woodcock, to her springes flies;
Is tamely caught, and while he lies and coos,
Sucks falsest poison from her wanton eyes;
Thinks it is love her viper breast that heaves,
And to the smiling Siren's voice gives ear;
Trusts to her oaths, her fraudful tears believes,
His be the worst of ills, the worst of torments here.

101

"And by that name tremendous be it sworn;
Which to pronounce not even spirits dare,
That naught this curse and my resolve shall turn,
Till pointed out by fate, a constant pair,
United by love's chastest, fondest dart,
And proof alike to bliss and woe supreme,
With hearts unsevered, though their bodies part,
Shall by their innocence this harlot's guilt redeem.

102

"And should this pair of guiltless souls and pure,
Give all for love, and under every pain
Unmoved the strokes of harshest fate endure,
Faithful, with water to the chin remain,
And in the flames choose rather to be cast
Than faithless even for a throne to be;
When this, Titania, when all this has passed,
May you and I once more each other see."

103

He spoke and vanished from her sight; in vain
She with a voice of tender love implored
And called him back into her arms again;
E'en though himself now rued the hasty word,
Spoke in his anger, yet could naught unbind
His solemn oath, until as it requires,
What wholly seems impossible to find,
Appear two lovers such as he desires.

104

From that time forward to this very day
In his own shape he never would appear,
But still has chosen, as the people say,
Now a high mountain, now a forest drear,
Now a deserted vale for his abode,
Where he delights lovers to plague and sunder.
That on the contrary, he has bestowed
Blessings on you alone, is truly like a wonder.

105

Here brought the squire his story to a close;
And Huon takes Amanda by the hand;
"If Oberon and his queen for their repose
Only" (says he) "a constant pair demand,
Then is Fate's work just bursting to effect.
Did not his hand our wondrous union fetter?
Us,—else a foe to love,—his cares protect.
The proofs!—Oh! let them come, the sooner still the better."

106

The fair, with looks where all her soul was shown,
For answer lays his hand upon her heart.
When for him she so much had given and done,
What was there left for language to impart?
And now a scene of ecstasies ensues
At which how oft soe'er he nods his head,
The good Cherasmin, of his tale to lose
At once the fruit, has no small cause to dread.

107

True—the chaste veil of innocence yet hides
Their growing danger to the gentle pair;
As yet their tenderness pours forth its tides
More freely, the more pure its sources are.
A newer pair in love's affairs was never,
And hence their lot was by a hair suspended:
For, all their happiness to blast forever
On one forgetful moment still depended.

Book the seventh

1

Meanwhile the elements, as Oberon sways,
All favor our heroic, tender pair,
And at the close of seven clear pleasant days
Them to the harbor of Lepanto bear.
Here, as the knight on his arrival finds,
Prepared to sail two light-winged vessels lay;
One, waiting for Marseilles propitious winds,
And one for Naples just about to weigh.

2

The young lord, who Cherasmin's vigilance
And mentor-look a little tedious thought,
Was much rejoiced at this kind hit of chance
And straight to make the most of it he sought.
"Friend," quoth he, "there may pass a year and day
Before in Paris I myself can show.
Thou know'st to Rome I promised first to go,
And to this duty must all else give way.

3

"Yet, I am anxious Charlemagne should see
I kept my word— My subject liege thou art;
What I cannot, accomplish thou for me;
Ascend the vessel ready to depart
Bound to Marseilles. To court then hasten straight;
And there, to make the Emperor relent,
This casket with the teeth and beard present,
And to him what thou hast beheld, relate.

4

"And say that nothing shall my steps delay
When the Pope's holy blessing I shall bear,
The Sultan's daughter at his feet to lay.
Farewell, old friend! the wind blows fresh and fair.
They just weigh anchor— Luck thy course attend!
And when my charge thou hast performed, to Rome
Thy course to seek me in the Lateran bend,
And who knows but we both together there may come."

5

The faithful old man looks with glistening eyes,
Shakes his gray head and would most gladly take
The liberty for this unkind surprise
To his young lord remonstrance smart to make.
Yet he restrains himself—although 'tis plain
He thinks the casket without harm might wait
Until the knight himself were in a state
In person his account to give to Charlemagne.

6

Yet as his prince and friend was on it bent,
What could he do but to depart consent?
He kissed Amanda's hand and to his breast
The dear young hero strained with moistening eyes,
Whom as it seemed his presence now oppressed.
At last, tears trickling down his beard, he cries:
"Sir! dearest Sir! may all God's blessings rain
On you, and may we soon and joyous meet again!"

7

The knight's heart beats when now between his friend
And him he sees the deep still wider spread.
"What have I done? Where has my rashness led?
Where with his lord did ever man intend
So well as this? In dangers how he stayed
True at my side! How cruel his reward!
Who now when reason fails shall lend me aid?
And who against myself in future be my guard?"

8

Thus secret he exclaims, and to himself
And Oberon swears (for though concealed to view,
Around his brow the softly fluttering elf
He feels in fancy) all he can, to do,
With glory, love and duty's strife to fight.
Cautious, he keeps from his Amanda far:
By day casts o'er the main his mournful sight,
And gazes all night long upon the polar star.

9

Amanda sees him, in whose bosom lies
Her heart, thus changed, and is the more perplexed,
As she no reason for it can devise.
Yet, at her want of charms to cheer him vexed,
In tenderness, much more than in her pride,
She naught but gentleness and patience shows;
While the strange evil hourly grows more wide,
And day and night robs both the lovers of repose.

10

One night, about the time when in the skies
Arcturus sparkling sunk on Thetis' breast,
Hushed into silence was the bustling noise
And like a wheat-field by soft Zephyrs pressed,
Ocean scarce moved. The people, to a man
With all their senses in deep slumber closed,
The wine digested, in their veins that ran,
And even at the helm secure the steersman dozed.

11

E'en Fatme, at her lady's feet to rest
Had sunk— Oh! Huon, from thine eyes alone;
Alone, oh! Rezia, from thy anxious breast
Is sleep yet banished— The poor souls atone
For love's sweet poison— How its blazing brands
Burn in their blood— And oh! they are so nigh!
Between them a partition only stands,
Nor can they heave unheard a single sigh.

12

The knight, to whom his passion long suppressed
Became a torture, whom each bitter tear
Which from Amanda's eyes his harshness pressed,
Burnt at his heart, sighed out so loud and drear,
As if he breathed his last— With love and shame
She who an hour had strove, could not forgo
At length to ask what thus convulsed his frame,
And tender consolations to bestow.

13

In a white night-gown, with an angel's charms
His room she entered, while soft pity beamed
In her chaste look. Her timid open arms
Before him like an opening heaven seemed—
But now so wan, so deadly pale, his face
Grew red as fire: his pulse, which scarcely crept
Lazy and spiritless, doubled now its pace,
And like a fish in glassy water leapt.

14

But Oberon's word again straight casts him down;
And by her kindness bold already grown,
When to his bosom he the fair would strain,
Quick from her kiss and breast himself he flings;
Attempts to fly, then stops, then comes again
In haste, and just as to her arms he springs,
Starts off, while round him frantic looks he throws,
As if resolved at once to shorten all his woes.

15

She sinks upon the bed—high beats her heart
Through the soft yielding garb, and streams of tears
Fall from her eyes, by love weighed down with smart;
The sight no longer human nature bears.
Half senseless now (come of it e'en the worst!)
He takes her up; his lips intensely glow
And suck the dew of love with scorching thirst,
While of his loosened heart the streams unbounded flow.

16

Rapt by her love, the fair too on her part
Forgets resistance and yields up to bliss;
Straining and strained in transports to the heart,
Heedless she quaffs the long unwonted kiss.
The copious draught that from her lips of fire
His mouth insatiate drinks, his reason drowns.
The maddening heart emboldens fierce desire,
And oh! in Hymen's stead their union Cupid crowns.

17

Straight the sky blackens: quenched is every star,
Ah! happy souls! unnoticed by their eyes.
With tempest-laden pinions from afar
Unchained, the raging tribe of rough winds flies.
They hear it not!— In darkest anger veiled,
Beside them Oberon rushes on the spot.
They hear him not!—thrice has the thunder pealed
With threatening voice—alas! they hear it not!

18

Meanwhile bursts forth and whistles in the shrouds
An unexampled storm from every side.
Earth's axle cracks, the bosom of black clouds
Pours streams of fire; the sea roars far and wide.
The foam-capped waves in swelling mountains rise.
In course unsteered the staggering bark is tossed;
In vain to storm-deaf ears the pilot cries.   [lost!"
Loud howls throughout the ship: "Woe! woe!—we all are

19

The fury of the winds that spurn all bound,
The welkin like a hell, one fiery flame;
The ceaseless cracking of the vessel's frame
Which in the lowest deep by turns seemed drowned,
And soaring up to heaven, upon the head
Of waves, to spray beneath her dashed, to dance;
All this, enough to frighten up the dead
Could not but rouse at last our lovers from their trance.

20

From the loved arms she starts aghast away.
"Almighty God!" she cries, "what have we done?"
The conscious knight implores the guardian fay
For aid and pity, though for her alone.
In vain! for Oberon, now a judge severe
Is at his bar relentless as the grave.
The pledges of his favor disappear:
The cup and ivory horn.—— He hears but will not save.

21

Called by the captain now together came
The crew— "You see," said he, "our perilous state;
At every pulse by water, wind or flame
The ship is threatened with the worst of fate.
I ne'er saw such a storm— Heaven seems to death
For one man's guilt perhaps to doom us all.
To stop one criminal's devoted breath,
On whom the avenger's lightning seeks to fall.

22

"Let us by lot then ask of Heaven to show,
Which is the destined victim by it sought.
Is there among you one who dreads the blow?
Where all must perish, no one hazards aught"—
He spoke—to his proposal each agrees;
To hold the lots the chaplain brings an urn;
Around him all the crew are on their knees;
He mutters a short prayer—then bids them draw in turn.

23

With boding soul, but firm, undaunted heart
The knight, his looks on Rezia fixed, draws near;
And while she, chilled with terror stands apart
A statue pale—he draws—(Oh! Fate severe,
Oh! Oberon!) with cold and trembling hand
The lot of death— All silent on him gaze.
Bloodless, he reads; attempts not to withstand,
But the severe decree of destiny obeys.

24

"This, Oberon! this work is thine," he cries.
"Spirit incensed! I feel, I feel thee near,
Although yet undiscovered by mine eyes.
Thou toldst me this! thou gav'st me warning clear.
Just is thy doom! no pardon I implore
But for Amanda. Her forgive and spare!
She was not guilty—thy resentment pour
On me alone and I with patience all will bear.

25

"You, whom my death preserves, one pious tear
Give to the youth by luckless fate pursued.
I die not guiltless, yet my life was fair—
One moment, by the poison sweet subdued,
My word too rashly promised, I forgot.
Forgot the warning, in my fearful sense
That now too late resounds—the general lot
Of mortals, weakness—was my sole offense.

26

"The lovely fault I never can regret;
Though harshly punished I disdain to moan.
Is love a crime? then Heaven my sins forget!
My heart in death no duty else can own.
What else but love on thee can I bestow,
Oh! thou, who all to me for love didst give?
No watery grave can quench this sacred glow;
No! in thy Huon's shade immortal it shall live."

33

Canst thou their death unpitied, Oberon, see?
Thou who so late their friend, their guardian wast?
Thou seest—thou weepst—wilt thou relentless be?
He turns and flies!— Alas! their die is cast!—
Fear not!—the ring suspends them on the wave,
And both unhurt shall reach the nearest strand.
Their lives the strange mysterious ring shall save,
By Rezia received from Huon's hand.

34

No element can quench his vital ray
Who holds this seal of Solomon the great;
With it, through flames unscorched he makes his way.
Is he in prison? every bar and gate
Flies at his touch— If instant he would fly
From Trent to Memphis, the ring lends him wings.
This Talisman will every power supply
To him around whose finger once it clings.

35

Its powers will make the moon desert her sphere,
And at his pleasure in a viewless cloud
In open market and with sunshine clear
From spirits even, will the holder shroud.
If any one before him he would bring
Be it a man or beast, a ghost or shade,
He needs for summons only press the ring
And straight it must appear—his nod must be obeyed.

36

In earth and air, in water and in flame,
This wondrous ring the spirits all obey.
The wildest monsters at its sight grow tame,
And Antichrist draws near it with dismay.
Nor is a might on earth or in the skies,
From him who stole it not, this ring to wrest.
Its boundless powers to guard itself suffice,
And shield the hand by which 'tis rightfully possessed.

37

The ring, Amanda, saves thee on the main;
Thee and the man to whom love's holy band
And thy strong arm, thy tender bosom chain;
Who knew not how, but on an island's strand
Thee and himself again, oh! wonder! found.
Chance truly for you a rough bed has chose;
One mere volcanic ruin seems the ground,
Nor can your eyes on leaves, or aught of green repose.

38

This was not what the lovers first perceived,
In moments with tumultuous raptures fraught.
Thus from the billows wondrously retrieved,
Thus beyond hope unhurt to dry land brought.
Safe, free, alone, embraced, themselves to find,
This happiness immeasurably great
Makes all around them vanish from the mind:
Yet were they soon called back to feel their hapless state.

39

Wet to the skin, how could they out of hand
Forbear, themselves upon the shore to strip?
High was the sun, deserted was the strand,
And while on rocks their hanging garments drip,
Where shall they from the sultry sunbeam go,
Which thy soft skin, Amanda, stings and parches?
The gravel burns their feet, the pebbles glow
And ah! no tree, no bush, a shelter for them arches!

40

At last the young man's fearful eye detects
A rocky cave; with her he to it flies;
And for a bed some withered moss collects
And sedge (for need must anything suffice).
Then by her side himself upon it throws;
Sighing they gaze, and from each other's eyes
Soft solace suck for all their present woes
And all that threaten them in future to arise.

41

Oh! Love! sweet comforter of human care,
Delicious ravishment of wedded souls!
What other blessings can with thine compare?
How dire the change that o'er this couple rolls,
How sudden the transition, and how great!
Once fortune's darlings, from a throne now hurled,
Scarce with their lives they shun the stroke of fate,
Yet might their bliss excite the envy of the world.

42

The proudest hall in royal splendor dressed
Has in Amanda's eyes not half the charms
Of this wild grot—and, to her bosom pressed
He is a God—immortal in her arms.
The withered moss on which their limbs repose,
To them feels softer than the richest bed;
And yields a sweeter scent than had the rose,
Lily or jasmine, fragrance o'er it shed.

43

Alas! the dear delusion cannot last,
However cherished by their hearts' desires.
Two hours indeed insensibly have passed,
Yet nature other food at length requires.
Who here shall serve them?—from this desert strand
To cheat their hunger nothing can be drawn;
And Oberon, alas! withdrew his hand,
Incensed, from them away—the golden cup is gone.

44

With feet unwearied the young man ascends
The cliffs around and gazes far and wide.
A frightful mass of rocks and clefts extends
Before his weeping eyes on every side.
There, clad in green, invites no flowery mead,
No tree with golden fruit there stands displayed;
Scarce here and there a thistle, briar or weed
Strews o'er the barren ground a scattered, scanty shade.

45

"Then must I," he exclaims with frantic air,
"Must I return" (and bites his lips with pain)
"To her, with hands thus comfortless and bare,
For whom alone my life could worth retain?
I who on earth am now her only stay,
Whose heart and every pulse to her belong,
Have not the power but for a single day
So much as to assist her being to prolong.

46

"Art thou then doomed to perish in my sight,
Thou fairest work of Nature's hand divine?
Thou, perish, who art in this wretched plight
For me alone! for me didst all resign!
To thee whose stars so fair a promise gave,
Ere by Heaven's anger to my bosom driven,"
(With anguish here the knight began to rave)
"Not e'en what hunger craves to satisfy is given."

47

He cried aloud, with keen excessive smart;
Then sinking down, in fearful stillness lay.
At last a gleam of faith revives his heart;
From black despair he tears himself away,
Plucks up fresh courage and with zeal renews
His search, long vain— The sun-beams melt in gold
Upon the deep—when oh! delight! he views
Before his eager eyes the fairest fruit unfold.

48

Half under leaves, half glowing in the sun
He sees this fruit which stalks with broad leaves bear
Along upon the ground like melons run,
Sweet to the smell and painted wondrous fair.
For all his pains how rich this meed appears!
To break the fruit off, with what haste he springs!
To Heaven his eyes with gratitude he rears,
And joyous transports to his speed add wings.

49

Three mortal hours the fair herself had found
Far, on the strand, from him who was her all,
Alarmed at all she sees—at every sound—
Her heart the very stillness tends t' appal.
Of this long interval a part had fled,
With arm unused, in bringing from the shore
Sedge, sea-weed, moss, of love to deck the bed,
And strewing it in heaps upon the cavern's floor.

50

This work exhausted her last feeble strength,
Now fail her knees, she sinks upon the shore;
And lies, with gasping palate, all her length,
By hunger gnawed, by thirst yet tortured more.
In this wild spot, of everything bereft,
What anguish racks!—whence Huon's long delay?
Misfortune should he meet?—Some beast of prey?—
The mere idea robs what life she still had left.

51

The dreadfulest event that can arise
Her fancy to her in warm colors paints.
In vain to struggle with her fears she tries,
At every wave her heart within her faints.
Yet, feeble as she is, she climbs a steep,
Panting, and gazes round in every track;
And as the sun's last rays shoot o'er the deep,
She spies him—yes! 'tis he!—her Huon is come back!

52

He sees her to'wards him stretch out her arms,
And shows from far the fruit with golden rind;
Not that in Paradise had greater charms,
Which erst seduced the mother of mankind.
To the last beams the sun declining shed
As he holds up in triumph his fair prize,
They paint its glossy skin with flame-like red,
While Rezia scarcely trusts her joyous eyes.

53

"Thus then takes Heaven compassion on our woe!"
She cries, a large tear glistening in her eye;
And straight, before the tear begins to flow,
Into her arms she feels her Huon fly.
Her feeble tone, as trembling on his breast
She sinks half lifeless, bids him speed his care.
They sit—and of no other knife possessed,
His sword he uses the fair fruit to share,

54

Here from my hand the trembling pencil drops.
Canst thou such woes, too cruel Spirit, view?
And mock their miseries and defraud their hopes?
Bitter as gall, and rotten through and through
Was the fair fruit—and pale, the cheated pair
As death's last agonies, with stiffened eye,
All comfortless upon each other stare,
As struck by thunder from a cloudless sky.

55

A stream of bitter, raging tears now springs
From Huon's eyes; such fearful tears they are
As from thick blood and glowing eye-balls wrings
With quivering lips and chattering teeth, despair.
Amanda softly, but with spirits broke,
With languid cheek, with lustre-faded eye,
And lips as dry as glowing cinders spoke:
"Let me," she whispered feebly, "let me die."

56

"Upon thy bosom even death is sweet,
And thanks to the avenger, whose fierce ire,
Harsh as it is, this comfort leaves me yet"—
—The words, half stifled, on her lips expire.
She sinks, as droops the lily to the storm,
On the knight's breast—him love and fear impel.
He springs up raving, round her throws his arm
And bears the lovely burden to the cell.

57

"One drop of water, righteous God!" he cries
With half impatient, half imploring tone.
"The load of guilt on me, me only lies,
Oh! let thy anger fall on me alone!
Be nature all a grave, a yawning hell
To me— Her only spare!—In mercy's name,
Oh! lead my darksome feet to trace a well
Merely to light again of her dear life the flame."

58

He goes to search once more, and swears that first
Himself amid these rocks will find his grave,
With hunger sooner perish and with thirst
Than empty-handed come back to the cave.
"He," (cries he weeping) "whose compassion hears
The ravens when to him for food they cry,
His fairest creature cannot hate; his cares
Will surely, surely not with hunger let thee die."

59

Scarce has he spoken, when he seems to hear
Not from him far, the rippling of a stream.
He listens to it with attentive ear;
It ripples on—his eyes with rapture beam.
He searches round and in the twilight dim
Soon finds the spot—then snatches from the shore,
Instant, a shell, the cordial dew to skim
And hastes her gasping breath to Rezia to restore.

60

With greater ease the blessing to dispense,
The fair herself he carries to the stream.
Though only water—to her dying sense
To trickle down her throat new spirits seem.
Each draught heart-strengthening as wine descends,
And sweet as milk and soft as freshest oil;
Of food and drink at once it serves the ends
And in oblivion sinks all pain and toil.

61

Refreshed and strengthened all their faith revives,
Their ardent thanks to him they offer up
Who for the second time now saved their lives;
Fondly embrace, and after a last cup,
Beside the spring upon cool moss reclined,
The sweet consoler of all human woes
Creeps o'er them slow, their sinews to unbind,
And in the gentle arms of slumber they repose.

62

The morning twilight scarce begins to peep
Round Huon's brows, when up from Rezia's side
He springs—renews his search and many a leap
Ventures where steeps abrupt the rocks divide;
Hunts every corner, bearing still in mind
Not to forget the way back to the cell;
And sorrowful, the island all to find
Unfit alike for man or beast to dwell.

63

Leading at last southeastwards from the cell
At a small bay, a crooked by-path ends;
And in a bush, amid a rock-girt dell
A palm-tree loaded with ripe fruit ascends;
Not lighter tŏwards' Heaven directs its flight
A suffering soul, from fervid flames just free
And purgatory's pains, than now the knight
As if he scaled the skies, climbs up the tree.

64

His pockets full no sooner can he break
Of the sweet fruit, than down he springs and flies,
As if he ran a racing roe to take,
When she awakes, the charmer to surprise
On whom his thoughts are constantly bestowed.
Still gathered in herself the fair reposed
In slumber soft; her cheeks like roses glowed,
And scarce her garment held her bosom half enclosed.

65

In raptured gaze, the purest joy of love,
He seems the Genius of the sleeping fair;
With greedy fondness leaning from above
Long stands on her angelic form to stare
And charms still new. 'Tis she who for his sake
Renounced a bliss, which others to acquire
Without condition, joyously would make
A sacrifice of all they worship or admire.

66

"For love, thy forfeit, Rezia, was a throne;
And wherefore?—thou deliciously wert bred,
Where all the pomp of gorgeous Asia shone
And on a hard rock now must lay thy head;
Heaven's arch thy canopy, thy bed but sedge;
Bare to the storm, exposed to every ill,
And deem it bliss where thorns scarce spread a hedge,
E'en this wild fruit to find, thy hunger's rage to still.

67

"And I, condemned by Fate's severe decree
On all I love my miseries to shed;
From dire mischance instead of shielding thee
Have brought this deep distress upon thy head;
Wretch! and is this the meed I then bestow
For all what thou for me hast given and done?
Thy all on earth, what can I for thee do?
When to myself is left my naked life alone."

68

This torturing thought at last broke out in sighs
And waked the charming sleeper from her rest.
What first she saw was Huon, in whose eyes
Joy and love's ecstasies but half suppressed
Deeper affliction. In her lap he strewed
The mellow fruit he gathered from the tree.
One shell of water, and this meagre food
A banquet fit for Gods to her appeared to be.

69

Yes, fit for Gods!—for on her Huon's breast
Lies not her head? the fruit did he not break?
To pluck it, robbed he not himself of rest
And leapt so many a cleft o'er for her sake?
Thus love insists all credit to allow
To him, nor heeds what she for him has done.
And to disperse the clouds that shade his brow,
She teaches her fine eyes to beam with joy alone.

70

He feels this generous tender overflow
In the deportment of his lovely fair,
And with a tearful eye and cheeks in glow
Sinks in her arms.—"Oh! must I not despair?
Not hate myself?—not curse each star that shed
Upon the night which gave me life, its ray?
Not curse the light when first my infant head
Wailing upon my mother's bosom lay?

71

"Thee, best of women, thus cast down to see
From every bliss through me, through Huon's crime;
From every bliss that smiled at home on thee;
From every bliss that in my native clime
I taught thy hopes with Fancy's hues to paint.
Thee, thus degraded to this wretched fare—
Yet see thee suffer all without complaint;
Indeed it is too much!—'tis more than I can bear!"

72

Amanda, with a look which Heaven displays
And full of what her breast can scarce contain,
Beholds him— "Let me never hear," she says,
"From thy loved lips those hated words again.
Thyself accuse not of this drear event,
Nor him accuse who from the realms above
These woes to try us, not to punish, sent;
He tries but those he loves, and with a father's love.

73

"For, tell me, since that dream, our passion's germ,
Hath not whate'er befell us proved it still?
The founder of our union thou mayst term
Fate, Providence or Oberon at will,
Suffice it that our ties a wonder formed;
That but a wonder, naught our lives could save.
Who brought us out of Babylon unharmed?
Who warded from us off the overwhelming wave?

74

"And when at death's last verge we from the flood
Thus beyond hope escaped, what other might
Has to this moment our kind savior stood?
Sure from his breast have I this dreadful night
The water drawn, which in my writhing veins
Once more has kindled life's expiring flame;
And sure this meal too, which our lives sustains,
Prepared by secret hands to us propitious came.

75

"Had fate to our destruction set the seal,
Why to relieve us all these favors sped?
What my heart tells me, I believe and feel—
The hand which us through all this darkness led
Will not abandon us to woes a prey.
And from her anchors were e'en hope to fall,
To the last gasp be this our steadfast stay:
A single moment may reverse it all.

76

"Suppose the worst, suppose the hand, our shield
Until this hour, should wholly disappear.
That year succeeding year no help should yield
And that thy tender, faithful Rezia here
Should find her grave upon this desert strand.
Far be it from me, what I did to rue,
Should the free choice again before me stand,
With joy would I thy steps to wretchedness pursue.

77

"All I possessed I willingly forgo;
Thy fondness and my heart will all requite,
And deep as Fortune plunges me in woe,
While thou art left, no envy can excite
She who in gold and purple deems her blest.
Thy pangs alone thy Rezia can depress;
One sorrowing look, one sigh escaped thy breast
Sharpens a thousand fold the stings of my distress.

78

"Of what for thee I did or gave, talk not.
'Twas for myself, 'twas what my heart bade give
And tenfold death were not an harsher lot
Than for Amanda without thee to live.
Our mutual love will help us both to bear
However cruel destiny's decree;
Though hard, though insupportable it were—
Here, take my hand! with joy I'll suffer it with thee.

79

"Still as the sun shall rise or shall descend
With all thy toils, my labors shall combine,
My arm is strong, and shall unwearied lend
In every work its constant aid to thine.
The love shall brace its nerve, that bids it rise
And the least service cheerfully return.
While for thy bliss and comfort I suffice,
To change my happy lot with any queen I'd spurn."

80

Thus spoke the best of women, and impressed
With tender lips the seal of what she said.
The magic of this kiss the cliffs confessed,
The flinty ground in Huon's eyes displayed
The beauties of Elysian fields once more.
His eyes no trace of indigence behold,
With pearls bespangled over seems the shore;
The cave a marble hall, the rocks all burnished gold.

81

He feels his bosom swell with spirits bright;
What world is worth a woman such as this?
With rapturous, heaven-breathing, high delight
Her open breast he presses close to his.
"Earth, deep, and thee, O Sun! all seeing, I adjure,"
He cries: "I swear it by this breast I strain,
Of truth and innocence the altar pure,
That instant be my last, when I my heart profane.

82

"Yes! if this heart, where burns thy holy name,
To virtue and thy worth prove ever base,
And howsoever long the trial's flame,
By weakness pang thee, or itself disgrace,
Or, dearest woman! ever tire, for thee
The worst of toils and dangers to defy:
Then hurl, O Sun! red lightening against me.
Then every refuge, earth and deep deny."

83

He spoke, and with a kiss his words repaid
The angel-wife— They glory in their love,
And in the firm resolve each other aid:
Severely as Fate's lord their hearts may prove,
With steady patience, and steel-tempered soul
To keep themselves reserved for better days;
And blindly trust that gracious power's control
Which still in their defense, so often silent sways.

84

On the same day with nicest ken the ground
They searched together, where their palm-tree sprung,
And like it five or six besides they found
Which here and there with golden clusters hung.
The joyous pair, like children, in their store
Possess in fancy an exhaustless prize;
And as they rove the palm-tree valley o'er
Day after day in joyful frolic flies.

85

But their stock failed—a leaden-footed year
Must travel round, their harvest to restore,
While daily new, their wants, alas! appear.
Love deems itself with little blessed, though poor.
Out of itself needs but what nature's laws
Require to spin the thread of life along;
Yet, when this fails, want doubly cruel gnaws,
Then must the spell dissolve, however strong.

86

With roots which hunger's rage alone could eat,
Are they compelled to feed full many a day.
Oft when the youth returns with weary feet,
Are berries, from the brambles snatched away,
A bird's egg plundered from the nest on high,
A fragment of a fish from ravens torn,
All, niggard chance allows him to supply
Her wants who with him all his miseries has borne.

87

Yet want of food is not their sole distress:
They miss a thousand trifles day and night,
Which though despised by those who them possess,
Without them, with a thousand wants we fight.
Besides with such light garments as they wear
With wind and rain and tempests how contend?
How bear the buffet of inclement air?
How from them five long months the frosty winter fend?

88

Now the grove's honors are the season's prey.
Already whistles o'er dry leaves the wind;
In hoary vapors veiled, the solar ray
Its genial energy has all resigned.
The sky and deep are blent; the billows roar
Upon the strand, which scarcely breaks their shocks.
Oft rage-befoamed they burst their fetters o'er
And dash with silver spray the forehead of the rocks.

89

Need drives our couple from their peaceful place,
Up in the mount— Yet wheresoe'er their sight
They turn, gaunt hunger stares them in the face,
And with his withered form bars up their flight.
A new event too comes amidst their cares
With fear-fraught pleasure and delicious smart
To charm and torture them—already bears
The fair, three months, a pledge of love beneath her heart.

90

Oft, silent to her breast, her consort's hand
She strains, while tears her smiling eyes bedew.
Between them weaves itself a second band;
A still, soft wish, replete with bodings new
Her bosom swells—a sympathy obscure,
Deeper than ever, comes her heart to move;
A foretaste of maternal pleasures pure,
Glows, thrills through all her frame, and sanctifies her love.

91

This pledge to her a further pledge contains
That she will never lose his tender cares,
Who all his creatures o'er his wide domains
Loves as a father— Willingly she bears
The burdens of her state and still conceals
From Huon's sight, nor seems to him distressed;
Naught in her cheerful eye but hope reveals
And feeds the confidence expiring in his breast.

92

His mind had not forgot the solemn vow
Which he to Heaven and his Amanda swore;
And hence, his duties being doubled now
With deeper weight upon his bosom bore.
What else was needed to transpierce his heart
With poisoned daggers than this moving view?
Should Heaven the hoped-for aid not soon impart,
With him his tender wife and babe must perish too.

93

Full twenty times a day the youth ascends
For weeks, the rocks behind the cell that rise,
And o'er the deep an anxious look extends:
His latest hope— In vain he wastes his eyes
O'er the broad bosom of the boundless main,
With straining sight a vessel to descry.
The Sun arose, the Sun went down again,
Bare was old Ocean's breast, no vessel could he spy.

94

One thing, which seemed impossible, remained.
(What so, to him who struggles for his all?)
Had on his head each hair a death contained,
The whole combined his heart could not appal.
This rock, by Oberon his exile doomed,
To him was yet unknown upon one side.
A fearful mass of cliffs and ruins gloomed
Its guard, and seemingly all human feet defied.

95

Now, that he feels of want the cruel stings,
They are but hills that he with ease can scale.
And even were they Alps, sure Love has wings.
Perhaps the bold adventure will not fail.
Perhaps his stubborn soul to force its way
Through these wild Nature's ramparts may succeed;
To fields conduct him with fair harvests gay;
Or to compassionate and friendly beings lead.

96

To spare his lovely wife a load of cares,
He shuns the worst of dangers to disclose,
Which for their common safety he prepares
To meet— Silent she bears her share of woes.
At parting, nothing but farewell! they say—
Such is the fullness of their burdened hearts;
Yet Huon's eyes a confidence display,
Which like a sunbeam through her sorrow darts.

97

Now at the foot of mountain crags he stands,
While like a world in ruins lie around
A Chaos rude of dross and cindered brands,
Where burns a fiery mountain underground;
Mingled with rocks which hideous to the sight
Broke thousand-fold, with savage grandeur rise;
Now drive down deep into the realms of night,
And now soar upwards till they pelt the skies.

98

Despair alone a passage here could break;
Oft on his hands and knees he needs must creep
And stepping places like the chamois take
Oft on the edge of precipices steep.
Across his way now rocky fragments stand
And choke both path and light— Back he must go.
Now dropping, snatch a shrub that tears his hand,
And barely saves him from the gulf below.

99

Reft of his strength, refuse his limbs to stir?
His spirits Rezia's image calls again.
Hard breathing, he stands still and thinks of her,
And feels new vigor shoot through every vein.
This true heroic courage meets reward.
The path before him opens by degrees;
And with the hardships, 'ready past, compared,
The struggle that remains is perfect ease.

Book the eighth

1

The knight had now attained the first ascent
And sees before him, like a rocky hall
O'er which high-arching aged fir-tops bent
In twilight still, a valley straight and small.
The weary, breathless wanderer shudders here
While his resolved, yet tottering step pervades
Of solitude the sanctuary drear,
He feels as had he reached the silent realm of shades.

2

And soon a gently-winding foot-path leads
Descending slowly to a narrow bridge,
Deep under which a foam-white stream proceeds,
Rolling a torrent o'er a rocky ridge.
Fearless he steps upon the rising ground
To which the bridge conducts, and soon perceives
Himself enclosed within a mountain round
Which every issue out insensibly bereaves.

3

The path which brought him to this spot he found
Snatched as if by enchantment from his sight.
In silent anguish long he searches round
Till through the shrubs appears an opening light,
Where a small passage as he shortly finds
In perpendicular direction bent
Amidst the rocks as round a spindle winds
More than a hundred paces in ascent.

4

Breathless he scarce had reached the topmost stair
When to his eyes a Paradise expands,
And with a long white beard and silver hair
A man of noble, earnest features stands.
A girdle binds his russet garment round
Whence hangs a lengthy string of beads unrolled.
A person such as this, in this place found,
'Twas natural at once for what he was to hold.

5

But Huon, weak with hunger, tired and stiff,
In these wild heights where he so long had sought
A human face in vain, and on each cliff
That glooms around him could discover naught
But hoary fir trees waving o'er his head;
By this white beard at once astonished, thinks
He sees a vision risen from the dead,
And to the earth before his presence sinks.

6

The hermit, struck with little less surprise
Than Huon's self, starts back, but soon again
Collected, speaks: "Oh! hast thou, as thine eyes
Announce, the hope redemption to obtain
Out of thy pains, what can I for thee do?
Thy guilt how expiate, tortured spirit, tell!
That port of bliss how open to thy view,
Where, in eternal rest the pious dwell?"

7

Pale and emaciate as with care and need
Sir Huon seemed, the aged Sire's mistake
Was but too easy to commit indeed;
But soon their eyes an explanation make—
And when our knight the hoary sage informs
What brought him here (his looks suffice to tell)
Straight as a son he clasps him to his arms,
And kindly bids him welcome to his cell.

8

And to a fountain of fresh water brings,
Which, pure as air, as lucid crystal clear,
Forth from a rock beside his cottage springs;
And while his thirst he quenches, resting here,
Hastes to his little garden to descend
With his best fruit the stranger to supply;
Which for his care, himself to plant and tend
Yields in profusion, a benignant sky.

9

And ceases not his wonder to attest
How any wingless mortal could ascend
Th' enormous rocks his cottage that invest,
Where he has deemed full thirty years to spend
In solitude complete as in the grave—
"That a good angel guards you, let it teach.
But what most urges now, must be to save
The fair, and to her, comfort's hand to reach.

10

"A safer path, though veiled in shades so deep
That none without me would descry its track,
In half the time it took to scale this steep
Shall bring thee to her, and conduct both back.
What from this hut and garden you can draw
With honest heart is offered for your ease.
Sweet is the rest of virtue, though on straw;
And purer flows the blood on pulse and meagre peas."

11

The knight proceeds his cordial thanks to pay.
The hermit takes his staff, the way to show,
And, that returning, Huon may not stray,
Takes care the path with fir-twigs fresh to strew.
Before the golden sun in ocean sinks,
Amanda's foot the panting heights attains,
Where, as with thirsty, deep-drawn draughts she drinks,
The kindly stream of purest Heaven she drains.

12

Into another world she thinks the scene
Removed, and feels herself in fairy land;
No sky to her so blue, no earth so green,
No other trees so freshly leaved expand.
Here, where for shelter lofty rocks arise
And round the pleasant spot a circle throw,
Autumn itself the northern blast defies,
And figs yet ripen, oranges yet glow.

13

As to the Genius of the holy place
Before the sage with awe-struck breast she bends,
Nor scruples with a pious kiss to grace
The shriveled hand which smiling he extends.
Her overflowing heart cannot forbear
On him as on a sire her eyes to raise.
The second look already banished fear;
She feels as had she known him all her days.

14

That native dignity was in his mien
Which even through a cowl unhidden gleams.
Each living creature's friend, his eye serene
By steady habit, heaven-directed seems
Though age's burden his neck softly bends.
Upon his eye-brows inward peace appears,
And like a rock where never cloud ascends,
Above the toys of earth his radiant head he rears.

15

The world's black rust, the passions' traces all
Time from his brow had long since washed away.
Should at his feet a royal sceptre fall
Which he, for snatching as it dropped might sway,
His hand he would not stretch— His cheerful soul
Shut up against desires and fears and pains,
Open alone to truth's supreme control,
And Nature's voice, attuned to her alone remains.

16

Alfonso was his name before he fled
The world's rough wave— At Leon he received
His being; and, to princely service bred
With thousands ran, alike by shows deceived,
After that will-o'-the-wisp, before the hands
That hovers still, and, snatched at still retreats—
That glittering shade which incense still demands
And like the stone of fools the hopes forever cheats.

17

And having thus the fairest days of youth
To kings, in self-delusion's tumult lent,
With willing, ardent, unrequited truth
His blood, his treasures in their service spent;
From brightest favor's dawn a sudden fall
Unhoped for freedom from his fetters gave;
Yet happy, from the storm that wrecked his all,
His life at least upon a plank to save.

18

This storm had spared another treasure too
Which quite against the use of courtly life
Made all his loss good in Alfonso's view,
A friend, a cottage, and a tender wife.
Oh! leave me these! was all the prayer to Heaven
Which now to form, his blissful heart presumed.
What he entreated, ten years long was given,
Yet, to survive this also was he doomed.

19

Three sons, his youth's own image, of his age
The hope, amidst the pride of youth's career
The plague snatched from him in its sudden rage
And grief soon stretched the mother on her bier.
His last friend too, alas! he could not save;
He lives, and no one with him sheds a tear.
He stands alone; the world is but a grave:
The grave of all he held, of all that held him dear.

20

He stands a single, tempest-blasted tree;
Drained are the sources whence his pleasures flowed:
The hut, with what but anguish could he see,
So lately of his bliss the dear abode?
What is the world to him? an empty square,
Where Fortune whirls her wheel about its nave.
His last staff broken, what shall he do there?
He now has nothing more to seek—except a grave.

21

Alfonso fled, with nigh distracted thought,
Into this barren and deserted clime;
And on this rock found more than he had sought—
First rest, and with the silent lapse of time
Content.—With him an aged servant went,
The single soul left faithful, in his woes;
Who to forsake him never would consent,
And in a rocky cave their dwelling place they chose.

22

His heart insensibly from grief's black flood
Rose purified. While temperance and rest
With air serene and free refined his blood,
His sense unclouded, and cheered up his breast.
He now perceived that life's eternal stream
Even his wounds in healing balm could steep;
And oft the magic of one solar beam
At once brought back his soul from sorrow's lowest deep.

23

And when at last he this elysium found
By some kind Genius as for him placed there,
And thus intrenched with woods and rocks around
He felt at once relieved from all his care.
Waked from an anxious, dreamful, feverish night,
As to the twilight of eternal day:
"Friend," cries he, charmed at this unhoped for sight,
"On this fair spot, build we a hut and stay."

24

The hut was built, and shortly stored appears
For want, and then for ease as time proceeds;
Stored as befits a sage's latter years
Who always much less wishes than he needs.
For that Alfonso when his flight he planned
Took with him such utensils o'er the main
As want in his retirement might demand,
To every reader must of course be plain.

25

In labor and enjoyment thus he spends
Life's better autumn in this mild retreat;
The garden, source of his abundance, tends
With toil which had become to him a sweet.
Forgotten by the world, and as a play
Of childhood bearing all the plagues in mind
Its service brought him, while, to bless each day,
With conscious purity, health, virtue, rest combined.

26

Eighteen years after, died his faithful friend.
Now left alone his soul with steadier eye,
In silence wholly to that world could tend
Where all he once loved, dwelt beyond the sky.
Where, more than here, himself already dwelt;
Oft when to outward sense, in silent night,
To its first nothing flesh dissolves, he felt
Upon his cheeks unbodied touches light.

27

Deep from the hedges too he seems to hear
With shuddering joy, a quire of angels call,
Resounding tuneful accents to his ear.
His fancy feels the thin partition fall
Which scarce yet keeps him parted from his love.
His inward sense expands, the holy ray
Bursts from his breast— In radiance from above
His soul around him sees celestial visions play.

28

E'en when awaked, his sight entranced beholds
These visions still; for when returning day
Before him Nature's scene again unfolds,
The charm yet lasts— Of bliss a heavenly ray
Warms, fills, irradiates every rock and tree;
In every creature that now meets his view
His eyes the great Creator's image see,
As the Sun's image floats in drops of dew.

29

Thus in his soul melt Heaven and earth in one,
Insensibly, and wake an inmost light;
Thus, far remote from where the passions stun
Amidst the darkness of this holy night
The purest, inmost sense— But, who has sealed
My lips, presumptuous, with a viewless hand?
Nor lets them speak what must not be revealed?
Struck dumb upon the edge of this abyss I stand.

30

Such was the sage, to whom with filial awe
Amanda bowed— He too, unused so long
To see what still the secret heart must draw,
A human face—enjoyed with rapture strong
The dear, heart-moving, unexpected sight;
Pressed her soft hand with kind paternal air;
Embraced again his son with new delight,
And speechless looked his thanks to Him who sent them there.

31

And forthwith leads them to his seat of rest,
And to the fountain in his garden's bower,
With golden fruit and purple clusters dressed,
And all he has, straight places in their power.
"Nature," says he, "needs less than we suppose;
Who pines with little, him no wealth can sate.
Here, till the days of your probation close,
No one thing will you want, worth asking for of Fate."

32

He spoke; for to him the first look displayed
What neither he would ask nor Huon say.
For in their form and manners both betrayed,
Though misery half their bloom had stripped away,
If not the splendor of a royal birth
At least what even Fortune's boundless sway
Can never rob, of that pure sterling worth
Which inward, inborn goodness must convey.

33

Three times the day's autumnal light had rolled
Thus in the lap of this asylum spent,
And neither lover can the thought withhold
That this old man, who such kind aid had lent,
Is not a mortal, but a guardian sprite,
It may be, Oberon, who their fault forgot
(Harshly enough atoned for, in their sight),
Will soon again restore their blissful lot.

34

This fancy vanished slowly from the mind
And with it died, alas! with poignant smart
The hope it fed— Yet now, their hearts inclined
But the more strongly to a mortal heart.
The good old hermit's heart, how kind it was!
His inward sense how mild, how pure it shone!
Impossible! six days with him to pass
And to him longer keep themselves unknown.

35

Their host forbearing still to ask, the youth
Whom gratitude and confidence impel,
His name and rank with unreservèd truth
And all his history proceeds to tell,
Since he had slain the son of Charles the Great
At Montlery, until this very hour:
By what an order Charles had meant his fate,
And how he sped the work with Oberon's aiding power.

36

How, by a dream, the thread of life was spun
Which at the first glance bound him to the maid;
How, with her, he escaped from Babylon,
And the severe injunction on him laid
By his exalted friend, which, spurred by love
When in a hapless moment he forgot,
Against them rising, how all Nature strove,
And Oberon's favor turned to vengeance on the spot.

37

"Blest," said the noble hermit, "blest is he
Whose fate at once is kind and harsh as this:
The smallest fault unpunished will not see;
Blest he! for sure the purest earthly bliss
Awaits him. Trust me, Oberon's wrath so dread,
Against such hearts cannot forever burn.
Unseen, his eye still hovers o'er thy head.
Deserve his grace, my son, and soon it will return."

38

—"And how deserve it? by what offering still
His wrath?" says hastily the knight again.
"Perform it, harsh as it may be, I will.
What can I do?"—"Of free accord, abstain!"
Returns the sage—"Wherein thou didst offend—
This only can atone"— The youth turns pale—
"I feel it," softly blushing said his friend,
"But know the heart I call thus nobly to prevail."

39

The young man's bosom swells with generous pride,
"Here! take my hand"— No other word he spoke
And after being two long winters tried
Bore witness to himself he never broke
The tacit vow— And say, what battle's rage
Could yield a triumph like this self control?
Yet feared he oft to blush before the sage,
And needed oft the check of Rezia's steadier soul.

40

"Naught," said the hermit, "can so fully tend
To keep the senses true to duty's laws,
As under toil their stubborn necks to bend;
And nothing from the path of virtue draws
Like idle reveries." These then to prevent,
His axe in hand, the knight without delay
At earliest dawn into the forest went
And spent in felling wood the livelong day.

41

Another cottage for the fair to raise
And spread the roof and walls with moss and earth;
Then for the chimney that must always blaze,
And in the needful plenty for the hearth
The gummy pine to find and split up light
And all along the cottage walls to heap;
This and much else employs at full the knight,
But helps him better too, when night comes on, to sleep.

42

At first his wishes small success obtain,
The hatchet, in the knightly falchion's stead,
The hand unpractised grasps at first with pain.
A boor in half the time the work had sped.
Yet he soon learns—use forms the master's hand;
And when beneath the toil his sinews shrink,
One thought that Rezia's wants the work demand,
Sustains them and forbids his fainting heart to sink.

43

While in the forest Huon tires, his friend
The sage, whose steps beneath the heavy load
Of eighty years are scarcely seen to bend,
Remains not idle; though from his abode
He seldom ventures far—no pleasant day
Flies o'er his head but sees him busied there
In garden labors passing time away,
While on the little hearth to tend, is Rezia's care.

44

There might one see (though if the angels bright
Gaze not in silence on their image fair—
Who sees her here?) with visage blithe and light
But thinly shaded by a cloud of care,
How this king's daughter to each duty mean
Of household small concerns herself applies.
What she has never done, scarce ever seen,
How quick she catches it! how all succeeds she tries!

45

Oft by the cistern at her cottage door
Her taper arm, as white as snow, she bared,
Nor of her skin, so soft enameled o'er
To lose the polished gloss one moment feared.
The sweet reward, the kind paternal sage
And much loved husband by her toils to place
Beyond the reach of want's extremest rage,
Gives to her meanest task both dignity and grace.

46

And when the sage as he from toil returns
Sees her (he too is of the angels bright)
And blesses her—oh! then her bosom burns
With purer, deeper feelings of delight
Than ever Bagdad gave; and when arrayed
In stars, night on the hearth collects them all,
And on her lovely visage, half in shade
From the brisk fire, the flames reflected fall:

47

Then with a silent, rapture-swelling soul
The youth upon his charmer glues his eyes;
Down his dark cheek sweet tears of transport roll
And all desire within his bosom dies.
To him she seems a being from above
Sent for his comfort, and how blest is he!
That such perfection he may dare to love,
And in each tender look himself beloved to see!

48

Between them oft the kind old hermit sat
While in her left hand Rezia held his right;
And thus they listened, hearing him relate
Some portion of his life through half the night,
As memory serves;—their souls, in all he tells
So warm an interest take as he proceeds;
His warmth it kindles, his narration swells,
And tale insensibly to tale succeeds.

49

To charm the fiend of sadness when he scowls
O'er all the cheerless fields, in silence chill,
And lurks in snowy clouds on wings of owls,
Sir Huon shows upon a harp his skill
Which in a corner he by chance had found;
Long since disused, untuned and scarce half strung,
Yet seems the soul of Orpheus to resound
From the harsh scrannel wood, when with it Rezia sung.

50

Attracted by a lucid winter's day
Oft when the distant ocean smoked with cold,
And dazzling snow thick on the mountains lay,
Which now the sinking sun-beams dipped in gold,
Attracted by this lustre, glaring bright
In the pure stream to bathe of frosty air;
With what fresh strength it braced their sinews tight!
How cheered it all their hearts and freed their souls from care.

51

Insensibly thus winter slips away;
Now from her lengthy slumbers earth awakes
And decks herself afresh in green array;
No more the forest a dumb ruin shakes,
A desert where the shafts alone stand bare,
But lofty columns arching overhead
Of Nature's temple now stand full and fair,
While crowding leaves on leaves, a lovely foliage spread.

52

Her bosom Nature decks with flowrets fair,
The garden and the meadows laughing blow;
The song of birds makes vocal all the air,
The rocks are garland wreathed, and purely flow
The trickling drops again from crystal streams
Down the fresh moss. The thickening hedges ring,
As all night long beneath the moon's pale beams
The nightingales their tuneful descant sing.

53

As now Amanda's term draws daily near,
She seeks retirement, seeks some place of rest,
Where in the hedge, thick boughs a shelter rear;
There oft she leans with boding thoughts oppressed
Against a tree in bloom, and joys to hear
The universal life with which 'tis fraught;
And as it hums and buzzes in her ear,
Clasps with forestalling bliss a lovely child in thought.

54

A lovely child on whom the mother's love
With lavish hand bestowed each pleasing grace;
With what delight she let her fancy rove
In its first fond instinctive smile, to trace
Its thanks for every bitter pang she felt
And bore with pleasure for its sake alone;
With what delight on each fair feature dwelt
The image of the sire, soft blending with her own.

55

Insensibly this dream of dear delight
To anxious terrors was compelled to yield;
And silent sorrow, which from Huon's sight
She scarcely could conceal, and yet concealed.
"Oh! Fatme"—oft she thinks and checks a tear—
"In this distress wert thou but by my side!"
Rezia! be cheered! the Fate that led thee here
Long since for thy relief was careful to provide.

56

The fairy queen, Titania, since the day
When unexpectedly by scorn and heat
She lost o'er Oberon's heart her gentle sway,
Had in this mountain chosen her retreat.
By him forsworn with such a dreadful vow
As wheresoe'er heaven's boundless arch is spread,
No spirit dares to break, she feels that now,
With him and with his love her bliss is wholly fled.

57

The hasty deed she now repents too late,
Of one rash hour— With visage dyed in shame
She feels her fault—her treason feels, how great!
No less against herself, than Oberon's flame.
Pride would withstand her tenderness in vain,
How gladly, could it but her fault atone,
His feet with tears of penitence to strain
Would she beyond the bounds of Heaven have flown.

58

But oh! he swore, in water nor in air
Nor where in flowery hedges balsams rain,
Nor where in caverns the lank griffins' care
Guards magic hoards, to meet her ne'er again.
E'en to himself repentance came too late,
Bound down forever by his solemn word.
T' appease him sees she not one open gate,
The sole one left alas! what hope can that afford.

59

'Tis closed forever— For, a youth and fair,
Such as ne'er was, nor e'er will be, can break
Alone its bars—of man's frail race a pair
To find, whose truth no tempests' rage can shake,
No charm delude, no trial e'er impair.
Impossible!—then to the latest age
Her tear-charged eye she turns in deep despair
And nothing can her wretchedness assuage.

60

The fairy frolics odious now she finds,
The dance by moonlight, and the lovely May,
In roseate garb. No myrtle garland binds
Henceforth her brows— Of joy the mere display
Tears open all her wounds— Through vacant air
She hovers in a tempest to and fro:
Finds nowhere rest, and with sad looks of care
Seeks for a place to suit her mind worn down with woe.

61

At last, this isle amidst the deep she spies,
A vast, enormous mass of ruins drear;
Its sable color first attracts her eyes,
Her wandering progress thitherwards to steer.
It suits her gloom; she darts down from the sky
And chooses a dark cavern, there to moan,
And undisturbed, her life away to sigh
And turn amidst the rocks, if possible to stone.

62

Seven times restored has been the youth of earth,
By her unnoticed, since the beauteous fay
Led this sad life— As on an altar's hearth
Upon a stone, expecting death she lay.
Day springs and falls, in vain the glorious sun
Sheds magic light on all the rocks around,
Should every stream of joy towards' her run
At once, yet in her heart would no delight be found.

63

One thing a shade of comfort to afford
Amidst her ceaseless woes alone remains:
Perhaps the state of her lamented lord
Is like her own, or harsher still his pains—
For, sure he loves her yet, and if that be:
Doomed by himself to cause her torturing care
And his own torments—oh! how wretched he!
So wretched—she forgives him readily her share.

64

Yet as the great consoler, Time, has power
For mental wounds true balsam to dispense,
How deep soe'er they burn; at length the hour
Came for Titania, when her blunted sense
Clears by degrees—more patient she endures;
Again in green her fancy stands arrayed,
And as Hope's flattery once more allures,
What seemed impossible, her morning dreams now made.

65

In horror now these gloomy caves she held,
Where she before had joyed to be concealed.
Part of the cliffs her nod at once dispelled,
Before her bloomed a new Elysian field.
At her light call three sylphids bright appear,
A sister triplet, on her to attend;
Urged more by love than duty, with her here
Charming her griefs away, their days to spend.

66

This paradise which thus Titania rears
Amidst these craggy rocks is just the spot
Where the old sage had dwelt for thirty years;
Unknown to him, her throne was in the grot
Whence, through the bushes that angelic song
Came floating to him on the breath of night.
'Twas she who flitted by his side along,
When on his cheeks he felt aerial touches light.

67

Our lovers, from the moment when their fate
Had cast them on this isle too, she surveyed;
And day by day, inquiries of their state
Both morn and eve had regularly made.
Oft stood she, when themselves alone they thought
Unseen, beside them, to observe with care;
And what she heard and saw, suspicion brought
That this might be her long expected pair.

68

The closer still she kept them in her view
The more she felt her heart with hopes inspired;
If this be not the pair supremely true
And trial proof, as Oberon required,
Then is the hope to find them ever vain—
Henceforth she holds them as her eye-balls dear,
Determined, with her little fairy train,
With aid invisibly the lovely wife to cheer.

69

The hour drew near— Impelled by anxious dread
About among the bushes Rezia roves,
Which round the huts a mingled fragrance shed
That seems the morning incense of the groves;
She wanders forward as the by-path winds
Until she finds herself before a grot,
Which a light web of wreathing ivy binds
O'er whose dark gloss the sun his early radiance shot.

70

Oft had Alfonso and his aged friend
Before this strove to enter there, in vain;
Nor on our knight did more success attend
When he had tried admission to obtain,
To mark the wonder— Nothing had they seen
But by a strange resistance felt opposed,
As if a door invisibly had been
Upon them, as they tried to force their passage, closed.

71

Straight, wondrous horrors came their breasts to strain,
Silent they slipped away, nor ever more
Ventured to make the like attempt again;
Whether the fair herself had tried before,
Appears not, but she now could not withstand
The thought that first to her this place was meant
To be disclosed—then shoved with gentle hand
The twigs of ivy by, and in she went.

72

Anon strange shiverings thrill in every vein,
She sinks upon a seat of moss and rose;
Shoot following shoot she feels a cutting pain,
Her bones and marrow shake with torturing throes.
It passed—soft languor next her limbs pervades,
A seeming moonshine plays before her eyes;
And as they swim in giddy, deepening shades,
Her senses soft dissolve, till fast asleep she lies.

73

In sweet confusion now before her soul
Fair glimmering forms arise and pass away,
Or wondrously within each other roll.
She thinks three kneeling angels to survey
With secret mysteries to aid her wants.
A woman, whom light's rosy tint infolds,
Beside her stands, and when for breath she pants
Close to her lips a bunch of roses holds.

74

A last short, keen, though partly softened pain
Now seemed her high-distended heart to break:
The forms are fled, her sense is lost again,
But tuneful echoes cause her soon to wake,
Wafting away and dying on her ears:
She looks: no more the sylphids charm her sight:
Alone, the queen of fairies now appears
And smiles before her eyes in rosy splendor bright.

75

And in her arms a new born infant lay
Which to the fair she reached; and straight was flown
As in the breeze of morning melts away
A nightly cloud from breath of blossoms blown.
Instant awakes Amanda from her dream,
And stretching out her arms with ardor strains
Still of the rosy garb to snatch the hem;
In vain! she grasps at air, and quite alone remains.

76

But soon, oh! how unbounded her surprise!
Her bliss, oh! how unutterably great!
She scarce can trust her feelings and her eyes;
She feels herself delivered of her weight,
And on her bosom pants a lovely boy.
Fresh as the morning rose, as Cupid fair—
With what a tremor of delicious joy
She feels her bounding heart tŏwards' him bear.

77

Yes! 'tis her son! with tears of rapture wild
She presses to her lips his little hand;
Nor can be sated looking at the child.
The child already seems to understand
The mother's thought; at least, oh! let her deem
This comfort to enjoy—his bright eyes look
So speakingly at hers!—His lips too seem
Each kiss she gives them, from her mouth to suck.

78

She hears the silent call—(how swiftly hears
A mother's heart)—and follows it untaught.
With bliss, which angels, leaning from their spheres
To look at her, could angels envy aught,
Might view with envy, to her breast she lays
The lovely suckling and its instinct guides;
Her heart the impulse of full joy obeys,
And tender sympathy pours forth in all its tides.

79

Meantime her Huon in the groves around
Two long and anxious hours had for her sought.
Him, as with fruitless search he trod the ground,
At last his wandering footsteps hither brought.
The unapproachèd grotto he draws near;
Unchecked goes in— Oh! what a moment this!
At Rezia's breast he finds a love-god here,
And she, sunk deep and swallowed up in bliss.

80

You, to whom Nature, at life's entrance, gave
That ample substitute for every joy;
That treasure, matchless on this side the grave
Which all the wealth of India cannot buy;
That richest gift in all her wide control,
Which follows e'en to better worlds your hopes:
A feeling heart, and pure, unspotted soul—
Look here and gaze—the sacred curtain drops!

Book the ninth

1

To Fatme now, 'tis time our eyes to turn,
Whom when the lovers leapt into the main
We left on board the ship, alone, to mourn
Her lady's fortune and her own in vain.
Robbed of all comfort weeps she night and day
And wails, and tears her hair, and rends her breast.
Alas! a single breath has swept away,
Forever swept away the fabric of her rest.

2

What will become of her thus left alone
On board a ship, amidst a curbless race
Of sailors rough, who mock her every groan
And with bold looks and maddening wine-flushed face
Devour their prey?—Oh! what will be her fate?
But on the second night a lucky storm,
In pity of her unprotected state
Came with fierce rage the face of ocean to deform.

3

Despair at once unnerved the heartless crew;
Drifting at random long the vessel went
Westwards or southwards as the tempest blew,
Till when its rage in seven dire days was spent,
The captain finds her wrecked on Tunis' coast,
And of this accident, which thus befell
Quite out of time for him, to make the most,
Concludes here Fatme for a slave to sell.

4

Scarce four and thirty times had Fatme seen
The lovely May her flowery garb unfold,
And one of those long-blooming forms had been
Who fade not easily, who late grow old;
And who with charms of solid weight combine
A dimpled cheek, a fire-enlivened eye,
Which, when youth's splendors cease to shine,
E'en then, a pleasing substitute supply.

5

Chance to the place the Sultan's gardener brought,
Where one poor hundred sequins was to draw
This precious prize— It claimed regard, he thought;
Drew near, examined, and a treasure saw.
This flower, he thinks, will his Gulistan crown,
Without at all consulting his gray hairs;
The gold is fetched and instantly paid down;
And what she cannot change, with patience Fatme bears.

6

Meanwhile, still favored with propitious gales,
His course prescribed the faithful squire pursued,
And scarce had safely landed at Marseilles
When swift as if his life had on it stood,
A steed he mounted, straight to Paris flew
And reached Mount Martre as night's shadows fled;
Where, as the sleeping town lay full in view
A sudden scruple shot across his head.

7

And with himself communing, "halt!" he cries,
"Before we ride another step, my son,
Think what you are about— Your pate, so wise,
Should have considered this at Askalon,
Though as the wind in Huon's sail then blew
Your time to make objections was but short;
Yet, to be candid, honest friend, with you:
You should have struggled then in quite another sort.

8

"For, be it said between ourselves, 'tis plain
This embassy has not a spark of sense.
We never were much loved by Charlemagne,
At this then how much will he take offense!
To pot, no doubt, the precious casket goes;
For truly, all this goat's hair to display,
And these same grinders, from what jaws, God knows,
Your Excellency sure would make but little way.

9

"Ay! if Sir Huon with a stately band
Of guards, and so forth, should himself appear,
And with the Caliph's daughter by the hand
Should enter and accost his Highness here,
And with a proper set of bows and cringes,
Such as a knight, a duke and peer befit,
On a red velvet cushion with gold fringes
Present the things—that might do something, I admit.

10

"The solemn splendor of the long parade,
The Sultan's daughter at the bridegroom's side,
Pride, pomp and circumstance, all come in aid
And lend their share to make it smoothly glide.
Charles has no base on which a doubt to build;
The proofs are all in sight, are in his hands:
The knight his word has like a man fulfilled,
And freely what no right can controvert, demands.

11

"All this, Cherasmin, will to ruin run,
Unless you wiser than your lord should be;
Consult your wits for what is to be done;
At all events, the best thing I can see,
Is, with your box to slink off soft and fair
Before you are observed, and smartly drive
To Rome, the port where pious souls repair
And where meanwhile your lord may probably arrive."

12

Thus spoke his better Genius to the squire,
And finding after he the thing revolved,
That prudence nothing better can inspire
Against the measure, finally resolved
The shoulder-blade to Paris straight to show,
And spur to Rome with all the speed he can.
Then soon behind him leaves the Alpine snow,
Arrives, and first of all visits the Lateran.

13

In vain the sentries at the gate he tires
With questions numberless about his lord;
In vain of all the front-hall train inquires;
No man can of knight Huon tell a word.
From house to house he hunts the town all through,
The hospitals and churches all in vain;
And paints his person o'er from top to toe
To every man he meets—'tis all but fruitless pain.

14

Six tedious, endless weeks he wastes away
In still deluded hopes, nor will permit
Himself or others to repose one day,
Still asking if his Prince were not come yet.
And finding it of no avail to wait,
Of the Basque nation the great oath he swears,
To hunt his knight up, in a pilgrim's state
As far and wide as Heaven an azure mantle wears.

15

What could he do? his cash was at an end,
And of the casket but one pearl to use,
(Which as a present from his fairy friend
As tenfold raised in worth, Sir Huon views)
He sooner would consent himself to flay;
A pilgrim neither gold nor silver bears,
But finds it easy, half the world to pay
With a few muscle-shells and pious prayers.

16

Thus through the world for two long years and more
The faithful old man begs his wandering way;
Unwearied roams the hills and valleys o'er
And makes at every port and isle a stay;
After his lord and lady still inquires
At every place in vain, till him at last
Fate, and an impulse that his hopes yet fires,
Before the gardener's door at Tunis cast.

17

And being tired, and with long fasting weak,
Upon a bench of stone his limbs he spread,
There in the shade a little rest to seek.
A female slave meanwhile brings wine and bread.
She views the pilgrim with astonished gaze,
Alike her features all his thoughts employ—
"Cherasmin!" "Fatme!" crying in amaze
Upon each other's neck they fall with tears of joy.

18

"Oh! Fatme!" cries the pilgrim—"can it be?"
Long had Cherasmin lost a hope so sweet;
"And is it truly Fatme that I see?
How strange, at Tunis thus again to meet!
What wind has blown you to these heathen lands?
And where is Huon and his charming fair?"
"Oh! friend!" exclaims the nurse, and wrings her hands—
"They are— Ah! woe is me!—to ask forbear."

19

"What sayst thou?—God forbid!" the old man cries—
"What are they? Speak!" "Cherasmin, oh! they are—"
She can no more—her voice its aid denies—
"They are?—Oh! God!" he sobs—"unhappy pair!"
And weeping like a child o'er Fatme stood.
"In the full bloom of youth!—'tis too severe
But long before I boded nothing good!
Fatme! the trial was too hard, 'tis clear."

20

As soon as Fatme finds her breath restored,
Minutely she relates the piteous tale,
From his departure to the night deplored
When by the livid glare of lightnings pale
Amanda thrust herself through all the crew,
Thick urging upon Huon, as he stood—
Raging with love, her arm around him threw,
And with him headlong plunged into the furious flood.

21

And thereupon a full hour they sat
Prompted by pure affection, to lament
And weep together the disastrous fate
Of the most lovely couple ever sent
To grace the world— "No, never," oft she cries,
"Shall I another such a woman see."
"Nor I," Cherasmin in like tone replies,
"Beside a prince like him again shall ever be."

22

And having made her thrice at least repeat
How all had happened, he at last perceived
A feeble gleam, his hopes indulging yet,
That from the deep both lovers were retrieved.
That Oberon had left them to their fate,
The more he thinks, the less can he suppose;
For all his favors to them demonstrate
(He thinks) a secret plan, a purpose fixed disclose.

23

This glimmering of hope beams o'er his heart,
As in deep night a distant taper glows.
From Fatme he resolves no more to part,
But with her joined in bonds of common woes
To wait at Tunis here Fate's final doom,
As she suggests, put staff and garb away,
A spade and slave's vest in their stead assume
And in the royal garden work for daily pay.

24

While Fatme and the honest squire bedew
With tears—as were it of their love the tomb—
Their flowery field, to Huon's sorrowing view
The third return of spring unfolds her bloom
Since in that spot so dreadful yet so fair,
His trying fortunes, banished him retain.
His valiant heart cannot as yet forbear
Fondly to wish itself amidst the world again.

25

The little Huonnet, a compound fair
Of all the father's strength and mother's charms
As ever goddess at her bosom bare,
And born quite otherwise to use his arms
Than in the forest with an axe to go
And fell the wood, now aggravates his pain.
Thy angel too, in sleepless nights of woe,
Hears oft, Amanda, thy still tears complain.

26

Thus in the bloom of youth, both deeply feel
Nature against their severed state protest.
His heart the fires of high-souled valor steel
And boundless goodness glows in Rezia's breast.
These virtues ask a like unbounded sphere;
In vain would they before the sage control
With eyes averted the unwilling tear,
Their smiles deceive him not; he reads the secret soul.

27

And though long since this world to him be naught,
He makes their case his own, weighs what they lost,
Weighs all their dues, and all their birth had brought,
Feels from their breasts, and holds the tears but just
Which they, from love, to hide before him strive—
Nor their unwilling impulse views with blame;
But only cheers them still to keep alive,
While fate impedes their bliss, hope's silent flame.

28

One evening, when the daily work was done
They sat, all three, before the cottage door
(Upon her lap Amanda held her son)
And viewed the star-bespangled heavens o'er;
While on the wonders of the scene they gaze
With secret boding, awe their bosoms burn;
And silent looks of thanks to Him they raise,
Who thus created them their eyes to Heaven to turn.

29

And now the sage in yet more moving tone
Began to speak than he had done before
Of life on earth, as of a dream alone,
And of a wafting to *true being* o'er.
A breath of heavenly air already flies
Around, and seems to raise him as he speaks.
Amanda feels it—shadows veil her eyes,
A half-unbodied form her thought already seeks.

30

"To me, already from the other shore
They reach" (he adds) "the hand: *my* race is run.
Yours scarce begins, and much, much sorrow more
And many sweetest joys beneath the sun
(They often but to greater woes prepare)
Await you, while you still draw near the end.
Both turn to dreams; both vanish into air
And nothing leave behind, your passage to attend.

31

"Naught but the precious treasure, in the heart
Collected, truth, and inward peace, and love;
And the remembrance that no joy or smart
From duty's path could ever make you rove."—
Much more like this he speaks, and when to rest
They all retire—as of them he takes leave,
They feel him strain them warmer to his breast
And in his eye a glistening tear perceive.

32

On this same night, by dark forebodings led,
Titania skyward looked, for much she feared.
She stood and gazed and in the future read—
And from her cheeks the roses disappeared.
She called her lovely sylphs, with her to see
What evils Fortune at that instant brewed;
And with what lines of deep calamity
Amanda's stars in gloomy junction stood.

33

Then in thick shades involved, she swiftly flies
To the soft bed between the almond trees,
Where with her child the Sultan's daughter lies—
Whose slumbers interrupted oft she sees
By ill-presaging dreams. Her gentle hand,
Amanda's strong disquiet to allay,
Her bosom touches with a rosy wand,
While the unconscious boy she softly steals away.

34

Returning with her lovely spoil—you see
What cruel fortunes o'er Amanda lower;
"Haste then"—(to her attendant nymphs says she)
"Transport this infant to my fairest bower,
And of him, as of my own son take care."
Then to each Grace, her nimble hands convey
A rosebud from the wreath about her hair.
"Begone," says she— "Already dawns the day.

35

"And every day and hour, as time shall fly,
Look on your buds, and when before your view
They change to lilies, then conclude that I
And Oberon are reconciled anew.
Then hasten, hither Rezia's son to bring;
Her woes shall end with my returning joy."—
The nymphs bowed lowly down, and on the wing
Of a soft cloud, bore off the lovely boy.

36

The gloomy shades of night had scarcely fled
When with an anxious, restless, trembling heart
Amanda sought her friend, whose rocky bed
Was from the hermit and her far apart.
With such an haste she goes as to forget
Upon her son beforehand to look round
(What since his birth had never happened yet),
Beside her, as she deems, in slumber bound.

37

Strolling the garden o'er, she finds her friend
And both together take their silent way,
Concealing what their bosoms apprehend,
To the small cell in which Alfonso lay.
How her heart beats, on drawing near his bed!
Breathless he lies, his hands across his breast;
With paleness over all his visage spread,
Yet quiet calm and pure in every line expressed.

38

"He only sleeps," said Rezia, while she lay
With gentlest touch upon his hand, her own—
But finding it all cold as lifeless clay
And in his veins the pulses silent grown,
On the stiff corpse she sinks, but cannot speak
Till streams of sorrows bursting from her eyes
Descend and bathe his venerable cheek:
"Oh! father! hast thou left us then?" she cries.

39

Again she rose—on Huon's bosom fell
And now they both cast down themselves with awe;
Silent, before the purest soul's cold shell
And in full draughts the painful pleasure draw
Of weeping— Often press his hand, to go,
The last sad tribute of affection warm;
Yet still remain with pangs unfelt of woe,
As chained by magic to the much loved form.

40

It seemed as if they saw upon his face
The dawning twilight of new life arise;
And round his brows reflected beams could trace
Of lambent radiance shooting from the skies.
The earthly clod to spirit seemed refined
And on the placid lips, yet scarcely closed
From the last blessing they had left behind,
A scarce perceptible but steady smile reposed.

41

"Seems it not," cries the knight, while upwards roll
His ravished eyes—"as if a beaming ray
Shot down from yonder world upon the soul?
The dignity of man, until this day
I never felt—nor ever to my sight
Seemed life on earth so much a dreary cell,
A passage merely to the realms of light—
Never for all good works such strength my bosom swell.

42

"Such cheerful vigor my heart never knew
For every sacrifice and every strife;
And every trial bravely to fight through.
—Suppose much grief, oh! my beloved wife
Await us yet—it brings us to the goal—
Naught shall dismay us, naught this faith abate."
Retiring, thus the hero spoke his soul,
And straight was taken at his word by Fate.

43

For, as their exit from the cell they made,
Returning hand in hand, and raised their eyes,
Oh! God! to what strange world are they conveyed?
Where are they? and what scenes before them rise?
Gone is their paradise, forever gone
The grove, the hedge, the fields that bloomed around!
Oh! can it be?—They stand as turned to stone.
Not even of the spot a trace is longer found.

44

They stand upon a precipice's edge
And wheresoe'er they look, with horror wild,
Surrounded by a hanging rocky ledge—
No spire of grass, where once their garden smiled—
Gone the dark grove in which the tuneful strains
Of nightingales were wont their ears to charm.
Naught but a mixture horrible remains
Of craggy cliffs, black, dismal and deform.

45

For what new scenes of wretchedness prepares
This dreadful spectacle before them spread?
"Alas!"—(they cry, and turn with eyes in tears
A mournful look towards' their sainted dead)
"For him this hill was dressed in spring's attire;
This Eden decked, which for his sake alone,
We have enjoyed—Nature and Fate conspire
Once more to ruin us, when he is gone."

46

A sigh suppressing in her breast that rose,
Amanda softly says: "I am resigned."
Unhappy fair!—the day that brings these woes
Has yet reserved the dreadfulest behind!
She hastens to the infant, whom so late
She fancies to have left in slumber's ties.
With this last comfort, the worst blows of Fate,
While he is at her bosom, she defies.

47

Quick to the bed she flies—and back again
Staggers, as thunderstruck—the boy is gone!
The bed is empty too, where he had lain!
"Were the doors open?—could he rise alone
And seek her?—Oh! God! should aught of ill
Befall him?—horrible!—yet, did he stray
Perhaps not far"—(this fancy flatters still)
"Or only to the garden found his way."

48

The garden? that is now a ruin wild;
Away she rushes and with lips nigh stiff
Calls by his name aloud and seeks her child
In deadly fear, o'er every cell and cliff—
The father, summoned by her cries, would speak
That comfort which he needs himself, in vain—
"Sure if among these winding rocks we seek
We safe and fresh shall find him soon again."

49

Two hours already fruitless is their pain—
In vain, loud calling, climb they every steep,
O'er all the hills around them roam in vain
Amidst the rocks, through every crevice creep—
Down every precipice at least to spy
His grave, they turn their sorrow-laden eyes.
Alas! no trace of him can they descry
And from the rocks resound alone their piercing cries.

50

The strangeness of the thing, that of his age
A child should lose himself in such a place—
Exposed to no wild beast's devouring rage,
Nor to man's often still more savage race,
Sharpened their terrors, yet their hopes it fed—
"It must be so! He has but strolled away;
And tired with wandering, on some stone his head
To sleep in innocence of childhood lay."

51

Amid the rocks they now their search renew.
Each shrub, each corner that may hide the child
Again with eagle eyes is hunted through;
At last they ramble down, with anguish wild,
However small the chance, upon the strand
To find alive the darling of their heart;
There amid swampy brakes and hills of sand
Insensibly, they strayed, themselves apart.

52

Amanda soon with terror seems to hear
A strange unusual noise, that seems to sound
Like voices— But it died upon her ear
And as, on listening, near at hand she found
A fall of water, with stupendous roar
Over an arching rock a passage break,
And dashing down, in foaming torrents pour,
She deems what first she fancied was mistake.

53

Of greater danger naught she apprehends—
Her infant's life employs her thoughts alone;
And suddenly, as round a hill she bends
And scarcely by the water-fall is gone,
By a rough tribe of tawny, swarthy men
Amazed, she sees herself encircled round;
While in the bay a galley meets her ken
Behind a lofty reef, and by her anchors bound.

54

To take in water they had anchored here
Shortly before, and still were busied so,
When they beheld with hasty steps appear
A woman, as the first glance serves to show,
Formed e'en the fairest of the sex to shame.
They stand, for wonder, rooted to the place,
At meeting in the desert wild, a dame,
A match for goddesses in beauty and in grace.

55

The sight of beauty softens even brutes;
The very tigers crouch before her charm—
Yet these feel naught—their robber sense computes
The value of the fairest female form
Alike in flesh or marble, with cold blood,
Just at the market price, like merchandise—
"This prize will make ten thousand sequins good,
As easily as ten"—the captain cries.

56

"Come! seize her, boys! a score of costly bales
To us at Tunis were not worth this face.
The king, you all know, loves such nightingales
And his whole Harem cannot show a grace
To match this wild one—Queen Almansaris,
Though fair, were scarcely fit her train to bear—
How will the Sultan's bosom burn at this!
No!—chance could not provide us better fare."

57

While thus the captain speaks, Amanda stands
And thinks on what she must determine here—
"Are these men foes?—flight, to escape their hands
To me of no avail can be, thus near;
Courage perhaps, and prayers their hearts may gain;
Let me then go and to them speak, as friends,
As saviors, whom in pity of our pain
Kind Heaven, and our good fortune hither sends."

58

Thus, with firm, dauntless step, and with an air
Where quiet innocence and candor reign,
Up to the pirates goes the noble fair;
But deaf to her entreaties they remain.
That language which all hearts can understand
Has o'er their iron, brutal souls no sway—
The captain nods and straight the savage band
Surround, seize, hurry to the ship their prey.

59

The rocks, resounding with her piteous cries
At last her danger to the knight reveal.
Dismayed, distracted, to her aid he flies,
And, soon as intervening trees conceal
No longer what it is, as need inspires,
He snatches the first knotty club at hand,
And swift as from black clouds celestial fires,
Darts down in vengeance on the pirate band.

60

His lovely wife, struggling with blood-stained arms,
Herself from robbers' fangs to disengage:
This sight the oak club in his hand soon warms
And spurs his passion to a tiger's rage.
Strokes following strokes as thick as hail-stones fly,
And rushing down, on head and shoulders storm;
He seems a God— Fire sparkles from his eye,
Already seven strong Moors have sunk beneath his arm.

61

Confusion, shame and rage, their prey so fair
Thus by one man snatched from them to behold,
Spurs all the rest upon the knight to bear,
Who braves them all, with untamed fury bold.
While he can lift his arms, 'till as he fights
His club drops from him, numbers press around,
And though he raving strikes, and thrusts, and bites,
O'ermaster him at length, and strain him to the ground.

62

Amanda, with a shriek that rends the skies,
Sinks in a swoon, thinking she sees him slain—
Part of the people then bear off their prize
While raging, on the strand the rest remain,
And snort revenge upon their fallen foe.
Too kind they think it, instant death to give—
"No!" cries the captain—"to prolong his woe,
The worst of deaths to suffer—he shall live."

63

They drag him deep into the woods along,
So distant from the strand, his loudest cries
No ear can reach, and bind with cordage strong
About his neck and back, his arms and thighs
Fast to a tree— Beneath his load of woe
The wretched man, weighed down in deep dismay
Looks up to Heaven, while shouting as they go
To Tunis with their spoil, the pirates speed their way.

Book the tenth

1

The day was sunk, and night (no longer passed
Amid the sweet, confiding, cordial smile
Of love and friendship) had in pity cast
Her gloomiest shade around the desert isle,
Where songs of joy no longer wake at morn
From the deep silence of her calm repose;
But where one man, abandoned and forlorn,
Of patient sufferance the sad example shows.

2

Him, shaded in a cloud the fairy queen
Hears from the wood, at distant pauses sigh;
She sees him, silent, pine with anguish keen,
And from him turns her pity beaming eye.
In vain her heart with soft compassion swells;
A stronger charm, with unresisted hand
Her flight across the shore from him repels,
Where, flying, she beholds a gold ring on the sand.

3

Amanda, struggling with the pirate crew
Had, undiscovered, dropped it from her hand;
Titania, snatching it, the signet knew
Before which awe-struck, all the spirits stand.
"Fate's measure soon will fill," she joyous cries;
"The stars shall soon appease thee, spouse adored!
This ring, which joined us once in wedlock's ties,
Shall for the second time soon crown thee as my lord."

4

Meanwhile on board the ship, with no small pain
Amanda from her swoon to life they brought,
And when she opened to the light again
Her eyes, with dull, despairing languor fraught,
The captain fell before her on his knee,
Entreating her no more at heart to moan.
"I only speed your happiness," said he,
"A few days more shall seat you on a throne.

5

"Dread naught, for to protect you and to serve,
Is all we have to do— Our king alone,
Almanzor, to possess you can deserve.
His charms are equal, Fairest, to your own.
He your soft sway will from the first glance prove,
And to your charms you'll joy to see him yield"—
He spoke—and all suspicion to remove,
Reached her a costly veil, her beauties to enshield.

6

"Death! instant death!" (proceeds he with an air
And tone which makes the people all turn pale)
"Shall punish him whose insolence shall dare
But lay his finger on this sacred veil.
Her as a precious jewel henceforth view
Of which Almanzor can alone dispose."
He spoke and knelt, and from her sight withdrew,
That undisturbed she might enjoy repose.

7

With stiffened gaze and tearless eye the fair
Hears not his speech, nor aught around her sees;
Unmoved and by misfortune stunned, sits there
Her hands across her brows, and on her knees
Her arms supported— Too intense her woe
To be expressed— E'en her strong heart must faint
Beneath the weight—alas! this latest blow
Is too severe—she sinks, yet sinks without complaint.

8

She looks for comfort round, but none can find,
For all is hopeless, gloomy as her soul.
The world itself is changed, and to her mind
Appears no other than a murderers' hole.
Upwards she looks to Heaven, but even there
No comfort gleams, no angel kind remains.
Thus, hovering on the borders of despair,
To raise her as she sinks, death only power retains.

9

In pity he his withered hand extends,
The wretch's last, best friend— With him she goes—
Down to the silent land of shades descends,
The land which neither pain nor sorrow knows;
Where the free soul no more is galled with chains,
Where this world's scenes, like dreams of children flee,
Where nothing of it but our hearts remains
And where her eyes again, whate'er she loved shall see.

10

In silent sufferance like a lamb she lay,
That bleeds beneath the knife, and death implored:
When in the dead of night Titania
With comfort came— A viewless rain she poured
Of slumberous dews, the sufferer's heart to raise
And lull her outward sense to soft repose;
Then in a dream the lovely queen of fays
Displays herself, and bright in rosy radiance glows.

11

"Up! and take heart!—thy son and husband both
Yet breathe—are not forever lost to thee!
Recognize me—and know that Oberon's oath
Your truth will have redeemed, when thou shalt see
Me for the third time— You will end our pain
And with our bliss yours too will be renewed"—
With this, the Goddess melts in air again,
But rosy fragrance waves where she had stood.

12

Amanda wakes, and by the fragrant smell
And rosy splendors which but slowly fade,
The godlike woman knows, who in the cell
Alike unhoped for, once had lent her aid.
While shame and gratitude her bosom fill,
She snatches the new solace of her woe;
This pledge that Huon and her son live still
And with it sets at naught Fate's direst blow.

13

Knew she, alas! what for her bliss concealed
To her remains, how her unhappy friend
Fast to an oak by seven-fold cordage held
This comfortless long night was doomed to spend,
How would it break her heart!—and he, the while,
Who sees through darkness, the good angel, stays—
Stands on a rock's point, at the source of Nile,
Where shines the sun with never clouded rays.

14

With earnest look tówards' the island cast
Where Huon pines, the prince of Spirits stands;
Hears his low sobs upon the distant blast;
Looks to the morning star, and with his hands
Covers his face and sighs—among the bands
Of Spirits who attend him everywhere,
And wait, in rings or single, his commands—
One now, his special confidant, drew near.

15

Pale and unlustrous, comes with silent gaze
The sylph tŏwards' him, and his eyes in tears
Inquire what woe upon his bosom preys;
To ask aloud from reverence he forbears.
"Look up," said Oberon—and full in sight
Just then, with outstretched wings above them flew
A cloud in which as in a mirror bright
Poor Huon's image struck the Spirit's wondering view.

16

Sunk in the deepest woe, forlorn and bound
In the wild desert wood he stands and sighs,
His bosom bleeding at each open wound,
And the long tedious death of martyrs dies.
His tortured soul too in this hopeless state
His feelings thus contribute to inflame.
"Have I, hath Rezia merited this fate?
Of higher beings are our woes the game?

17

"How small a share in my dire sufferings take
These objects all around? How quiet all!
No grain of sand will flutter for my sake,
For me no leaf will from the forest fall.
No being feels for me— To cut my ties,
Can but a single pointed pebble need;
Yet all the lapse of time no hand supplies
To lend it motion for the friendly deed.

18

"And yet, oh! thou, who hast so oft from death
Unhoped for snatched me; if thy will it were
To turn my woes away, thy smallest breath
Would turn to hands each twig these forests bear!"
—A holy shuddering all his bones pervades
As gleams this spark of Heavenly flame serene.
The cords fall off—he reels with eyes in shades
And falls in arms that hold him up unseen.

19

The sylph to whom his monarch had displayed
The sad disasters of the faithful pair,
It was, who thus unseen lent Huon aid—
The child of light, that vision could not bear.
"Alas!" he cried, with inward grief oppressed,
And sinking at his feet; "canst thou survey
Thy favorite, though guilty, thus distressed,
And from his sufferings turn thy noble heart away?"

20

"The future, to earth's children is concealed,"
Replies the king—"and we ourselves, my friend,
Are but Fate's slaves—in holy darkness veiled
High above us, his hidden ways extend.
Whether with willing or reluctant hearts
His impulse we must in the dark pursue.
Thou seest the gulf which me from Huon parts,
One thing alone for him am I allowed to do.

21

"Fly hence, unbind him, and to Tunis bear
And set him down, in just his present state
Before old Ibrahim's door, who in his care
Has the king's garden, near the city gate;
Close to the door, upon the bench of stone
Place him, but stand not to his sight revealed;
Go with all speed and hasten back anon,
And to him be thy lips in awful silence sealed."

22

Not swifter flies an arrow through its track
Than comes the sylph to aid our hapless knight,
Unties his bonds, and with him on his back
O'er land and sea pursues his airy flight,
Until arriving at old Ibrahim's sill,
He lets him down upon the bench of stone
As on a bed of feathers soft and still;
While Huon thinks it all a dream alone.

23

To make it sure, he looks with deep surprise,
And all he sees persuades him it is so.
"Where am I," dreading to awake, he cries,
Just as a cock at hand begins to crow.
Anon a second and a third succeeds,
The silence flies, Heaven's golden gates unclose.
The God of day drives forth his fiery steeds
And all around the hut with life and motion glows.

24

Now creaks the door, and from it with a spade
Comes a gray-bearded man of stature high,
But whose fresh cheek the rose's tints displayed;
And both, what neither can believe, now spy,
Sir Huon in a slave's vest sees his squire;
And in his turn the good old man beholds
His long lost lord, arrayed in such attire
As little promise of good luck unfolds.

25

"And can it be?"—they both at once inquire—
"My dearest lord!"—"My friend!"—"That here we meet?"
While nearly mad with joy the faithful squire
Clasps Huon's knees, and weeps upon his feet.
The hero bends himself to raise his friend
And on his cheek a cordial kiss bestow.
"Thank God!" Cherasmin cries—"my sorrows end,
Since now, that you are still alive I know.

26

"What blessèd wind hath brought you to this shore?
Yet this is surely not the place to tell—
Before we thus together at this door
Are seen, dear Sir, come with me to my cell.
My nephew Hassan you must henceforth be"
(He whispers in his ear), "a youth in trade;
Who from Aleppo sailed, the world to see,
And barely with your life, escape from shipwreck made."

27

"Alas! yes! naught is left me," Huon sighs,
"Except a worthless life"— "Time will give more,"
Cherasmin opening his small cell replies,
And entering with the hero, shuts the door.
"There, take a seat," says he, and on a plate
Brings him the best his little stores contain,
Bread, olives, wine, his appetite to sate,
And at his side sits down and bids him cheer again.

28

"That after all the ugly tricks which Fate
Hath played us, dearest Sir, we meet once more
Thus unexpectedly near Tunis' gate
Before the gardener Ibrahim's cottage door,
Is a sure sign that Oberon still is kind
And will together bring us all in course;
The best, be sure, as yet remains behind,
But as Amanda's pledge, at least we have the nurse."

29

"What sayst thou?" cries Sir Huon full of joy—
"She is a slave," the honest squire replies,
"To the same Ibrahim who gives me employ.
How will she feed on you her eager eyes!"
And thereupon he to the knight relates
All since they parted he has done and borne,
And what inducements urged him, fully states,
With unaccomplished charge from Paris back to turn.

30

How in the Lateran for him he sought
And after waiting many weeks in vain
His little stock of cash to nothing brought,
And then with muscle-shells o'er land and main
Had, as a pilgrim, begged his way around
Till hither brought at last by lucky Fate,
Where unexpectedly he Fatme found
Who bound herself with him for better times to wait.

31

"The casket I brought with me," adds the squire,
"The present of the dwarf at Askalon,
By great good fortune yet remains entire—
For, I perceive, the horn and cup are gone—
Dear Sir!—forgive me this imprudent prattle;
I see my ill-timed freedom galls the sore.
The joy of finding you thus makes me tattle;
But you know all my heart, and now not one word more!"

32

"I know thy faithful soul," the prince replied—
And warmly pressed his hand—"my worthy friend!
Thou shalt know all— I naught from thee will hide;
But first of all, thy aid for one thing lend.
The casket thou hast kept is richly set—
Dost thou not think the gems were best applied
With speed an horse and arms for me to get,
And knightly ornaments at Tunis to provide?

33

"Scarcely twelve hours ago, a pirate band
Snatched Rezia from me on a desert shore,
While I alone was with her on the strand,
Unarmed—to this land her perhaps they bore,
Morocco, Fez, or certainly some place
Where there may be a hope to sell her high—
But never shall a Harem boast that face,
Though I the whole world o'er, to save my treasure fly."

34

The old man ponders all in silent thought—
"The place, where you received this heavy blow
Is then," quoth he, "not far from this remote?"
"That's more," returned Sir Huon, "than I know.
It may be three months journey or still more.
I know not who (a Spirit it must be)
Me with unbounded swiftness hither bore
From where the pirates tied me to a tree."

35

"No arm but Oberon's did this, 'tis plain,"
Exclaims the squire— "So I myself believe;
And as a pledge" (returns the knight again)
"That he will do still more, the whole receive.
How terrible soe'er it was to part,
To see my wife in robbers' fangs, how dread!
Yet this new wonder, friend, o'er all my heart
New life, new hope, new confidence hath shed.

36

"That man were wholly heartless, all of stone,
Void of all feeling, and unworthy quite
That Heaven for him should make its wonders known,
Who with but half the prodigies in sight
That I have witnessed, still a doubt could breed
And yield his soul to lowly-minded fear—
Though my dark path through fire or flood should lead,
Yet shall my truth and courage persevere.

37

"But, good Cherasmin, go this very day;
If possible, a sword and steed provide—
From both have I too long been kept away—
Though truly—by my loved Amanda's side.
But far from her, the blood within my breast
Seems like a pool to stagnate—think on't, friend!
Till from these heathens their fair spoil I wrest,
Her life and all my bliss may on one hour depend."

38

The old man with this ardor to comply
Swears every nerve this very day to strain;
But new misfortunes soon his zeal defy,
And render that same eve his efforts vain.
Such oft-repeated shocks, blow after blow,
At length subdued the sinews of the knight;
Feeble and restless, with a fever's glow,
In sick, distracted dreams he passed the night.

39

The images which in his mind abound
Take life— He thinks to fight with hostile swarms,
Then sinks exhausted down upon the ground
And strains his lifeless infant in his arms.
Now buffeting the waves, his lovely bride
He scarce can keep from sinking in the main;
Now to a tree by bands of robbers tied,
He sees her bleeding strive to break from them in vain.

40

Worn down by rage and pain, upon the bed
He rolls with stiffened eye— In his distress
Cherasmin's knowledge stands him in good stead.
For squires were wont in those days to profess
With knighthood's art, the art of healing too;
Cherasmin by his sire had first been taught;
And from his travels many a secret knew
Which from the lips of knights and sages he had caught.

41

Soon as fair Hesper whitens in the sky,
With his dear lord he leaves the faithful nurse,
With tender care for his relief to ply,
And to the silent garden takes his course;
There seeks out herbs, whose wondrous powers and use
He learnt on Horeb in a hermit's cell;
And strains them out and mixes up a juice
The strongest fever's rage in little time to quell.

42

Already on the second night, soft sleep
Upon Sir Huon's brows begins to sink,
And as their watch true love and duty keep
With him, and amply give him cooling drink,
He feels himself recovered the fourth day,
So that when Cynthia gives Night's face a glow,
He can assume his laborer's array,
And with Cherasmin to the garden go.

43

They from the hut had gone but little way
When them among the rose-trees Fatme sought
(Who near the Harem oft was wont to stray
To pick up news) and tidings with her brought
Stronger to cheer the blood in Huon's veins
Than all the cordials Tunis can supply;
Assuring them that scarce a doubt remains
But their adored Amanda must be nigh.

44

"Where is she?—where?"—in transport Huon cries,
And starting with impatience—"Fatme!—say!
Where didst thou see her?"—"See her?" she replies,
"I did not that!—but I my life will lay
That your Amanda landed here this eve—
Hear what the Jewess Salome declares:
Which for undoubted truth you may receive—
This moment she came down the inner Harem's stairs.

45

"A little space ere even-tide," says she,
"Was seen a vessel, sailing to'wards land;
Swift as a bird can fly she cut the sea,
And a fresh breeze appeared her sails t' expand.
When on a sudden, from unclouded skies
A livid flash of forky lightning came;
And kindling as the blast began to rise,
The vessel soon was one devouring flame.

46

"To quench it no man thinks in such distress—
Out of the flaming jaws of death to break,
All who have strength to spring, together press
And to the pinnace straight themselves betake.
The wind soon parts it from the vessel's side,
It drifts tŏwards' the shore; but near the strand
A sudden blast o'erwhelms it in the tide;
It sinks within a furlong of the land.

47

In vain to Mahomet the people cry
And from the cruel flood their lives to save,
In vain of agony the struggles ply—
One woman only floats upon the wave.
No danger seems upon the deep to dwell
For this fair object of Heaven's tender care;
Unhurt, unwet, the billows as they swell
As on a chariot her tŏwards' the dry land bear.

48

"Just then it chanced the Sultan with his queen
Upon the terrace of the palace stood,
Whence the wide waste of waters may be seen—
And for the issue looked tŏwards' the flood.
Soft zephyrs onwards seemed the fair to blow;
Yet, not to trust too much a wonder's aid,
At the queen's nod, an hundred slaves now go
And to their necks, to help the woman, wade.

49

"The king himself came, say they, to the strand
And from an Idshoglan received the fair,
Who from the foaming surges to the land
Upon his nervous back the lady bare.
No person, what he said indeed, could hear,
Yet seemed he much civility to offer;
And having neither time nor freedom there,
His heart to her at least in every look to proffer.

50

"Thus much is sure, however that may be"
(Adds Fatme), "that Almansaris displayed
Much kindness to the lady from the sea,
And many handsome offers to her made.
And though, no sooner had Almanzor seen
The lovely stranger, than she stole his heart—
Yet, in the summer-palace of the queen,
This very now, she holds a room apart."

51

While Fatme speaks, joy, terror, love and pain
Painted by turns on Huon's visage play;
The more he thinks, the more he deems it plain—
It must be Rezia, for 'tis clear as day
That Oberon, though hidden to their eyes
Guides of their destinies again the reins—
"Well, friends!" quoth he, "what now you think, advise!
To fix what yet is to be done remains."

52

"The lady from the king by force to wrest,
Is more than Roland to advise would dare"—
Returns Cherasmin—"though I hold it best
Ourselves with arms in secret to prepare
Ready to be for good or evil fare—
But let us now of skill the trial make.
To dig you blush not— How, if as you are
With our old Ibrahim you should service take?

53

"Even suppose he shy at first should be,
Look at you sharp, and wisely shake his head;
That would give no concern, Sir knight, to me;
Before a diamond, many a doubt has fled.
Be this my care—before another day
You in a gardener's apron must be dressed;
Spite of all obstacles athwart the way—
To time and Providence leave all the rest."

54

This project being by our knight approved,
They put it in effect with speed and care,
And soon old Ibrahim's heart so far is moved
As Huon for his nephew to declare;
His sister's son, come from Damascus' plains
Where raising flowers had long been his employ;
Thus Huon soon with much address sustains
The noble office of a gardener's boy.

Book the eleventh

1

The golden Hope that spreads o'er Huon's breast
Her glistening wings, of her whom he adores
Shortly to find himself again possessed,
Youth's fairest splendor to his looks restores.
The mere idea that his love is here,
That this same gentle breeze which cools him now,
Haply just kissed those lips to him so dear
Or comes from fluttering round Amanda's brow.

2

That these same flowers which for the Harem's fair
He culls and braids in garlands fresh and gay,
Are destined to adorn Amanda's hair
Or on her bosom breathe their lives away;
The thought alone with transport fills his heart;
Again his cheek the blush of rapture dyes,
Desire and Hope new life and joy impart
And give their former radiance to his eyes.

3

Day in these climes the place of night supplies,
And still is wasted in the arms of sleep;
But when the winds of evening first arise,
Sir Huon, whom love's visions cheerful keep,
On every shade for his Amanda calls—
The night he knows is spent in watching here;
Yet that no man within the garden walls
Must after sunset venture to appear.

4

The fair are wont then, by the moon's mild ray,
In little circles, or by pairs till morn
Along the arbors in full bloom to stray;
And if the queen the lovely train adorn,
Then song and instruments combine with dance
Dull night to speed— Then in the silent grot
A bath anon succeeds, tŏwards' which t' advance
(Decorum's law, so stern) Almanzor's self dares not.

5

Yet could our knight not see his lovely spouse
(Within the Harem, as he thought, confined)
Unless he longer than the rule allows
Should in the garden stay at night, behind.
Three restless nights already had he spent
Sheltered amidst a copse's foliage green,
By which the passage from the Harem went—
Had watched there, listened, gazed, but not Amanda seen.

6

Implored by Ibrahim, Fatme and the squire
All at his feet, no longer to expose
His life and theirs, he purposed to retire
On the fourth evening just at day-light's close.
He thinks the coursers of the sun too fleet,
And lingers till they wholly disappear;
Then as he turns a hedge to make retreat,
Before him stands Almansaris, quite near.

7

Leaning on one of her fair nymphs she came
Amidst the fragrance of a cool alcove
To seek refreshment from day's scorching flame—
A nightgown, light as if by spiders wove
In flowing folds her body scarcely veils;
A golden girdle clasps her bosom round,
Which heaving still the thin restraint assails
And with impatience sweet, attempts to burst the bound.

8

The plastic hand of nature never made
A model for a Venus more divine
Than this fair body, which in shape displayed
To nicest eyes alone, that waving line
Which flows with matchless grace, and forms precise
Between too little and too much the mean.
No!—Such a form, not even Joseph's ice
Without dissolving down to tenderness had seen.

9

Whatever wonders we in Grecian art
As images of perfect beauty see,
This form possessed in every single part.
'Twas Helen's bosom, Atalanta's knee,
And Erigone's lip, and Leda's arm;
But when she once the wish for conquest feels,
No sculptor's skill can ever reach the charm
Before which every heart submissive kneels.

10

Then to the whispering air her breath imparts
The very soul of amorous delight.
Her eyes are full of Cupid's keenest darts,
And woe to him who with them dares to fight!
For e'en against that fiery, languid eye
With some success himself should he defend,
How could he that enchanting mouth defy?
How with its fascinating smile contend?

11

How, that transporting Siren voice control
Which bids the inmost chords of feeling rise?
Bears sweet illusion to the secret soul,
As if she floated upon wanton sighs.
And if perchance ere Wisdom can take heed
Your treacherous senses with her leagued appear,
And the last moment of mad riot speed;
Who, to his fall, oh! say, were then not near?

12

But stay!—perhaps uncertain or remote
Is yet the shipwreck which we deem so near;
Flight, which might else the wisest plan be thought,
The queen so nigh, could be no resource here;
Though a true gardener's boy in Huon's room
Had fled— By good luck, should the dame inquire,
A basket full of fruit and flowers in bloom
He bears upon his arm, an answer will inspire.

13

The lovely queen at this unusual sight
Here at this hour surprised, can scarce draw breath—
"What dost thou here?"—inquires she of the knight
With such a look as had been certain death
To any other of old Ibrahim's race;
But Huon with his eyelids downwards bent,
Falls on his knees with reverence and grace,
His basket as an offering to present.

14

"Beyond the hour that closed the garden gate
To all like him, he stayed for this alone,"
He said—"and if his boldness was too great
His head must for his hasty zeal atone."
But while the handsome culprit prostrate lies
Before her, milder projects she revolves.
She looks upon him with complacent eyes
And, with reluctance, to proceed resolves.

15

The fairest youth her eyes had ever seen—
Like heroes fair, with dignity and grace;
A stranger by complexion and in mien,
Clad like a gardener, seemed quite out of place.
How gladly would she to converse advance
But that decorum's rigid law restrains—
She nods to bid him go; yet seems a glance
To follow him, that much, oh! very much contains.

16

Silent she sauntered on, and turning round
Her lovely neck, the stranger still to see;
Her nod too soon obeyed, with anger found.
"Is he too weak to understand," thought she,
"Th' explaining look?—or is that beauteous form
Without a soul?—Is that eye's fire a cheat?
Can he be chilled by danger's threatened storm?
Or was his purpose here another fair to meet?"

17

"Another?"—Suddenly this doubt reveals
What to herself she blushing scarce dares own—
Still Huon's image on her fancy steals—
She roams all night the arbors up and down,
Lists to each breath of air amid the dark,
To every leaf that flutters on the breeze.
"Hush!"—to her confidante says she—"and hark!
Methought I heard a rustling through yon trees."

18

"Perhaps the handsome gardener may be there,"
Says the sly maid— "Unless I much mistake,
His life without a scruple he would dare
Here, in the background, leaning on a brake,
Another look of paradise to snatch
And with sweet rapture his soul once more to feed.
What if we softly creep along and catch
The fair offender in the very deed?"

19

"Peace! foolish girl," the Harem's queen replies—
"I think thou rav'st, bewildered in a dream."
Yet instantly with tripping feet she hies
Towards' the tree from which the rustling came.
'Twas but a lizard, creeping through the bush—
The queen upon her nosegay bends her head,
And half-breathed sighs that from her bosom rush,
Confirm what in her looks Nadine had read.

20

At variance with herself she sighs and frets
And bites her lip and mutters something low.
At the fourth word, what she would say, forgets—
Then chides Nadine for comprehension slow
And not divining what she should divine—
In love, in one word, is this fair forlorn.
Her nosegay finds it—for without design
'Tis plucked out leaf by leaf and all in pieces torn.

21

Already lasts this evil three days long
And thrives upon resistance and restraint—
Each night, each morning sees it grow more strong;
For when the rays of evening twilight paint
The motley window, from her room she sallies
And like a nymph, with tresses half unbound
Wanders o'er all the garden bowers and alleys
Wherever Ibrahim's nephew could be found.

22

But vain is all the waiting of the queen—
Vain her impatience—from what cause soe'er
The handsome gardener can no more be seen—
Thy pride all sinks, unhappy princess, here.
"But wherefore," thinks she, "torment thus endure?
Why from Nadine what gnaws thy breast conceal?
She has observed it long ago, be sure,
And secrecy no serpent's bite can heal."

23

Thus, to seek comfort from a friendly heart
She thinks, but flattery is what she needs.
Nadine was mistress of that courtly art—
Not all the cooling juices Afric bleeds
Can so refresh the blood within the veins
Of her who burns with love's intensest fires,
As this friend's counsel and her tender pains
Soon in her net to draw the man whom she desires.

24

With the doors closed, and at the midnight hour
'Twas easier henceforth the youth to bring
To those apartments where the lady's power
Was uncontrolled, since openly the king
Was to his love for Zoradine resigned—
(For such was here the lovely stranger's name
Who, rescued from the raging flame and wind
So lately hither by a wonder came).

25

The nurse in her conclusion had been right:
It was Amanda whom Titania's hand
Had snatched by lightning from the pirates' might
And brought uninjured upon Tunis' strand.
What happened when she came to land, you know.
How the king's fickle heart at once she gained
And what an envious and dissembled show
Of tenderness, Almansaris had feigned.

26

The sun perhaps had never shed his ray
Upon a man whose charms the king's excelled,
And he so well his merits could display
That every female heart at once they quelled.
Here for the first time vain is all his art;
Only one man in all the world is known
To Zoradine, for whom she has a heart—
No eyes, no thought has she, except for him alone.

27

The cold, yet modest, unaffected mien,
The dignified reserve, exempt from pride,
The noble boldness, candid and serene,
With which she keeps at such a distance wide
Him who can here command, that scarce he dares
E'en by a silent look express his flame;
Seeing all this, Almansaris declares
Seduction's masterpiece should be its name.

28

Wont, at her will the Sultan's heart to wind—
Him, and the Harem uncontrolled to sway;
Thus, by a stranger, could she coolly find
The sceptre wheedled from her hands away?
She lends indeed a smiling look to hate,
Nor to suspect the lovely stranger seems;
Yet every spot within the Harem's gate
With swarms of hidden eyes, to spy her actions teems.

29

But since love's sharpest dart from Huon's charms
Hath to the lady's proud heart found its way,
A softer passion jealousy disarms,
And love of pleasure masters love of sway.
To quaff his kiss is all she wishes now,
Only to vanquish him her pride aspires.
Let at the stranger's feet the whole world bow,
If she but in her arms clasp him her soul desires.

30

By the king's orders was in haste prepared
Part of the Harem distant from the queen;
Who now herself with zeal the purpose shared
With more distinction to treat Zoradine.
This, her true rank a sort of duty made,
Though by herself not yet avowed it be;
Since the first glance to every eye betrayed
That she was wont above her naught to see.

31

While thus Almansaris with courtly art
Tries an unwelcome witness to remove,
The Sultan, having now resigned his heart
Without restriction to his present love,
Himself concerns not in the smallest wise
About his queen, or how her time she spends;
But free space leaves her, projects to devise
For which an hundred hands the Harem lends.

32

Meanwhile our hero, deeply grieved in mind,
That having gone round seven successive days
The walls where his Amanda mourns confined,
(For that she mourns, his own heart boldly says)
His wife to see, so much as through a grate
Or but the print of her light foot to spy,
(Sure among thousands he could find it straight)
His stern, inexorable stars deny.

33

Towards' his friends he turns in cruel pain:
"Sure, if you love me, you can find some way
Within the Harem but one mouth to gain
My name to whisper in her ear, and say
That I am near"— "Stay! something strikes my mind,"
Exclaims the nurse— "Send her a Maneh there,
Go—in the garden, all the flowers you'll find;
I understand this language to a hair."

34

And at her word the handsome gardener goes
And forthwith brings a wreath of myrtles fair,
With lilies, jasmin, daffodil and rose;
Then from his locks she bids him pluck a hair,
And, braiding with the hair a thin gold thread,
Ties up the posy with a love-knot gay,
And in the midst a leaf of laurel spread,
On which entwined were scrawled an H and A.

35

"Dash it," says she, "with ginger water o'er
And it will be the prettiest *billet-doux*
That ever lady on her bosom bore.
Sir knight—shall I translate it here for you?"
"Thanks," quoth Sir Huon, "lose no time—but go—
Thou canst not soon enough an answer bring—
May love protect thee and success bestow;
We will expect thee here, beside this cooling spring."

36

She goes—but as the inner Harem stands
Closed, that she there no entrance can obtain,
The nosegay runs through many servile hands
Till by Nadine's mistake picked up again;
(For thus in all affairs of mortal men
Chance, uninvited, meddling, still is seen)
She, after many questions, how and when,
Bears it in joyous triumph to the queen.

37

As Ibrahim's female slave the letter brought,
Suspicion could upon no other bear,
Than on the handsome gardener youth, she thought—
As sure it seems, that of the Harem's fair,
Meant for the loveliest it must have been;
And after what had passed so late ere this,
What could the intertwining letters mean?
What else but Hassan and Almansaris?

38

But even were a rival in the way,
Albeit quite incredible it seems—
To rob by force from her the charming prey,
She only as a prouder triumph deems—
The jealousy these thoughts at once excite
With passions of a milder tone combines,
No longer than until the following night
To wait the victory for which she pines.

39

Meanwhile without suspicion of deceit
The nurse comes back, nor can her joy suppress;
With panting breath and cheeks that glow with heat,
And quite transported at her own success.
Her looks, e'en distant, like the sun's appear
Through clouds, as from his face they pass away.
"What will you give" (she whispers in his ear)
"For opening Heaven to you, Sir knight, this very day?

40

"Yes! your Amanda you this day shall see—
Open to you, near midnight, the small gate
That leads tŏwards' the myrtle grove will be—
Follow secure the slave who there shall wait,
Where'er she goes and no deception dread—
She will conduct you safely to the place."
—Poor Fatme troubles not with doubts her head
But on the way relies, of which she found the trace.

41

"How much, oh! Fatme! to thy cares I owe,"
Exclaims the knight—"I shall my love behold!
This very night! and though my way should go
From her to instant death a thousand fold,
Thy words would scarcely give me less delight."
—"I feel" (Cherasmin cries) "my spirits swell—
The stars are kind; you will succeed, Sir knight,
To get your lady free, and all will yet be well.

42

"Three days but give me secretly to freight
A bark, which safe at anchor in a bay
Not distant, only for your nod shall wait
When all is ready for the flight, to weigh.
Your little casket is with jewels fraught
Which for our purpose ample means supply.
With gold, Sir knight, the world may all be bought.
Turned by a golden key all padlocks open fly."

43

While, till the moment of his bliss shall rise
Our knight counts instants by his pulse's beat,
And while his pulse each moment swifter flies
And fiercer still grows his impatient heat,
The charming queen with not more patience sighs,
For triumph at the midnight hour prepared.
Chance kindly to her plans his aid applies
And frees her on all sides from what she feared.

44

In the king's palace a great feast prepared,
In honor of the lovely Zoradine,
At which the Harem ladies all appeared,
Gave open field on her side to the queen.
That she herself as wholly useless deems
At this festivity, could not displease;
But very natural the headache seems,
Which at command upon her comes to seize.

45

Hark! the hour calls! the handsome youth draws near
The garden gate, and through the bushes steals—
He pants—how beats his heart with love and fear!
When in the dark a tender hand he feels
Grasp his, and draw him on with gentle powers;
Silent, he follows it without delay,
Through narrow, often crossed, dim-lighted bowers
Till now, before a gate, it from him slips away.

46

"Where are we?"—whispering, with both his hands
He taps the door— It opens—a faint ray
(Such as where ivy-shaded myrtle stands
In vernal hedges, glooms expiring day)
A seeming endless range of chambers shows,
While imperceptibly the feeble light
Becomes a gleam, and spreading as he goes
The gleam bursts out, in utmost radiance bright.

47

Amazed and dazzled, splendor to behold
To which, whate'er he saw before was mean,
So much is lapis lazuli and gold
In proud profusion lavished o'er the scene,
With all, Golconda's richest mine supplies;
Yet seek for *her,* his eyes unsatisfied—
"Where is she?" sighs he loud; and as he sighs,
Quick as a lightning's flash a curtain draws aside.

48

Up, rustles on both sides the rich brocade;
And what a scene before his sight unfolds!
A lady on a golden throne displayed,
Such as a sculptor's raptured fancy holds
The queen of love— Twelve nymphs, all young and fair
As Cupid's sisters, form in groups around,
As twilight's gleam, more nobly to declare
The rising triumph of the Sun is found.

49

While rosy silks scarce shade their limbs, they seem
Around their lady's feet, in posture low,
Like clouds which in a youthful poet's dream
About the car of Cytherea flow.
In richest garb herself, the costly load
Of jewels only served to make it sure
That howsoe'er in varied hues they glowed,
Her native lustre they could not obscure.

50

Sir Huon (still the gardener Hassan called)
On looking up, Almansaris straight knew;
And staggered back, astonished and appalled;
What was this dazzling and voluptuous view
To him, where his Amanda was not seen?
She whom alone his heart and looks here sought—
While by a natural mistake, the queen
That he was dazzled by her splendor thought.

51

Now, with a smile, descending from her throne,
She takes him by the hand and seems prepared
Upon her beauties to depend alone,
And lay aside the pomp which round her glared.
Still freer by degrees her conduct grows—
Her eyes a tender, blazing fire display—
Which to his breast electrically flows,
While pressing soft his hand, she bids his heart be gay.

52

His looks emboldening, something seem to say:
She nods—the nymphs withdraw—his heart is gone—
He scarcely dares his eyes upon her lay—
The scene is changed—a second curtain drawn,
And by the queen into another hall
Her bashful and reluctant swain is led,
Where wreathes of rose and myrtle deck the wall,
And with refreshments stands a table spread.

53

The loveliest music hails their entrance there;
From strings and voices rings the soul of joy—
He seats himself right opposite the fair,
As she commands him, while, with boldness coy,
The languor in her swimming looks that lies,
And fond impatience glowing on her cheeks
Confess his triumph—though from Hassan's eyes,
As from a lurid cloud, a gloomy glimmer breaks.

54

His looks indeed, no longer timid, rove
Bold o'er her charms, but not as she desires—
Not with the languishing delight of love,
Not glistening with the beams of luscious fires.
With absent mind he seems her to compare,
And every beauty, by degrees revealed,
But livelier paints Amanda's image fair,
And must, ashamed, to her chaste graces yield.

55

The sparkling cup she reaches him in vain,
With love's whole quiver, shooting from her eyes;
Not sweeter smiling midst the heavenly train
At the most joyous banquet of the skies
Young Hebe held to Hercules's lips
The nectar bowl— In vain—with aspect chill,
He takes the goblet from her hand and sips,
As felt he poison o'er his tongue distill.

56

The lady nods, and straight the sister-quire
Of nymphs, who formed around her throne a ring,
Begin a dance which might new souls inspire
Into the dead upon a bier, or bring
To ghosts their bodies— Now in groups entwined,
Now pair by pair again, his eyes behold
The loveliest forms in thousand postures wind,
And freely all their wanton charms unfold.

57

Perhaps too clearly all these arts reveal
The purpose, sensual desire to raise—
Be it—thinks she—provided he but feel
How rich the spectacle that beauty plays!
How lovely the soft waving of the arm!
How the joints whirl! how swings the pliant hip!
Their eyes half-closed, with what a languid charm
As if in sweetest death, they slowly backward slip.

58

Our hero's senses, taken by surprise,
Howe'er reluctant, at this flame grow warm;
Till with an effort, closing both his eyes,
He calls the potent check of Rezia's form:
Of Rezia's form, as at the solemn hour
When of her kiss his lips th' impression bore;
And by the Lord of Nature's boundless power
The oath to her of love and truth he swore.

59

He swears in thought the tender vow once more,
Before this holy form, upon his knee,
And straight it seems as if an angel bore
A shield before his breast, to such degree
The darts of pleasure forceless from it sink;
The queen, who watched whate'er his looks betrayed,
Now clapped her hands, and with a silent wink
An end of this luxurious dancing made.

60

And though she scarcely can forbear with pain
By force the young man's feelings to assail;
And in her arms his marble bosom strain,
One trial more she fancies cannot fail.
She takes her lute and with enchanting grace
Leans on her sopha, while love's purple dye
Adds almost magic beauties to her face—
Thus with the Muses' aid, oh! who can aught deny?

61

With what a rapid and tumultuous flight
Her rosy fingers fill with soul the strings!
From her wide, open, flowing garb, how light
Her snowy arm in wavy motion swings!
And, from a bosom which a sage's brain
Might madden, when the mighty feelings pour
In tuneful song, oh! how can he refrain
From falling on his knees, the goddess to adore?

62

Sweet were the tones, and much the sense expressed.
Of a poor shepherdess it was the lay,
Who long concealed a flame within her breast
But yields at last to its relentless sway,
And, blushing, to the youth who caused her pain,
His triumph, and her sufferings avows—
The book did such a song indeed contain,
Yet, as she sung, sings none but with like ardor glows.

63

Here to victorious Nature yields proud art,
The doves of Venus only thus can coo—
So strongly spoke the feelings of the heart!
So clear her voice the beauteous tones ran through!
The frequent, gentle, interrupting sighs,
The reddening cheeks, the panting bosom's toil,
All, all a foaming, dashing torrent flies
Of fiercest passions which within her boil.

64

In the excess of what she felt, at last
Drops from her hand the lute—her arms expand—
But Huon, shuddering catches it in haste,
E'en as it falls, and with intrepid hand
Like one inspired, strikes out in forceful strains
The answer—owns, another has his heart;
And adds, not Heaven or earth a power contains
That can on him prevail, to act a traitor's part.

65

His tone is firm, and stern his look appears;
The fair enchantress owns its strong control;
Her cheeks turn pale, her eye-balls swim in tears,
Pride, with desire now struggling in her soul.
She takes in haste her veil—she hates the light,
The spacious hall can scarce contain her ire,
She coldly on the rebel turns her sight
And with a nod commands him to retire.

66

Upon the hills the dawn began to glow,
When to his friends our knight returned at last;
With pallid terror in his face of woe
They read too clearly half of what had passed.
"Unhappy woman!" he to Fatme said,
Who to the ground in shame sinks almost down;
"Oh! where were all thy wits and senses fled!
Yet, I forgive thee nurse!—thy error was my own."

67

And having told them what had passed that night,
He catches by the breast the faithful squire
And to him swears that not all Afric's might
Shall longer keep him from his heart's desire;
But, that as fits a knight, with sword and shield,
Into the palace he will fight his way,
And force the Sultan, Rezia to yield—
"Thou seest with what success" (quoth he) "at skill we play."

68

Long at his feet Cherasmin begs in vain
That for three days more he would consent
His restless, hot impatience to restrain
And in concealment wait for the event;
Nor by a step which e'en in valor's sight
Were desperate, Rezia's life and his expose;
Engaging in that period, for the flight,
To raze whatever obstacles oppose.

69

And Fatme too, upon her knees implores
And pawns her head within that time to trace
A way to her the hero's soul adores—
And swears no second fraud shall shame her face.
The knight himself concludes, howe'er he burns,
That not the best, which passion recommends;
He gives his word, and to his work returns,
And waiting the result, his garden tends.

Book the twelfth

1

With Cupid's fiercest ardors in her breast,
Meanwhile the queen on damask pillows lies,
Seeking in vain a single hour of rest.
"And can it then be possible," she cries,
"Or was last night's event a sordid dream?
A man, Almansaris, to scorn thee dares?
Thee can behold, and feel another flame?
Thee can despise, nor to avow it fears?"

2

Her veins to frenzy with the thought all swell,
And boundless vengeance to herself she vows.
How she detests him!—Not a monster fell
But in more lovely colors, Fancy shows,
Than this ingrate—how long?—two minutes more,
And of her anger not a trace remains—
Now, she would drain his blood at every pore,
Now to her breast the youth with rapture strains.

283

3

She sees him now in all his charms again,
He seems a hero!—scarce a son of earth—
It cannot be—the first of mortal men
From Ibrahim's father never drew his birth.
How easy, in his manner and address
To trace what he to hide would strive in vain!
Where did the hand of Nature e'er impress
The stamp that marks a king, on any brow more plain?

4

He, only he, is worthy here below
To taste celestial pleasures in her arms;
And, will no thunderbolt then crush the foe
Who by enchantment holds him in her charms?
—"But now, Almansaris!—be bright and gay!
Let him his peacock pride a little spread!
Nay, let his hero-ship resist thy sway—
'Twill o'er thy victory but brighter glory shed.

5

"Despair not yet, but storm at once his heart
With every charm true beauty can supply—
And every foreign weapon lent by art
More certainly to touch his bosom try.
Let him behold and feel what Gods desire!
And even should all this his breast not move,
Then, should he still disdain thee,—rouse thine ire,
And the delicious joys, O Queen! of vengeance prove."

6

Thus, from a handmaid's lips, in whispers low,
The demon speaks, who on this earthly ball,
Sits with full quiver and imperious bow
And with his magic goblet maddens all.
Yclep'd by many who no better know
The God of love, but let each youthful dame
Take notice here, to shun a world of woe,
That Asmodeus is his real name.

7

The queen, in whose warm blood already creeps
An urchin sly, against this outward foe
Much less upon her guard than ever keeps—
His breath inflames and feeds her fervid glow.
Scarce has she made a show (the forms to save)
Of struggling, but the demon gains the day—
The smooth-tongued chambermaid, his organ brave,
Proceeds at once with art the plan to lay.

8

Oh! from the lightning rob its wings of fire
Ye hours! and hither bring the moment sweet!
Ye creep too slow for languishing desire
However rapidly your pinions beat.
Yet not alone the queen now seconds weighs,
Patience to Huon too a torture seems—
He, through three lazy, loitering, hated days
Of his Amanda still, awake or sleeping, dreams.

9

The second morning, to the keen desire
Of the fair Harem's mistress at length came—
Came, breathing roses and with locks of fire
A herald sure, her triumph to proclaim.
Already from the myrtles thick entwined
Which here the fairest of all grottoes gird,
The gentle whispering of the morning wind,
And of ten thousand birds the choral notes are heard.

10

Yet is the sanctuary of repose
Here in the grot, beneath the myrtle grove—
Here in eternal twilight, only coos
To her soft mate the amorous turtle-dove.
Where these thick bushes a sequestered seat
To solitude in dark concealment gave,
Oft would the queen at silent morn retreat,
To bathe her, in the cool, refreshing wave.

11

The knight was summoned by the morning ray,
While all yet slept, to pluck the basket full
Of flowers, which he, with each successive day
Was for the Harem's use, obliged to cull—
When panting to him came a negro slave,
Commanding him forthwith to deck the grot,
And to spur on his zeal the notice gave
That a fair lady meant to bathe upon the spot.

12

Surprised, our hero the command obeys;
The largest basket fills with many a flower,
And Flora's motley treasure all conveys
In haste towards' the designated bower.
Far is suspicion from his mind remote,
Yet a strange horror falls upon his breast,
When at his entrance in the myrtle grot
A secret arm appears, his progress to arrest.

13

His basket he sets down, in deep amaze,
But instantly collects himself again,
And at his terror smiles—the glimmering rays
Of dubious light which through the foliage strain
And in this gloomy labyrinth contend
With darkness visible, this childish fear
He thinks have caused; and now his footsteps bend
Towards' the deep recess, in light that still grows clear.

14

Here, such a daylight reigns, as sly desire
Would choose for stolen pleasures when she pants—
Not twilight's gloom, not day's meridian fire,
But lovelier for what of both it wants.
'Tis like the moonshine when her silver light
Through rosy arbors melts to pallid red;
And though no danger threatens here the knight,
He wellnigh deems it all, a spell around him spread.

15

Here, where in every corner roses flaunt,
What Huon least can comprehend of all,
Is that of flowers there should still be want;
But while his wandering eyes on all sides fall,
Who shall the feelings of his soul describe
When on a couch reclined, in soft repose,
A nymph of Mahomet's celestial tribe
The purest beauty's brightest splendor shows.

16

Down from above, a beam of magic light
Upon her, like a flood of glory streams;
And from the darkness all around, more bright
The lilies with her bosom's whiteness shames.
His eyes such beauties never saw before
As in her attitude unfolded were.
Not all that changed the thunder's God of yore,
Into a bull or swan, could with these charms compare.

17

The gauze which round her as a shadow light
Over an alabaster statue came,
Transparent veil! seemed destined to unite
With nakedness itself the charm of shame.
Apelles! Titian! from your nerveless hands
The pencil here would fall—dull pen, begone!
Trembling, enchanted, here Sir Huon stands
Though to have closed his eyes had been much better done.

18

At sight of objects thus divinely fair
In pleasing error he one moment sinks,
And deems his own Amanda must be there.
But this good fortune soon too mighty thinks,
Draws nearer, and beholds in all her charms
Almansaris,—turns, flies, and in his flight
Feels two smooth, round, elastic, milk-white arms
Clasp him in close embrace, and hold him tight.

19

Since Joseph's days, no man so hard a fight
Had ever fought—the noble fight of truth;
Of love's fidelity and virtue bright,
With beauty, grace and fiery, wanton youth.
His will from culpable delight is pure
But oh! her fond entreaties how withstand?
Her glowing, frantic kisses how endure?
How, to her bosom pressed, resist the straining hand?

20

Where is thy lily sceptre, king of Fays?
Where, in this peril is thy potent horn?
To thee, to Rezia, to each Saint he prays
For aid—and aid is timely to him borne.
For just as every nerve begins to fail
And, for resistance to deny its aid:
Against the furious wanton's hot assail,
The opening door Almanzor's self displayed.

21

He, raging like a wounded beast of prey
At feeling passion for a scornful fair,
An hour since, in the garden came to stray,
Still by her image haunted everywhere.
Chance to the myrtle bower his footsteps drew;
There the Sultana's voice he thought to hear,
And as the door on touching open flew,
Entered the grot, at once his doubts to clear.

22

The very demon who assailed so late
By his most dangerous priestess, Huon's truth,
Is, at a distance, by the Sultan's gait
Aware of the approaching royal youth.
"Help! help! oh help!" exclaims the quick-warned wife,
And instant changes her part for the knight's—
For her own person feigns she is at strife,
And with a ruffian fierce to save her honor fights.

23

Her half-rent garments and her frantic mien,
Her hair dishevelled, the young gardener's fear,
Who stood as if he thunder-struck had been,
This unexpected, shameless charge to hear;
The spot where by the king he was descried,
All seemed to him the criminal to show.
"Allah be praised!" the perjured traitress cried,
"That to Almanzor's self I my deliverance owe."

24

She shrinks beneath her veils with modest grace
And instantly contrives a train of lies,
And tells with innocence's tone and face
How this detested Christian in disguise,
Here, where she came, a cooling bath to take,
In her retirement to surprise her dared;
And how she scarcely from his grasp could break—
When by the happiest chance the king himself appeared.

25

To clear our hero from a crime so base,
One cool, impartial look would straight suffice,
But that one look, in his unhappy case
The judge on whom his doom depends, denies.
To save his life, his noble heart disdains,
Seeing a woman's shame the price must pay;
He yields his arms to undeserved chains
And silent, in his conscience finds his stay.

26

The Sultan, from ill-humor more severe,
Inexorable and unmoved remains—
"Let him," commands he to the slaves whom here
His orders call, "be led away in chains;
Into a dungeon for the night be thrown,
And at the Iman's call for morning prayer
Let the devouring flames his guilt atone,
And, curse-attended strew his ashes in the air."

27

Silent, the noble youth his sentence hears—
On the vile woman casts a flashing eye—
Then turns away, in chains, and disappears
With courage, virtue can alone supply.
No solar beam can ever pierce the gloom
The grave to gladden where he sits confined—
It seems the darkness of the final doom,
And every ray of hope is stifled in his mind.

28

Tired by the heavy blows of partial Fate,
Vexed to be still for Fortune's sport a ball—
He sighs to be released from such a state,
Nor can the torturing flames his heart appal.
Love helps him every terror to subdue,
And angel-strength to sinking nature lends;
"Till death, I swore, Amanda! to be true,"
(He cries) "and keep my vow: with life alone it ends.

29

"Oh! dearest wife! that my unhappy end
To thee forever hidden might remain!
To thee forever, my old faithful friend!
And I, unpitied my sad fate sustain!—
But when the charge against me you shall hear
And while my death your sorrows shall excite,
I but as justly punished shall appear
And with the pangs of grief, disgrace unite—

30

"This, righteous God! is more than I can bear;
Let the most cruel death my faults atone;
None I accuse—yet Oberon, hear my prayer!
And grant to him thou lovedst, this alone:
What I have done thou know'st—protect my fame!
Protect Amanda!—Tell her, 'twas my will
Not to shun death amid the raging flame
The holy vow of truth I promised, to fulfill."

31

He spoke, and felt new confidence expand
His heart in the belief that Oberon hears,
Till o'er him slumber's Spirit waves his wand,
That silencer of mortal pains and cares;
And though his only pillow is a stone,
Lulls into kindly dreams his weary sense—
Haply the guardian Spirit's hands alone
This pledge, that soon his woes will end, dispense.

32

One half the world with darkness yet lay crowned
When a low clattering wakes him from repose;
Hark! in the wards the ponderous keys turn round
And lo! the dangerous iron doors unclose;
On the black walls a pallid light is shed;
He hears one walk, starts up, and lamp in hand,
In gorgeous robes, the crown upon her head,
Beside him sees the royal wanton stand.

33

Her hand extending with sweet smiling eyes:
"Wilt thou forgive the fault of need alone?
Not of my heart— O best beloved!" she cries,
"On thy fair life, depends not then my own?
To rescue thee from danger here I come
In spite of thy resistance to my flame;
And from the fiery pile, the tyrant's doom,
To raise thee to the throne, thy merits claim.

34

"For thee to greatness love prepares the way—
Come! let its loudest trump thy name resound;
Accept this proffered hand without delay—
A nod shall bring the tyrant to the ground,
And at thy feet his people lick the dust.
The Harem is devoted to my will—
Then to Love's hands thyself securely trust,
And what he undertook, thy courage shall fulfill."

35

—"Forbear, O Queen! my sufferings to swell
With offers, I from duty must deny!
To speak it, wherefore thus my lips compel?
My life I never with a crime can buy!"
—"What madness ever could with this compare?
Wretch!—in the very sight of flames" (she cries)
"All bursting round thy pile, canst thou still dare
A sceptre and Almansaris despise?"

36

"Say that my blood can serve thee, mighty queen!
And by the joy with which it shall be shed,
At thy command" (returns he) "be it seen
Whether ingratitude my conduct led.
In thanks, my blood, my life I can impart,
But not my honor, not my plighted hand.
Me thou knowst not—remember who thou art
Nor of me things impossible demand."

37

By this resistance driven to despair
Almansaris unpractised leaves no art,
At every stage his virtue to ensnare
Or storm the courage of his stubborn heart;
Caresses, threatens—lost in love and pain
Falls on her knees his pity to implore.
Yet, his unaltered senses firm remain,
And pure the truth he to Amanda swore.

38

"Die then!"—with fury-stifled breath she cries;
"I, I myself, upon thy keen distress
And pains, will feed with joy my eager eyes;
Die! stupid victim of thy stubbornness."
—Her eye-balls flash—she execrates the day
When first she saw him—heaps with curses o'er
Herself, with quivering lips; then storms away—
Behind her clattering shuts the prison door.

39

Meanwhile had Rumor, ever prompt to tell
And aggravate a tale with misery fraught,
To Fatme and the squire, of what befell
Their lord the piteous information brought.
The handsome Hassan, with the Sultan's wife,
Had, in the bath, by him 'twas said been found.
For which the next day he must lose his life
And to the fiery stake, in the great court be bound.

40

Of Huon's innocence no doubt they made,
For the true state of things to them was known;
But even had he failed, he needed aid;
In cases such as this, true love is shown;
No time they wasted his hard fate to wail,
But straight concluded every risk to try
For his relief, and if it all should fail
With their dear lord themselves at least to die.

41

With spirit and address, ere dawn of day
The nurse contrives to shun the sentries' eyes
And to the bedchamber to make her way,
Where, dreaming of her knight, Amanda lies.
O'erjoyed, each other to behold once more,
Their transports for a time their speech suspend;
And the first words which Fatme's lips can pour,
Are Huon, and the news from Rezia's dearest friend.

42

"What sayst thou, golden nurse?" Amanda cries,
And falls upon her neck— "Is he so near?
Where is he?"—"Dearest princess," she replies,
And sobs and weeps— "Oh! what hath happened here!
For your sake threatens him a cruel death—
Help!—burst his chains!—break down his prison gates!"
—And then the whole affair, with faltering breath,
The knight's fidelity, the queen's revenge relates.

43

"Already" (cries she) "stands the pile in heaps
And Zoradine alone can save his head"—
Straight with a shriek of anguish Rezia leaps
With terror almost frantic, from her bed;
Round her thin night-gown a large kurdee throws
And, swift as lightning to the Sultan flies;
Through all the guard of slaves, who while she goes,
In silence ope the way, and gaze with deep surprise.

44

With cheeks, as lilies pale, and tresses thin
About her shoulders, floating on the breeze,
Regardless of the hour, she rushes in
And falls before the Sultan, on her knees:
"Oh! let me not, Almanzor, kneel in vain!
If to my life thy soul a value lends,
Swear then that my request I shall obtain;
Upon it all my life's repose depends."

45

  "Ask"—was the wondering, joyous king's reply;
"No longer leave in doubt my anxious flame;
To please thee, fairest, I can naught deny;
My wealth, my throne, my empire freely claim—
One thing alone must an exception make—
Thyself"— "To grant what I request then, swear!"—
The love-sick moor proceeds the oath to take—
"The gardener Hassan's life," quoth she, "O Monarch, spare!"

46

"What!" cries the Sultan with astonished mien,
"Sure a request so strange was never known.
What can that slave's life be to Zoradine?"
"Much! much! Almanzor, it involves my own"—
"A fever's frenzy, damsel, makes thee rave;
Nay, thou abusest beauty's boundless sway;
How can the life of such an abject slave
Who suffers for his guilt?"—"For truth he suffers, say.

47

"I know his heart; he holds his duty dear;
Upon his honor never stain was seen—
And yet, Almanzor—were his guilt e'en clear,
Avenge not his offense on Zoradine."
The king, with eyes where ill-checked fury beams,
Exclaims: "By these delays why torture me?
What secret from this odious riddle gleams?
What is the gardener Hassan's life to thee?"

48

"Know then, since need compels my lips to speak,
I am his wife; a tie in Heaven wove,
A sacred tie which naught on earth can break,
Connects my bliss forever with his love.
Us the severest blows of Fate oppress;
How soon the turn to thee may come, who knows?
Thou seest me wretched—honor my distress;
And, happy as thou art, relieve my woes."

49

"Thou, Hassan's wife, and lov'st him?—above all!
—The wretch is faithless to thy tender sighs"—
"He faithless? he?—the cause that wrought his fall
Could only from his steadfast faith arise."
"Nay, but I saw myself"— " 'Twas all a cheat
On him and thee"— The king, with angry brow
Exclaims: "Presume not on thy beauty, sweet,
Too far, nor stretch until it breaks, the bow.

50

"I can but pity thee: thy Hassan dies!"
"He dies? Oh! tyrant! when one word from thee
To give him life," cries Rezia, "would suffice?
And canst thou have the heart to tell it me?"
"The Harem's chastity he has transgressed,"
Says the king coldly, "and is doomed to die.
Yet, since thou wilt, let Zoradine's own breast
Alone pronounce his pardon, or deny.

51

"Thyself of mercy a bright sample show—
Oh! give me back my lost, my peaceful lot!
My crown and empire at thy feet I throw,
Give me thyself, and be his crime forgot.
To his own country let him be restored;
And heaped with gifts of royal worth besides.
Oh! grant the mercy by thyself implored;
One word his destiny and mine decides."

52

"Wretch!" with angelic wrath exclaims the wife—
"Know,—the brave man beloved by Zoradine,
Disdains at such a price to take his life.
Of me, O tyrant! is thy thought so mean?
The poorest wench that ever bore my train,
Thee and thy throne, would scorn thus dear to buy.
True,—thou canst ruin us; yet hence to gain
A triumph never hope!—I too, know how to die."

53

This noble spirit makes the Sultan start,
And while it kindles his desires the more,
With stronger power affects his coward heart
Than the entreaties she had urged before.
What said he not, her heart with love to gain?
How serpent-like about her feet he wound!
How her compassion he implored!—in vain!
Her soul alike unmoved by threats or prayers he found.

54

"Death will be welcomer," she still declares.
—With voice tremendous, by the prophet's grave,
Unless forthwith she will comply, he swears,
That nothing from his rage her life shall save:
"Hear my last word! by Allah's power divine!"
(The very front hall echoes his acclaims)
"Take the resolve and on the spot be mine,
Or with the traitor perish in the flames."

55

Silent, she views him with wrath-beaming eyes—
"Speak!" he repeats.—"From thy detested sight
Oh! free me then," the best of wives replies.
"Compared with thee, death's horrors are delight."
To give the cruel charge Almanzor calls,
While sparks of hell from his red eye-balls shoot.
Upon his face the chief black eunuch falls,
And swears the high behest to execute.

56

The horrid altar only waits the fire,
While crowds of people, thronging to the sight,
Fond of the pain such tragic scenes inspire,
Rejoice and shudder, weep and take delight.
For sufferance and for death united still
To the same stake of martyrdom are bound,
The only pair, whom Oberon, to fulfill
His solemn vow, had pure and constant found.

57

A pair of noble souls dissolved in one,
Inviolably true to love's first tie,
Who, rather than be faithless for a throne,
In the consuming flames resolved to die.
With sympathizing hearts and tearful eyes
The people gaze upon them from below—
Yet anxious lest some accident should rise
To interrupt the progress of the show.

58

Each other to behold, as bound they stand,
The comfort to the lovers is denied;
Yet with the purest bliss their hearts expand
And triumph over all that can betide.
The love which brought them hither, cheers their minds;
Tells them, the death which now shall end their woes
And round their truth immortal laurels binds   [chose.
Was what they might have shunned; was what themselves had

59

Meantime by pairs, with torches in their hands,
Twelve blacks drew near to where the altar stood—
Around it, all prepared they take their stands
And at the Aga's signal, light the wood—
—Straight, thunder peals, the earth appears to quake,
The flame expires, the cords snap short in two,
Which bound the faithful couple to the stake,
And, hanging at his neck, the *horn* meets Huon's view.

60

At the same instant when all this occurred,
Distant, and in two separate bands appear,
By trembling, anxious apprehension spurred,
There, queen Almansaris, Almanzor here,
She to save Hassan, and he Zoradine.
"Halt!" they are heard with all their strength to cry;
And rushing through the frightened crowd is seen
A sable knight who waves a flashing sword on high.

61

Scarce hath our hero, with delicious thrills
Perceived the pledge of Oberon's grace restored,
When straight he puts it to his lips and fills
With sweeter tones than horn had ever poured.
His noble heart disdains to put to death
The tawny, tattered, trembling coward crew;
"Dance! dance!" he cries, "till dancing rob your breath;
Be this the sole revenge that Huon takes of you!"

62

And as he warbles out the tuneful sound,
The motley mob the mad vertigo feel.
Those first of all who stand the pile around,
And round and round the ragged rabble reel.
Soon with his negroes mingles in the sport
The Aga—then succeeds whate'er has feet
Throughout the town, the Harem and the Court,
Down to the meanest porter in the street.

63

The king, reluctant, seizes by the arm
His queen, who struggles to resist in vain.
To whirl amidst the tumbling, gasping swarm,
An impulse drags which neither can restrain.
Soon is all Tunis filled with dire alarm,
No mortal in his place can still remain;
Not gout, not lameness can resist the charm,
Nor e'en the pangs of death, from dancing can refrain.

64

The lovers turn not on the farce their sight,
But hold each other long in close embrace.
Their souls in speechless, rapturous delight
Scarce to contain the mighty bliss have space.
The dreadful trial-dream at length is dreamed,
And naught remains but what adorns their joy;
Their fate is pacified, their fault redeemed,
Henceforth their union nothing shall destroy.

65

What cordial joy the good Cherasmin felt
When from his steed (the sable knight was he)
He saw the lovers' hearts in transports melt—
'Twas he, who like a tempest came to free
From the detested hands of heathens base
The tender, faithful and beloved pair—
And, should he fail, to finish in this place
A life which henceforth he no more could bear.

66

Quick he dismounts, and strains towards' the knight,
By Fatme followed, through the madding crowd;
Helps from their throne the lovers to alight,
And then receives them both, in triumph proud.
Great was the joy!—yet higher still it swelled,
When wafted on the bosom of the breeze,
The well-known swan-drawn chariot they beheld
Descending to their feet by slow degrees.

67

Anon they mount, and leave the moors to dance,
As long as suits the fairy monarch's views;
Albeit Cherasmin, sooner than thus prance,
To rasp or mine would for his own part choose.
The wind-borne chariot light and steady flies,
Softer than downy sleep, and swift as thought,
And with them cleaves o'er land and main the skies,
While silver clouds like fans around them float.

68

Already on the mountains and the hills
The twilight in uncertain vapor dips;
The realms of air a deeper silence fills,
And Cynthia's image o'er the waters skips.
The swans descending slowly from above
With sinking wings at length on land alight.
When, seemingly of evening twilight wove,
A glittering palace rose at once in sight.

69

Full in the middle of a pleasant wood
Amidst a hedge of rose-trees in full blow
High shooting all around, the palace stood,
And with its splendor made the forest glow.
In accent soft, and shuddering through and through,
The knight began— "Is not this spot the same?"
When quick the golden gate wide open flew,
And twenty virgins from the palace came.

70

With ever blooming cheeks, and fair as Spring,
In lily-white arrayed, the maids advance;
To hail the mortals favored by their king
And welcome their approach with song and dance.
Th' immortal meed of constancy they sung:
"Come!" said they, "and receive, O faithful pair!"
(To their sweet measures, clanking cymbals rung)
"Come! and of victory receive the garland fair."

71

To other worlds transported with delight,
The lovers hand in hand, pass through the quire;
When, like the morning sun, the Spirit bright
Before them stood in nuptial rich attire.
A boy no longer, as until this time
In sweet disguise they saw the fairy king;
But a fair youth, in never fading prime,
And on his finger flashed the magic ring.

72

And crowned with roses, by him they beheld
His queen, who with the moon's mild lustre shone—
Each in the hand a myrtle garland held—
"O faithful pair!" said they, in sweetest tone,
"From friendly hands receive this fair reward
Of victory the well deservèd meed;
And while you keep this proof of our regard,
Your hearts the purest bliss shall never need."

73

Scarce from their lips the words an utterance found,
When in the air a cloud was seen to bend;
And from its lap, while golden harps resound,
With lilies at the breast three nymphs descend;
And in her arms one held a beauteous child,
Whom, kneeling to the queen she handed o'er;
Upon the boy Titania sweetly smiled,
And hastened with a kiss the darling to restore.

74

While with triumphal songs the virgins strew
In rows, the way along, with roses bright,
The happy band the golden gate pass through,
And enter Oberon's mansion of delight;
What there it was their lot to see or hear
Was by them ever after veiled in shade—
But, while to Heaven they looked, a joyful tear
The secret longing of their souls betrayed.

75

In softest sleep the blissful dream dissolved,
Deliciously—and with returning morn
They found themselves with arm in arm involved
Upon a mossy bank, as newly born;
And in the hedge that shaded light the way
Four coursers fair, in trappings rich they found;
While all about, a glittering mixture lay,
Of arms and ornaments and raiment on the ground.

76

Our knight, whose bosom overflows with joy,
Wakes his old friend, while with a mother's eyes
Amanda seeks to find her lovely boy,
Who on the nurse's lap soft sleeping lies.
Cherasmin gazes round with ravished breast—
"Sir! in what land imagine you to be?
Come! from this stand, look forwards to the West,"
(He to Sir Huon cries) "and tell us what you see."

77

Albeit his mind to miracles was used,
On looking round him our heroic knight
Almost to credit what he saw, refused;
So strange the spectacle before his sight.
'Tis Paris yonder, they behold arise.
It is the Seine, upon whose banks they stand.
Sir Huon gazing, rubs his brows and eyes.
"Can then my destined term," he cries, "be thus at hand?"

78

Ere he can settle whether yet he dreams,
Before him a new spectacle appears;
In wildest uproar the whole city seems;
And while the sounding clarions fill his ears
Tŏwards' the open lists trots many a knight—
"My fortune still behind her leaves desire,"
Exclaims the youth—"here, if I judge aright,
A tournament is held—go, honest friend, inquire."

79

Soon is Amanda by the nurse attired;
For she had found in heaps before her feet,
In rich profusion all that was required
To show herself with pomp and grandeur meet
Here, in a land of strangers such as this,
To suit the splendor of her rank and charms—
Huon the while, with many a father's kiss,
Dandles the smiling infant in his arms.

80

With heartfelt joy he sees his consort fair
From foreign ornaments derive no aid;
And neither gain or lose by all their glare—
Whether a simple rose her bosom shade,
Or jewels veil her in excess of light—
Fair in herself, and ever breathing love—
These can lend nothing to her beauties bright,
Which, with the other, nothing can improve.

81

With information now the squire returns,
That for the fourth day the lists open stand,
Since Charles, whose rancor unabated burns,
A tournament had published through the land.
"And guess the prize to victory assigned
This day—no less than Huon's lands and fee;
For never hath it entered Charles's mind,
You, come with glory crowned from Babylon, to see."

82

"Up! arm me!" overjoyed Sir Huon cries;
"No other message could so please my heart;
Be what birth gave me, now my virtue's prize—
Let Charles, if I deserve it not, impart
To him who shall deserve it more, the boon."
Amanda smiles applause in silence sweet.
Her bosom beats his triumph high, and soon
She sees her hero stand in shining arms complete.

83

The knights and ladies now their steeds ascend
And draw tŏwards' the town— In deep amaze
Large crowds of people on their steps attend
And follow them, upon their pomp to gaze.
Soon as Sir Huon at the bar arrives,
He leaves his consort in Cherasmin's guard—
Salutes her—draws his beaver down and drives
Within the lists for tilting all prepared.

84

Loud plaudits follow him on every side,
Him, who in strength and dignity exceeds
The first of those who hitherto had tried
Their skill and fortune in these knightly deeds.
On a proud courser at the goal, his eyes
Upon our hero turns the knight askance,
Who the three former days had won the prize;
While from the palace look, with Charles, the peers of France.

85

Our youth, as knightly usages require,
To Charles bows lowly down, and to the fair;
Last, to the judges—then with dauntless fire
Up to the victor hastens, to declare
His purpose from him to bear off the prize;
He should have told indeed his name and rank;
But to exempt him from this rule, suffice
His splendid pomp, and oath, he is a Frank.

86

He weighs and chooses from a heap of spears
That which he feels weigh heaviest in his hand;
With perfect ease to swing it round appears
And takes with confidence at length his stand.
To all the Saints, and Oberon, her prayers
Amanda sends, with anxious, beating heart—
When now the trumpet's brazen throat declares
That the impatient knights have leave to start.

87

The knight who all the former days, to ground
His rivals had all brought, was fain to fret
That thus himself again compelled he found
His fame and fortune on this stake to set.
Of Döolin of Mentz this knight was son
And breaking lances was to him but game.
As from black clouds the livid lightnings run,
Down storming on his noble foe he came.

88

Yet, without even staggering in his seat
Sir Huon hit him on the breast a stroke,
Which laid him prostrate at his courser's feet,
And many of his ribs in falling broke.
This knight will no more for the prize contend,
Four servants bear him in a swoon away.
Loud shouts of triumph to the skies ascend,
And Huon stands alone, the victor of the day.

89

A short while yet he stays upon the spot
To see if any still dispute the prize;
And as no one appears, with hasty trot
To Rezia seated on her courser flies.
Her, Goddess-shining, to the palace leads,
And courteous, helps her from her steed descend;
Then with her up the marble stairs proceeds,
While all the people round with shouts the concave rend.

90

A veil, resembling a light silver cloud
Through which the searching eye would pierce in vain,
Shades Rezia's features—while th' unnumbered crowd
In streams tŏwards' the noble couple strains,
Anxious to see how this will all unfold.
Before them opens now the hall of state,
And by his peers surrounded they behold
In pomp imperial seated, Charles the Great.

91

Sir Huon takes the helmet from his head,
And enters, radiant as the God of day:
The princes all recognize him with dread
And Charles believes his spectre to survey.
The hero with Amanda by the hand
Says, drawing near with reverence to the throne—
"My liege! behold, again before thee stand
A vassal true, who comes to claim his own.

92

"For, the condition by thyself declared,
Of my return, with God, did I fulfill.
Lo! in this casket are the teeth and beard
For which I staked my body at thy will;
And let thine eyes in this fair lady trace
The Sultan's heiress, and my comfort dear"—
With this, the veil falls down from Rezia's face
And tenfold splendors o'er the hall appear.

93

An Angel, in celestial lustre bright
(But softened down, for mortal eyes to bear)
Appears to stand before their ravished sight;
So dazzling radiant, yet so lovely fair
Appears Amanda in her myrtle crown
And silver robes— The fairy queen descends
Unseen, to aid her charming favorite, down,
And every heart submissive to her bends.

94

Charles bids them welcome, with a friendly grace,
Descending from his throne— The peers around
Throng, the brave youth, as brothers to embrace
From such a task returned, with glory crowned.
In Charles's bosom his old rancor dies;
He kindly shakes the valiant hero's hand—
"Oh! may our Empire never want" (he cries)
"A princely youth like thee, to guard and grace the land!"

FINIS

ℐotes

ABBREVIATIONS: Roman numerals in the notes refer to cantos, Arabic numerals in italics to stanzas, others to lines. Thus: I, *25*, 2 means: Canto I, stanza 25, line 2.

W. refers to Wieland, his words, and quotations from his *Oberon* in the German original. A. denotes J. Q. Adams, usually accompanied by citations from his translations. S. refers to quotations and renderings from Sotheby's translation of *Oberon*.

MS I, MS II, MS III, and MS IV are, as in the Introduction, designations for the four manuscripts of Adams, his four successive versions of his translation of *Oberon*. MS IV, the last version, has been used for the text.

CANTO I (Book the first)

I, *1*, 1. *Hippogriff*. A poetic invention by medieval romancers (cf. Ariosto, *Orlando Furioso*, VI, 18), of a fabulous winged beast, a cross between a griffin and a mare, with the head, wings, and claws of the griffin, the hind parts of the horse. The super-powerful griffins in ancient mythology were hitched to the sun-chariot of Apollo, who was also the god of poetry. The hippogriff was meant to be even more madly inspiring than the winged horse Pegasus of the ancient Greeks.

— *1*, 2. *romantic land*. (W. ins alte romantische Land.) Within the last decade Wieland had made two trips into the land of knightly romance, in his *Idris und Zenide* and *Der neue Amadis;* now he is about to take his last journey (*Ritt*) into these colorful realms of "follies," madness, and magic. For Wieland's sources see Introduction, pp. xxxii–xxxvii.

— *1–8*. These stanzas give a sort of poet's introduction, with a vision of the whole action of the poem. For an outline of the plot in prose, see Adams's so-called Analytical Extracts in the Introduction, pp. lxxii–xcii.

I, *3*, 4. *Hesperia*. A name given by the ancient Greeks to Italy, the land lying toward the west, toward evening, the setting sun.

— *8*, 1. *sopha,* or sofa, of Turkish derivation. (W. Canapee, S. couch.)

— *9*, 4. *Bagdad*. Wieland wrote *Babylon* in this place, though he uses the two names, *Bagdad* and *Babylon,* as interchangeable, and his translators follow his example. Geography and chronology were arbitrarily violated in the medieval romances, and in the Huon de Bordeaux epic Babylon was even located in Egypt (Cairo) instead of in Mesopotamia.

Charlemagne (Charles the Great) ruled from 748 to 814 A. D. He was crowned Holy Roman Emperor at Rome in 800; the ruler of all Christendom, and a heroic figure in history and romance.

— *10*, 7. *Joppe*. Now Jaffa, Syrian city on the Mediterranean, where the pilgrims for Jerusalem usually landed.

— *11*, 4. *St. Kitt's*. W. Sanct Christophel, i. e. Saint Christopher, patron of ferrymen, martyred about 250 A. D.; probably born in Syria.

— *12*, 6. *His tongue of Oc (la langue d'oc,* in distinction from *la langue d'oïl*) is used here to denote the Provençal language.

— *12–15*. Adams considered these stanzas especially beautiful. Cf. his diary Nov. 20, 1799 (Introduction, p. lx).

— *14*, 1. Here MS II seems better than the revision in IV.

W. Was ganz natürlich war, däucht' ihm ein Zauberspiel.

A. (MS II) Though natural the view, 'twas magic to his mind.
Adams revised to give the line five feet instead of the six in the original.

— *21*, 2. *Lebanon*. A mountain range in Syria.

— *21*, 5–8. These lines furnish evidence (see Introduction, p. xxx) that Sotheby and Adams used different editions of Wieland's *Oberon*.

W. (edition of 1792)

> Kommt, ruhet aus, und nehmt vorlieb, so gut
> Als *Mutter Natur* uns hier mit eignen Händen thut.
> Mein Wein (er springt in diesem *Keller*),
> Verdünnt das Blut, und macht die Augen heller.

S. In peace repose thee, nor my welcome slight;
> And freely take whate'er I have, the cheer
> That *Nature* for her children caters here;
> Yet grateful to the taste when hunger wrings;
> And quaff my wine that in the *cellar* springs,—

W. (edition of 1796)

> Kommt, ruhet aus und nehmt ein leichtes Mal für gut,
> Wobei die *Freundlichkeit des Wirths* das Beste thut.

Mein Wein (er springt aus diesem *Felsen*keller)—
A. Come, take your ease, and of my humble food,
  Deign to partake, *its seasoning is good-will.*
  My wine ('tis from this *rock*) will thin your blood—
Sotheby translates *Mutter Natur* and *Keller,* while Adams translates
something else: *Freundlichkeit des Wirths* and *Felsenkeller.*

— *22,* 5. helmet's *band.* Here Adams goes back to a reading of
the first edition of Wieland's *Oberon,* which he found among the variant readings of his 1796 edition: "Da jener jetzt den *Lör* des blanken
Helms entschnallet." All later editions read: "Da jener jetzt den blanken
Helm entschnallet."

— *22,* 8. *Alquif.* A sage and great magician in the Spanish romance
Amadis of Gaul. Sotheby does not use the name *Alquif* found in all of
Wieland's editions; he often thus avoids an allusion not very familiar:
S. "The woodman bound in fascinating trance"—

— *25,* 5. Cheras'min. A. places the accent on the second syllable
throughout, W. and S. on the first: Sche'rasmin, Sher'asmin. The spelling of the name in the French original is Gérasme.

— *25,* 7. *Guyenne.* An old French province corresponding in the
main to the Roman Aquitania Secunda (southwestern France, with the
capital Bordeaux).

— *30,* 4. *Amory,* the name taken exactly from W. *Hautefeuille (31,*
1) is an invention by Adams, probably as a more noble-sounding name
than Wieland's *Hohenblat.* Charlot (little Charles) corresponds to W.'s
Scharlot, second son of Charlemagne. Sotheby uses Amory, Hoenblat,
Scharlot, Gerhardine (*32,* 1), which in W. and A. appears as Gerard.

— *31,* 8. *Montlery.* Montlhéry, a small town in the department of
Seine-et-Oise, eighteen miles south of Paris, famous in history for the
battle in 1464 between Louis XI and the League of the Public Weal.

— *34,* 7–8. W. Schon lange dürst' ich nach der Lust,
        Mein racheglühend Herz in deinem Blut zu kühlen.
S. adds a very poor ninth line to this stanza (not in the original):
    Thou, like this boy, shalt fall beneath my footstep dead.

— *35,* 2. *Diederic, Duke of Ardennes* (W. Herzog Dietrich von
Ardennen). Charlot, by falsifying his identity, removes the guilt from
Huon for wantonly killing the Emperor's son.

— *38,* 1. *Unweeting* (W. unwissend). Obsolete for "not knowing,"
variant form of "unwit(t)ing" (Spenser).

— *38,* 2. *Paris* was in the French romances the capital of Charlemagne, not Aachen (Aix-la-Chapelle) as in history.

— *44,* 8. *scapular.* (W. Scapulier). Though the word generally refers to a priestly garment, it has been suggested that W. here may have used it as equivalent to *rosary,* held on high by the abbot to restrain the drawn swords.

— *52, 5. Duke Nayms.* Wieland tells us in his "Glossarium" (1796 edition) that he took this name and character from the knightly romances that frequently lauded Duke Nayms of Bavaria as the wisest man of Charlemagne's court, but that he (W.) could find no confirmation in historical documents.

— *55, 8. laid,* instead of the correct grammatical form *lay.* Here poetical license prevails (forced rime with *surveyed*), and in most cases the necessity of the rime explains Adams's seeming occasional confusion of the tense forms of the transitive verb *lay* (laid, laid) and the intransitive *lie* (lay, lain), as also: V, *60, 3, laid* instead of *lain,* to rime with *said;* VI, *8, 2, lays* for *lies,* to rime with *days;* VII, *1, 6, lay* for *lie,* to rime with *weigh;* IX, *50, 8, lay* instead of *laid,* to rime with *away.* But to prove that Adams knew his grammar we have correct forms in: V, *54, 8,* "lay upon his bolster'd throne"; VII, *47, 2,* "in fearful stillness lay"; IX, *47, 3,* "where he had lain"; etc., etc.

— *56, 1. The sun is shared* (W. Die Sonne wird geteilt). An equally favorable position was given both contestants in regard to the sun and shade. S. misses the point: "Now flamed in cloudless heav'n the midday sun."

— *58, 7. Roland.* The champion of the Charlemagne legends who lost his life heroically in the defense of the rear guard at Roncesvalles in 778. The absence of the mention of Roland by Sotheby is one of the numerous bits of internal evidence that he used a different edition of Wieland's *Oberon* than Adams. See Introduction, pp. xxx f.

— *68, 7–8.* Adams's MS II has a smoother reading:

> Thus graciously inclined, it seemed to every eye
> Was nothing better than my doom to die.

But the final version changed the rime scheme from aabcbcdd to Adams's standard ababcdcd and gave the last line six feet.

— *69, 8. Sir Gawin.* Sir Gawain was often given the first place for daring, among the knights of King Arthur's Round Table, as here, above Sir Lancelot and Sir Tristan.

Canto II (Book the second)

II, *5, 7. Mahound,* or Mahoun (W. Mahom), an old form for Mahomet (Mohammed); also thought of by the medieval mind as evil spirit, devil.

— *9, 1.* An often quoted line in the original: "Wie selig wär's in diesen Hütten wohnen!"

— *12, 2, 8. Babylon* and *Bagdad* are used to denote the same city (cf. note to I, *9, 4*). Adams follows Wieland's example of using the two names in the same stanza, a convenient aid to the meter, which in the one place required a name of three syllables, in the other one of two syllables. Sotheby uses the same tactics.

— *13, 6. Holy Virgin.* W. "Unsre Frau zu Acqs" is an equivalent in meaning derived from Cherasmin's home in Gascony (explained at length in the "Glossarium").

— *14, 4. deer.* MS IV uses *deers* for the plural, a mere slip of the pen, because the correct plural is found in all other versions, MSS I, II, and III.

— *17, 1.* In his last version, MS IV, Adams, obviously by an error in copying, wrote the line "Thus speaking, to them he spurs up his steed," which does not read metrically. All other MSS, I, II, III, read as adopted in our text.

— *18, 6. Pan.* When all the forces of nature are quiet, in an awe-inspiring and terrifying stillness, the nature-god Pan seems dead. In his "Glossarium" Wieland relates the myth of the skipper Thamos, who in a dead calm at sea was instructed to shout thrice "The Great Pan is dead!" on his arrival on the coast of Epirus.

— *18, 8. mole-warp* (W. Maulwurf) or moldwarp—earth-thrower, *mole*.

— *20, 7. Ventregris!* A Gascon oath, equivalent to *Od's bodikins*.

— *23, 8. Manichean.* A religious sect, followers of Manes, a Persian, in the third century A. D. Here used opprobriously.

— *32, 2. St. Agatha.* A Sicilian virgin martyr, put to death under torture by the Sicilian governor Quintianus, February 5, 251.

— *32, 6. St. Antony* (Anthony, Antonius) lived about 251–356 A. D., called by Athanasius the founder of asceticism; the saint's day: January 17.

— *37, 5. rigadoons.* A gay, lively dance for two, which probably originated in the Provence. "Some high-paced jig, or hop-skip rigadoon, befitting the brisk lasses at a rustic merrymaking" (Hawthorne). Adams, in MS II, translates as follows (written in December, 1799):

> The horn he to his lips applies
> And blows the sweetest air. Forthwith a giddy vein
> Subdues the squire, who can from dancing not refrain
> But packs a toothless nun, with like desire who dies
> Her portion of the *reel* to take.

> He leaps and prances like a youthful goat
> So swift with her about, that veil and petticoat
> Wave wide in air around while all with laughter shake.

The rime scheme here is abbacddc, which Adams changes in IV (MS III is very similar to II) to his standard ababcdcd. This is an example among a host of others of Adams's skill as a versifier and his painstaking fidelity to the original. Wieland wrote:

> Er setzt das Horn an seine Lippen an
> Und bläst den lieblichsten Ton. Stracks übermannt den Alten
> Ein Schwindelgeist; er kann sich Tanzens nicht enthalten,
> Packt eine Nonne ohne Zahn,
> Die vor Begierde stirbt, *ein Tänzchen* mitzumachen,
> Und hüpft und springt, als wie ein junger Bock,
> So rasch mit ihr herum, daß Schleiertuch und Rock
> Weit in die Lüfte wehn zu allgemeinem Lachen.

Sotheby translated the stanza very smoothly as follows:

> He to his rosy lips the horn applies,
> And breathes enchanting tones of fairy sound:
> At once old Sherasmin in giddy round
> Reels without stop—away the spinner flies,
> Seizes a hoary nun without a tooth,
> Who dies to dance, as if the blood of youth
> Boil'd in her veins; the old man deftly springs,
> Bounds like a buck, while every caper flings
> Her veil and gown in air, that all laugh loud forsooth.

— *46, 8. Langon.* A small city on the Garonne, famed for its white Bordeaux wine (cf. the "Glossarium"). The humor that Wieland puts into the behavior and character of his Cherasmin is original with him. Cf. the Introduction, p. xxxv.

CANTO III (Book the third)

III, *1, 7. helm* for *helmet* is frequent in English poetry; for example:

> He wore, against his wont, upon his helm
> A sleeve of scarlet.
>
>   Tennyson's *Lancelot and Elaine*

— *5, 2. Angulaffer.* Wieland found the name of the giant Angoulafre in his source, Tressan's abstract, but invented other names for the prince, the princess, and others.

— *5, 4. Caffer* (W. Kaffer), Caffre, Kafir, Kaffir, infidels belonging to a warlike race that always resisted conversion to Mohammedanism, and therefore applied by Moslems contemptuously to unbelievers, including pagan Negroes and also Christians.

— *6, 3.* The German reads clearer: ". . . bevor sie sich so viele Treu zu krönen Erbitten liess." Adams's MS II reads: "Before her heart to crown such truth I could convince."

— *6, 7. the wolf* (W. Wehrwolf). The werewolf was supposed to be a mysterious, bloodthirsty man who could take the form of a wolf.

— *16, 7. Switzers* (W. Schweizer). Swiss guards, an anachronism in the mouth of Cherasmin, whose valor is limited by discretion.

— *18, 6. a lightly shaded place* (W. am leicht bedeckten Busen). MS II reads: "slightly decked with lace."

— *24.* Sotheby translated this stanza in his edition of 1798, but expurgated it in later editions.

— *27, 6–7. Pelion* and *Ossa.* Mountains in Thessaly. In the Greek myth Pelion was piled on Ossa by the giants who wanted to see and storm Olympus. (*Odyssey*, XI, 313–317.)

— *28, 1. Glycon,* of Athens, the sculptor of the Farnese Hercules, found in the baths of Caracalla in 1540, with an inscription by Glycon. It was probably executed in the first or second century A. D. but points to an athletic type of Lysippus (fourth century B. C.).

— *37, 1. Taurus.* A mountain range in southern Asia Minor.

— *40, 5. Juno's royal bird* (W. Junons Pfau). Reference to the eyes of the peacock's tail feathers.

— *53, 7–8.* MSS II and III read:

> To hungry stomachs, work of godlike hands,
> Since on it ready served the banquet stands.

— *55, 7. Gascoon,* of Gascony, also *boastful, gay.*

— *56, 1.* This line is exactly the same as Sotheby's and might lead to the suspicion that Adams had borrowed it. On examination we find that in MS II this line (written before January 14, 1800, i. e. eleven months before Adams saw Sotheby's translation) reads:

> *And imperceptibly* the gentle hand of sleep

Adams in his revisions (MSS III and IV), in order no doubt to reduce this first line of the stanza to his standard of five feet, changed the first two words to one word, "insensibly," and this was done in MS III, which was also written undoubtedly before Adams got the first glimpse of Sotheby's translation on December 4, 1800 (see diary entry). The word "insensibly" is used a great deal by Adams, and needed no suggestion from Sotheby; see VII, *43,* 3 (W. unbemerkt); VIII, *48,* 8 (unvermerkt); VIII, *51,* 1 (unmerklich); VIII, *55,* 1 (allmählig); etc., etc. The coincidence of the lines is therefore purely accidental.

III, *56, 7. Mara.* A famous German soprano, Madame Gertrude Elisabeth Schmeling (born in Cassel in 1749, died in 1833). She married the violoncellist Mara about 1771.

— *58, 1. at once.* Here the final revision led Adams into an error in translation, not found in the earlier versions. MS II reads:

> He slept till at the early cock's shrill crow

(W. Er schlief *in Einem fort,* bis, da der frühe Hahn)
The German means *continuously,* not *at once.* S. translates "unmoved;" not exact, since the German means "without a break."

— *61, 3.* In his editions after the first, of 1798, Sotheby expurgated a whole stanza here, from this line to *62, 3,* omitting thereby one of the most beautiful passages of the poem. Adams was conscious of the difficulties, revised at least three times, and succeeded in making his final version the equal of the German:

— *61.*   W. Stillschweigend schauten sie einander beide an,
> Mit Blicken, die sich das unendlich stärker sagten,
> Was ihre Lippen noch nicht auszusprechen wagten.
> Ihm ward in ihrem Aug' ein Himmel aufgethan,
> Wo sich in eine See von Liebe
> Die Seele taucht. Bald wird das Übermaß der Lust
> Zum Schmerz: er sinkt im Drang der unaufhaltbarn Triebe
> In ihren Arm und drückt sein Herz an ihre Brust.

— *62.*   Er fühlt der Nymphe Herz an seinem Busen schlagen,
> Der Glückliche! wie schnell, wie stark, wie warm!

In two places (*61, 2,* and *62, 2*) Adams translated closer to the original in MSS II and III, as follows:

> With looks which infinitely stronger say

and

> Ah! happy man! how quick! how strong! how warm!

Only in MS IV, the last version, does Adams occasionally feel bold enough to depart slightly from his original.

— *62, 3–4.* The storm in the dream is an omen of what will actually happen in Canto VII; it is a premonition of the disobedience of the lovers (as in the garden of Eden), by which they will forfeit for a long time the protection of Oberon.

— *62, 5.* MS III reads:

> Loud howling shake the tempests' raging swarm—
> W. Laut heulend bebt der Stürme wilder Schwarm;

— *66, 8. honest rimes.* As in German: "Träume sind Schäume," dreams are idle stuff. "Dreams are but interludes, which fancy makes" (Dryden).

Canto IV (Book the fourth)

IV, 2. Sotheby translated this stanza well in his first edition; later he expurgated it.

— 2, 7. *Genevra.* Guinevere, beautiful wife of King Arthur.

— 3, 3. *Medusa's* head, cut off by Perseus, had the power to turn to stone anyone who beheld it.

— 15, 2. *wall* (W. Gaden). *Gaden* (see the "Glossarium") is a small shop or chamber of a run-down house on a side street. Adams, in his first prose rendering in MS I, uses "chamber" not "wall" to translate the German.

— 19, 1. *Euphrates.* This river, 1800 miles in length, and its tributary the Tigris (1150 miles), drain Mesopotamia in that historical fertile valley in which Babylon and Bagdad were located. Babylon of ancient fame was built on both banks of the Euphrates. Its ruins lie to the south of Bagdad, the leading metropolis of the Middle Ages, located on both banks of the Tigris. The knightly romances display a very inaccurate acquaintance with geography; Tressan locates Babylon somewhere in Egypt, presumably in the neighborhood of Cairo.

— 20, 5. *Merlin.* A Welsh magician in Arthurian and medieval romances.

— 21, 4. *Garonne.* A river in southwestern France, the home of Cherasmin.

— 22, 1. *Thou little spot* (W. Du kleiner Ort). This was spoken from Wieland's own heart, a nostalgic allusion to his own beloved birthplace near Biberach (Württemberg), as he confesses in a letter to Sophie La-Roche dated February 4, 1780.

— 27. From here on Adams in his final version (MS IV) departs from his standard rime scheme, ababcdcd, in very many stanzas. He had standardized MS III, but apparently preferred a great many of the stanzas as he had originally written them in MS II with their greater freedom in versification and often consequent better literary quality.

— 30, 6. MS II reads: "E'en life enough to reach the journey's end to want." MS III reads: "Scarce to have life to reach the journey's end."

— 30, 7. *chine* (W. Rückgrat). Spine.

— 33. The rime scheme of this stanza is the pure Italian *ottava rima:* ababbcc, with three rimes. Adams does not use this rime scheme frequently in his translation of *Oberon,* nor does Wieland. Another instance is found below: IV, *44.* In both stanzas the last line has six feet, in imitation of Wieland, who in these stanzas has three rimes instead of his usual four. Other examples are IV, *52;* V, *3, 20,* and *69.*

IV, *36,* 4. *goody* (W. Mütterchen). Adams also uses "wife" and "woman"; see below, IV, *60,* 7. Sotheby uses "crone" here.

— *36,* 8. *Han* (W. Han). The "Glossarium" explains: A large public building in Mohammedan countries where travelers are lodged, though without meals.

— *38,* 4. *Baucis.* In ancient mythology, a Phrygian peasant woman, who, with her husband Philemon, entertained Jupiter and Mercury. Goethe adopts the names for his aged couple in the first scene of Act V of *Faust II.*

— *40,* 3. *Druses.* A Syrian stock inhabiting the fertile plateaus of the Lebanon range.

— *44.* For rime scheme see above, note to IV, *33.* MS III reads:

Yet was Prince Babekan, of all the rest
(He whom the Sultan for her husband meant)
Believed the man she could endure the best—
Not that her heart beat when he came and went;
For still the most she on herself could gain,
Was never purposely to shun his view;
But that she loved no other man, was plain;
The wedding day once past, love, thought they, will ensue.

Here we have the standard form of rime, ababcdcd, and six feet in the eighth line, but Adams adopted for his last version the model of MS II, or nearly so. MS II varies from MS IV in the lines:

4. Not that her heart beat more, whene'er he came or went:—
7. But that no other man her fancy pleased they knew—

These lines, 4 and 7, both have six feet, which Adams reduced to five. All this shows how Adams worked, with what skill and painstaking care.

— *54,* 8. *Bezoar.* A stone found in the stomach of the Bezoar-goat (indigenous in the Caucasus), of blue or gray color and pleasing odor, to which was ascribed extraordinary medical powers.

— *60,* 7. *This wife* (W. die Alte). In MS III Adams translated:

And yet, quoth Huon, 'tis apparent too,
This woman forged it not; 'tis fate the knot that ties.

— *61,* 8. *Dulcimain* (W. Dulcimene). Dulcinea del Toboso, sweetheart of Don Quixote. The calm, unheroic advice of Cherasmin is crowned in the original with a touch of humor, the garbled name of

Dulcinea forced into a rime with "Zähne," impossible to reproduce in a translation. Lines 6–8 in the German read:

> Dem Junker linker Hand ließ ich den Luftpaß frei
> Und dem Khalifen seine Zähne
> Und hielte mich an meine Dulcimene.

— 62. The unusual rime scheme of this stanza Adams takes from his MS II (three rimes: abaabbcc), which he had standardized to four rimes in MS III.

— 63, 3. *the hare-foot prince* (W. dem Hasen von Bräutigam).

— 65, 7–8. MS III: At once so near, so distant from the port,
One instant seems to him a never ending age.

Wieland: So nah am Port, so nah und doch so weit!
Es ist ein Augenblick und däucht ihm Ewig-keit.

Sotheby: So near the port!—so near, and yet so far!
One moment—yet that one—it seems eternity!

CANTO V (Book the fifth)

V, *1*, 6. *Hymen*. The Greek god of marriage.

— 2. MS III gives a version happier in some lines than the final version:

> She slept— Before her eyes the fairy power
> Wove visions new to soothe her drooping mind;
> She dreamt that by the moonlight in a bower
> Raised in the Harem's garden, she reclined.
> Sunk in love's phantasies, a pleasing woe,
> A timid soft desire her bosom swells,
> And tears of tenderness profusely flow,
> While on the youth adored her hopeless fancy dwells.

— 8, 7. Love as the *lion-tamer*. W. Der Löwenbändiger, der mich beschützt, ist sie (die Liebe).

— 10, 4. Well translated by Adams (W. Mit diesem hoff' ich Alles vom Geschicke). Sotheby misses the point: "This lifts me high above the reach of fate."

— 14, 1. *the matron* (W. die Alte). A. uses various designations for the mother of Fatme (see above, note to IV, *36*, 4), as *goody, wife, good mother* (same stanza, V, *14*, 6), *old wife* (*15*, 1). S. uses *crone, grandam*, etc.

— 19, 1. *Emirs*, Turkish princes of the Faithful.
Vizirs, highest ministers of state.

V, *22, 3*. *Iman* (W. Imam). The officer in Mohammedan mosques who recites the prayers and leads the devotions.

— *23, 8*. *elders* (W. Flieder). MS IV translates "alders," which is incorrect, but MSS I, II, and III all read "elders," and this reading was therefore adopted. S. correctly translates "lilacs."

— *24, 1*. *He slept*. MS II reads: "he dropped asleep" (W. Er schlummert ein). The old reading had six feet to the line, which A. changed to five in MS IV.

— *25, 5*. *the son of May* (W. der junge Mai). Perhaps a reference to Hermes, messenger of the gods, the son of Zeus and Maia, oldest daughter of Atlas.

— *30, 1*. The often quoted line: W. "Nichts halb zu thun, ist edler Geister Art." MSS I and II: "In doing naught by halves, brave spirits *take a* pride." The prose translation in MS I is more exact: "To do nothing by halves is the way of *noble* spirits." Cf. Introduction, p. xxv.

— *37, 1–2*. *Perseus, Gordon*. A reference to the wedding feast of Andromeda, when Perseus subdued his enemies with the sight of the "snake-entangled" head of the Gorgon horror Medusa. Cf. IV, *3, 3*, note.

— *37*. MS III ends with this stanza.

— *40*. Sotheby's translation of this stanza is not as close to the original and poetically not superior (cf. Introduction, p. xxi):

> S. " 'Tis he!" she wild exclaims: yet virgin shame
> Stops in her rosy mouth th' imperfect sound:
> How throbs her heart! what thrillings strange confound!
> When with impatient speed the stranger came,
> And, love-embolden'd with presumptuous arms
> Clasp'd in the sight of all her angel charms!
> And, oh! how fiery red, how deadly pale
> Her cheek, as love and maiden fear assail,
> The while he kist her lip that glow'd with sweet alarms!

— *42, 1*. *the soft reluctant fair* (W. die sanft bezwungne Schöne). Sotheby's translation uses the same words:

> S. Then, for the third time, at these words, again
> The bridegroom kist *the soft reluctant fair:*

In Adams's earlier versions, MSS I and II (written before Feb. 15, 1800), the reading slightly differs: "Thus speaking to the soft-*constrained* fair." "Constrained" is closer to Wieland's "bezwungne." Why did he change? Was he influenced by Sotheby? Though this part of MS IV was probably written before Dec. 4, 1800, when Adams first saw the Sotheby translation, there are other reasons why he need not have turned to Sotheby for suggestions. He wanted a word of three syllables for *constrainèd*, which might so readily be mistaken for one of two. The word "reluctant" which he used often elsewhere, as in this Canto V, *56*, 5, etc., was unmistakably of three syllables and fairly close to the original German in meaning. We may reject the assumption of any influence. See also note on Canto III, *56*, 1.

— *42*, 4–5. In this same stanza Adams does not repeat the error of Sotheby, who has the Sultan address his daughter instead of his slaves with angry words:

> "Thou suffer'st then—inexpiable stain!
> This Christian dog to shame thy nuptial day?"

W. "... ihr leidet, daß der Hund
Von einem Franken so mich höhne?
Ergreift ihn! Zaudern ist Verrath!"

— *46*, 8. *the wonder* (W. Wunderwerk). Adams frequently translates the German "das Wunder" with *wonder*, meaning *miracle, marvel*, as: V, *49*, 3; V, *63*, 8; VII, *37*, 5; VII, *73*, 5 and 6; X, *35*, 7.

— *47*, 1. *divan* (W. Divan). An Oriental government council.

— *47*, 2. *bashaws* (W. Bassen). Turkish pashas.

— *47*, 4. *a swarthy gelding* (W. einem Hämling). The "Glossarium" states that the word "Hämling" is derived from "hämeln," to mutilate (stümmeln). In MSS I and II A. translates "eunuch." S. incorrectly renders: "spruce courtier" (euphemism?).

— *48*, 3. *the mutilated crew.* This translates Wieland's "die Verschnittenen," which Adams found in the variant readings of the 1796 Göschen edition that he translated from. The 1796 edition used the word "Kämmerlinge." Sotheby, using a Weidmann edition of 1789 or 1792, correctly translates "eunuchs." Cf. Introduction, p. xxxi.

— *48*, 7. *aprons green* (W. *bunten* Schürzen). Adams used *green* for the rime. In the prose translation of MS I he wrote "motley."

— *53*, 8. *The kitchen scullion* (W. Der Stallknecht). Here Adams drew on his imagination. His original prose translation gave "hostler." Sotheby translates "groom." All MSS of Adams render "kitchen scullion," which adds color but is contrary to his usual exactness.

— *56*, 8. W. "Und eine Hand voll Haar aus deinem Silberbart." Sotheby tries to minimize the barbarity of the request by rendering: "And from your reverend beard a lock of silver hair"! But W. and A. remain true to the legend as handed down.

— *59*, 6. *Chan* (W. Khan). Oriental prince or ruler, later a title of respect.

V, *62, 6. that One is with me* (W. Einer), referring of course to his protector Oberon.

— *64, 2. Shaw* (W. Schach). Shah, king.

— *68,* 1. *Strained ... o'er* (W. übertäubt), *overpowered* in MS I (prose).

— *69,* 1. *A cry of joy* (W. Ein lauter Schrei des Schreckens und der Lust). Sotheby incorrectly translates "Lust" with "desire."

— *72,* 1. *risk* (W. die Wage). The "Glossarium" compares the word with "Wagestück," meaning *risk.* Sotheby did not have the benefit of this explanation and mistranslates: "Yet if this *dangerous flight* thy soul alarm" (W. Noch, Rezia, wenn dich *die Wage* schreckt). It is not the danger of the flight, but the great risk of leaving her home and all the comforts and luxuries of her youth and exchanging therefor dependence upon a stranger in an uncertain future—of all which Oberon eloquently reminds Rezia.

— *75,* 8. "Safe with you on the shore of Askalon *to land."* This is the reading of MS II. By a strange slip of the pen MS IV reads "demand" instead of "to land," which destroys all meaning.

W. Euch sicher an den Strand von Askalon zu bringen.

MS I. To bring you safe on Askalon's fair strand.

Askalon, ancient city of the Philistines, on the coast of southern Palestine; it was the scene of battles during the crusades, and was destroyed in 1270; now Asgalan.

— *76, 5–8.* MS II reads:

... Anon her timid sight
Upon her sire as stiff in death he seems to lie
She sinks, while in her breast soft sorrow heaves a sigh
And mingles bitterness with all her heart's delight.

— *82–86.* In these beautiful closing stanzas the translators seem to vie with each other in an attempt to equal the original, Sotheby with his ornate diction, Adams with greater simplicity and power, closer to the German spirit.

Canto VI (Book the sixth)

VI, *1, 2.* MS II reads: "And with her rosy hand unbarred the gates of day." Both this and line 6 were reduced from six to five feet in MS IV, but the rime scheme was not standardized, remaining aabcbcdd. Cf. Introduction, p. xlv.

— *1, 6.* MS II reads: "And by a gentle shock awaked our double pair."

— *3, 2–4.* See illustration facing p. 122. This is a reproduction of a copper engraving found in the Leipzig edition of 1789 (Weidmannsche Buchhandlung), named E4b in Kurrelmeyer's critical edition of Wieland's *Oberon*. The artist was J. M. Kraus (delineavit), the engraver Geyser (sculpsit).

— *5, 5–6.* The reading in MS II, with six feet, is clearer:

> ... while Fatme sought
> A place beside the knee of her young lady fair.

Adams frequently places the object before the verb to get the standard length of line (five feet) in MS IV, though his original may be very irregular, in this stanza varying between four, five, and six feet.

— *6, 6. Though not expressly asked by Charlemagne.* The Emperor (Canto I, *67,* 6–8) bids Huon demand four molars and a handful of hair from the beard of the Caliph, but does not ask him to bring the trophies back with him, believing that the anger of the Caliph would be sufficiently aroused to send Huon to execution at once. Tressan, in the *Bibliothèque,* clumsily has Huon extract the teeth himself from the severed head of the Caliph. Wieland lets spirit hands perform this operation unseen, nor is Rezia's father decapitated or presumably slain.

— *7, 8. pincers* (W. Pelikan). The name of an instrument for extracting teeth, curved at the end like the beak of a pelican.

— *8, 2. lays,* to rime with *days.* See note to I, *55,* 8. MS I contains Adams's first prose rendering: "there in the harbor *lies* a vessel," etc.

— *8, 4. Lepanto.* A seaport in Greece, at the mouth of the Gulf of Corinth.

— *8, 6. Salerno.* Ancient Salernum, Italian port on the Gulf of Salerno, southeast of Naples, famous for its medieval school of medicine.

— *9, 2. Sylvester.* Three popes had this name, but none in the age of Charlemagne. It was probably chosen because of its good rhythm.

— *9, 8. dissever* (W. trennen). Separate. Cf. "and thei dissevered and wente eche to his baner," *Merlin* (EETS, iii, 485). "Thus when flesh and soul dissever," Hymn.

— *14, 7. Garonne.* See note to IV, *21,* 4.

— *15, 2. Gascogne.* Gascony, province in southwestern France. Cf. note to III, *55,* 7.

— *20, 7. timid vent'rous look* (W. furchtsam kühnen Blick), *vent'rous* for *venturous.*

— *24, 5–8.* W. Er war an Glauben stark, wiewohl an Kenntniß
> schwach,
> Und die Theologie war keineswegs sein Fach;
> Sein Pater und sein Credo, ohne Glossen,

In diesen Kreis war all sein Wissen eingeschlossen.
A (MS II). His faith was strong; his knowledge weak, indeed;
Nor was theology his shining side, 'tis true.
His pater noster, and his unglossed creed,
It must be owned, included all he knew.

VI, *27, 2. athwart the way* (W. weiter nichts im Weg). MS II:
naught further in the way   Our hero sees.

— *27, 7. Basil's rule* (W. Ein Jünger Sanct Basils). The vows of
poverty, chastity, and obedience are supposed to go back to this Oriental monk Basilius (born in 329 A.D.).

— *28, 1. Amanda.* The *lovable,* the name that Huon selects for her
in Tressan's work, where her name was originally Esclarmonde.

— *32.* This stanza appears in Sotheby's first edition, 1796, but was
expurgated in succeeding editions.

— *33, 3. unpractised virtue* (W. unerfahrene Tugend).

— *34, 3.* By a slip of the pen in copying MS IV has *not* for *nought,*
correctly written *nought* (naught) in MSS I and II.

— *34, 8. to tell a tale.* From this point on, stanzas 35–84 inclusive
are omitted by Sotheby in all his editions. He says in explanation of this
violent expurgation in a footnote on p. 198 of the first edition (1798):
"Sherasmin's tale is sufficiently known to the English reader by the
January and May of Pope: yet, though I have omitted nearly the whole
of it, I trust that the part which I have inserted will clearly point out
the art and contrivance with which Wieland has interwoven into the
texture, and rendered essential to the completion of the main object of
his poem, the only incident in the story which could have induced him
to revive the subject.—The incident to which I allude is the presence
of Oberon and Titania in the garden scene: and with this I begin the
narrative." His stanza 34 in the third edition is Wieland's (and
Adams's) stanza 85. Wieland has told the tale with equal humor,
greater delicacy, and less wearisome driftwood than Pope or Chaucer.
Adams's translation follows his original with consummate skill. Cf.
Introduction, pp. xxviii–xxix.

— *35, 2. Calender* (W. Kalender). A mendicant dervish of Turkey
or Persia, who made his way by telling tales and jests.

— *35, 3. Bassora* (W. Basra). Busra, below the confluence of the
Euphrates and Tigris in Mesopotamia.

— *35, 5. Libanus' wilds* (W. die Kluft des Libans). Same as Lebanon, mountain range of Syria, north of Old Palestine.

— *36, 2. Tessino's banks* (W. Tessin). The river Ticino, rising in
the Alps and flowing through Switzerland (Canton Ticino, Tessin) and

Italy, through Lago Maggiore into the Po. Chaucer and Pope give Lombardy as the home of January.

— *53, 6. fingers' ends* (W. Fingerenden) is the reading of MSS I and II. MS IV, apparently by a slip, writes *end*.

— *70, 3. faith.* This is the reading of MSS I and II. MS IV, undoubtedly through an error in copying, gives the word *slave,* which makes no sense whatever.

— *70, 8.* W. Und ihrer List nichts gleich, als ihre Wankelmuth. The reading of MS IV is undoubtedly the best, but the variant readings are interesting: MS I: "Their falsehood equalled by their art alone." MS II: "Naught, say they, can her craft and fickleness exceed." Also, MS II: "Her falsehood equalled by her fickleness alone."

— *79, 6. a longing* (W. ein Lüstern). A craving. "Lüsternheit" (VI, *84,* 2) would be better translated by *craving.* "Sehnsucht" is German for "longing."

— *85, 1.* Here Sotheby begins again.

— *89, 8.* A footnote explaining a succeeding additional omission is here given by Sotheby (first edition, 1798, p. 201): "Here by the intervention of Titania, the woman's artifice prevails, and the indignation of Oberon at once breaks forth." Sotheby then omits stanzas 90–97, which give the conclusion of the story of January and May, all of them admirably translated by Adams. Sotheby begins again with stanza 98: "Titania! hearst thou?" says the monarch now.

— *98, 8. From this time forward you and I must part.* (W. Von nun an müssen wir uns trennen!) Sotheby does not translate this line but substitutes an unwarranted line of his own: "Hence! fly to haunts unblest, from love and me removed!"

— *98–104.* Wieland's motivation for the separation of Oberon and Titania is generally regarded as a master stroke. Adams shows his recognition of the poetical genius of Wieland even more fully than Sotheby by not attempting to improve on the original.

Basing the separation of the King and Queen of the Fairies upon a quarrel arising from the possession of an Indian boy, as in *A Midsummer-Night's Dream,* is not nearly as plausible or effective a motive as that of a moral principle involved, the question of human fidelity. A flagrant case of bad faith has been revealed before their eyes, about which the King and Queen took different sides and quarreled bitterly. Only the evidence of human fidelity can counteract the curse pronounced by Oberon. This is the keynote of the second part of *Oberon,* Cantos VII–XII, the finding of an equally outstanding case of a loving couple true to each other unto death. Only the sight of such conjugal fidelity can restore the bond between Oberon and Titania and their happiness. Hence their interest in Huon and Amanda.

Canto VII (Book the seventh)

VII, *4, 7.* *the Lateran.* Until 1308 the residential palace of the Pope in Rome, now the Lateran museum. The basilica of St. John Lateran ranks above all other Roman Catholic churches.

— *10, 2.* *Arcturus.* The brightest star in the northern constellation Boötes (the plowman), behind the Great Bear.

Thetis. A Nereid, wife of Pelius and mother of Achilles.

— *10, 4.* *Zephyrs.* The west wind, poetically any soft wind.

— *10, 7.* *in their veins that ran.* Meaning *that ran in their veins;* inversions are frequent, especially in MS IV, to get the rime or reduce to a five-foot line.

— *11.* This stanza appears in Sotheby's first edition (1798), well-rendered, but was expurgated in later editions.

— *12–13.* Both these stanzas are translated by Sotheby, but the last line of *13* is changed to: "Forbear! frail youth, forbear! relentless fates oppose."

— *14–16.* Then Sotheby omits stanzas *14, 15, 16.* These, the most passionate stanzas in the poem, are admirably rendered by Adams, very faithful to the German and matching the original in metrical skill and poetical power. Sotheby does not make these pointless expurgations in his first edition.

— *30, 4.* *borne away.* By a slip of the pen MS IV writes "born." All other MSS of Adams give *borne* correctly.

— *34, 6.* *From Trent to Memphis.* Trent (Trient) in northern Italy, since 1918. Memphis, the ancient capital of Egypt; its ruins are located twelve miles south of Cairo.

— *36, 4.* *Antichrist.* Cf. I John 2, 18. This personification of evil and blasphemy has perhaps caused Sotheby to expurgate this stanza, even in his first edition. No other reason is apparent. Adams, daily reader of the Scriptures, saw no necessity for omitting it.

— *37, 4.* MS II is slightly clearer:
And who, unweeting how, upon an island strand
Thee, and himself again, Oh! wonder! found.

— *37, 5.* *wonder.* In the sense of *miracle.* See note to V, *46,* 8.

— *41, 1.* Cf. Introduction, p. xxv.

— *72, 8.* W. "Er prüft nur, die er liebt, und liebet väterlich." Cf. Introduction, p. xxv.

— *75,* 6–8. Neither translation has reached the beauty of the original lines:

> Und wenn die Hoffnung auch den Ankergrund verliert,
> So lass' uns fest an diesem Glauben halten,
> Ein einz'ger Augenblick kann alles umgestalten.

— *80, 3. confessed.* In the sense of *avow, attest.*

> W. Und mit dem Kuß verwandeln sich die Klippen
> Um Hüon her;

— *87.* This entire stanza is omitted by Sotheby, even in the first edition, for no apparent reason. From this canto two stanzas were omitted in the first edition (36 and 87), in later editions six (11, 14, 15, 16, 36, 87).

— *99, 7. 'ready past* (W. bereits). Already past.

CANTO VIII (Book the eighth)

VIII. The rime scheme which Adams made his standard, ababcdcd, has been successfully maintained throughout this canto. The lines are of uniform length, five feet, except the eighth, which is usually an Alexandrine.

— *9, 3. His cottage that invest.* An inversion for *that invest his cottage.*

— *10,* 7–8. W. Glaubt, auch auf Heidekraut schmeckt Ruh und
Unschuld süß,
Und reiner fließt das Blut bei Kohl und Schoten.
Adams has kept the proverbial ring of the original well.

— *16, 1. Alfonso.* Thus spelled in MSS I and II consistently. In MS IV spelled *Alphonso* in Canto VIII, *Alfonso* in Canto IX, *37,* 4. W. uses the Spanish spelling with an *f,* adopted for this edition.

— *16, 2. Leon.* A province, once a kingdom and its capital in north-western Spain.

— *16, 5. will-o'-the-wisp* (MS IV: will-a-wisp, W. Blendwerk). Referring to princely service (Fürstendienst).

— *16, 8. the stone of fools* (W. Stein der Narren). Antithesis to stone of the wise (Stein der Weisen); alchemist's stone.

— *24.* This stanza is omitted by Sotheby in all editions, for no apparent reason.

— *30, 7. his son* (W. den neuen Sohn). MS I (prose): "his new son."

— *31,* 5–6. Cf. Introduction, pp. xxv–xxvi.

— *39, 8. steadier soul.* (W. Rezias standhaftern Ernst.) This is the reading of MS II. MS IV reads: "soft control," undoubtedly by mistake because it does not translate the German, and the rime is faulty.

— *41, 7. knight.* Thus correctly spelled in MSS I and II. By slip of the pen MS IV writes "night."

— *42, 3–5.* W. Die ungewohnte Hand greift alles schwerer an,
　　　　Und in der halben Zeit hätt' es ein Knecht gethan.
　　　　Doch täglich nimmt er zu, denn Übung macht den
　　　　　Meister;
These very quotable lines Adams renders with characteristic terseness well suited to Wieland's proverbial utterances. Cf. Introduction, p. xxvi.

— *63, 4. own.* This is the reading of MSS I and II, while MS IV has the word "lord" in its place (destroying the sense), evidently a mistake in copying.

— *64, 1–3.* W. Doch, da für jede Seelenstunde,
　　　　Wie tief sie brennt, die Zeit, die große Trösterin,
　　　　Den wahren Balsam hat:
Adams again translates with proverbial brevity.

— *79, 6–8.* This touching moment was illustrated by Johann Heinrich Ramberg, *Prachtausgabe von Wielands Werken* (Göschen), reproduced in *Kürschners Deutsche National-Litteratur,* Vol. 52, II, p. 153.

— *80, 4. wealth of India* (W. alles Gold der Aureng-Zeben). All the gold of the Great Moguls.

Canto IX (Book the ninth)

IX. Adams's adopted standard has been maintained throughout this and the remaining cantos of the poem: rime scheme ababcdcd; length of line five feet, except the eighth line, generally of six feet; iambic meter.

— *5, 2. sequins* (W. Sultaninen). A sequin is a Turkish gold coin, originally gold currency of the Venetian Republic valued at about $2.25.

— *5, 5. Gulistan* (W. Gulistan). The "Glossarium" tells us the word is derived from the Persian and denotes flower- or rose-garden.

— *6, 6. Mount Martre* (W. Märtrerberg). Montmartre, a height and quarter of the northern part of Paris, the name deduced from Mons Martis (Mars), subsequently named Mons Martyrum (martyrs).

— *14, 6. Basque nation.* People of the French and Spanish Pyrenees.

— *16, 8. Tunis.* The seaport capital of Tunis in North Africa. The ruins of ancient Carthage are to the northeast.

— *20, 6. Thick urging upon Huon.* Thickly crowding upon Huon where he stood.

> W. Rezia durch alles Volk, das dichte
> Auf Hüon drängt, sich stürzt,—

S. is here better:

> While Rezia seen by gleams of lightning pale,
> Amid the crew that round her Huon prest ...

— 29, 4. *true being* (W. Ins wahre Sein).

— 35, 2–4. W. Schaut eure Rosen an; und wenn ihr alle drei
> Zu Lilien werden seht, so merket dran, ich sei
> Mit Oberon versöhnt ...

This beautiful symbol is a poetic invention of Wieland.

— 40, 3. *brows* (W. Stirne). This is the reading of MSS I and II.
MS IV incorrectly copied "bows."

— 40, 8. *but steady.* This is the reading of MS IV. MSS I and II
read *untransient.* W. "Ein *unvergängliches* kaum sichtbars Lächeln
schweben." S. "scarce visible celestial smile."

— 55, 1–2. Note the terseness of Adams's lines in comparison with:
> W. Der schöne Anblick macht sonst rohe Seelen milder,
> Und Tiger schmiegen sich zu ihren Füßen hin:
> S. Oft beauty makes the sternest spirit mild,
> And tigers lose their fierceness at her feet:

Canto X (Book the tenth)

X, 2. This stanza furnishes conclusive evidence, besides telling instances given in the Introduction, p. xxxi, that Adams translated from
the Göschen edition of 1796, while Sotheby used the Weidmann edition
of 1792 (called C and E4 respectively by Kurrelmeyer in his critical
edition of *Oberon*). Lines 4–8 are quoted below to show how they
differ in the two editions:

W. (C)
> ... Denn, ach! vergebens schwillt
> Ihr zartes Herz von innigem Erbarmen.
> Ein stärk'rer Zauber stößt mit unaufhaltbar'n Armen
> Sie weg von ihm; und wie sie überm Strand
> Dahin schwebt, blinkt vor ihr ein Goldreif aus dem Sand.

(Adams translates "Ein stärk'rer Zauber," *A stronger charm;* also:
Her flight across the shore, and *flying,* not looking about, etc.)

W. (E4)
> ... Denn, ach! vergebens schwillt
> Ihr Herz von Mitgefühl! Ein eisernes Geschicke
> Stößt sie, sobald sie sich ihm nähern will, zurücke,

> Sie flieht, und wie sie nach dem einst geliebten Strand
> Noch einmal umschaut, blinkt ein Goldring aus dem Sand.

S.

> *In vain she ventures near*—a viewless hand
> Still drives her back—yet, as she leaves the shore,
> Her *last long look that rolls the island o'er*
> Darts on a ring of gold that glitters on the sand.

— *2, 3.* pine (W. verlechzen). This is the reading of MSS I and II. Through an error in copying MS IV reads "pace."

— *9, 4.* nor. MS IV reads "or," MS II "nor."

— *12, 3.* cell (W. Felsengruft). Cf. Canto VIII, *70–72.*

— *17, 3.* flutter (W. . . . kein Sandkorn rückt am Meer' Aus seinem Platz). MS II has a better reading: "No grain of sand will *start up* for my sake."

— *20, 1.* See Introduction, p. xxvi.

— *26, 7.* Aleppo. A city of northern Syria, important for its commerce and silk manufacture.

— *31, 2.* Askalon. Cf. Canto VI, *1, 3;* also note to Canto V, *75, 8.*

— *33, 5.* Fez. Northern capital of Morocco.

— *41, 6.* Horeb. A mountain in the peninsula of Sinai, Arabia.

— *42, 6.* Cynthia (W. der Mond).

— *49, 2.* Idshoglan (W. Idschoglan). The "Glossarium" tells us that this is a kind of page of the Turkish court; the highest class among them are especially devoted to the personal service of the Sultan. By poetic license Wieland transfers the same institution to the court of Tunis.

— *52, 7.* To dig you blush not. A reference to Huon's work on the deserted island, Canto VIII, *42,* etc.

Canto XI (Book the eleventh)

XI, *3, 6.* watching (W. die Nacht wird hier mit *Wachen* zugebracht). Wakefulness.

— *8, 7.* Joseph's ice (W. dem kältsten Josephsinn). Reference to Genesis 39, 7-12. Sotheby omits the reference to Joseph.

— *9, 1.* Grecian art. W. names the Greek sculptors Alkamenes and Lysippos.

— *9, 4–5.* Helen. The wife of Menelaos, king of Sparta, carried off by Paris, causing the ten years' Trojan War.

Atalanta. In the Bœotian version the princess, beautiful and swift of foot, who agreed to marry the suitor who could outrun her. Hippomenes alone succeeded by throwing in her way three golden apples given him by Aphrodite, which Atalanta stooped to pick up.

Erigone. Daughter of Ikarus, and beloved of Dionysius; changed to the constellation Virgo.

Leda. Mother of Helen by Zeus, who came to her in the guise of a swan.

— *10,* 5. *languid* (W. schmachtend). MS I (prose rendering): *languishing.*

— *11.* This stanza was expurgated by Sotheby after his first edition.

— *12,* 5. *room.* Used here for the rime (W. Stelle). MS I (prose) renders "place."

— *16,* 3. She (line 1) with anger found her nod obeyed too soon.

— *23,* 4. *bleeds.* Used for a rime; otherwise no justification.

W. Der Saft von allen Pompelmusen
Erfrischte nicht so gut . . .

Pompelmusen (grapefruit) translated "melons" in MS I (prose).

— *31,* 2. *witness.* (W. Zeugin.) This is the reading of MS II. MS IV by a slip of the pen reads "mistress."

— *33,* 6. *Maneh* (W. Mahneh). Also called Salam, the "Glossarium" tells us, among Turks and Moorish Saracens, a secret love-letter composed of flowers, spices, and symbolical trifles, each reminding of a quotation from a poet, or symbolical of some lover's sigh or prayer and having a code meaning.

— *34,* 8. A and H were meant by Fatme of course to mean Amanda and Huon, not Almansaris and Hassan.

— *36,* 5–6. Cf. Introduction, p. xxvi. Proverbial lines also in stanza 42, 7–8.

— *44,* 3. *Harem ladies* (W. Odalisken). *Odalisken* were white female slaves in the harem, capable of rising to the position of favorite.

— *47,* 3. *lapis lazuli.* A rich blue complex of minerals, used to produce ultramarine and also for decorative purposes.

— *47,* 5. *Golconda's richest mine* (W. Golkond und Siam). Golconda, a ruined city, was at one time famous for diamond cutting. Hence a mine of wealth.

— *49,* 4. *Cytherea.* A name of Aphrodite (Venus), from Cythera, near which she rose from the sea.

flow (W. fließen). MS IV erroneously writes "blow"; MSS I and II correctly "flow," adopted here.

— *55,* 5. *Hebe.* Goddess of youth and spring, daughter of Zeus and Hera, who gave her as wife to Hercules after his deification. Hebe was cupbearer to the gods until supplanted by Ganymede.

XI, *57*. Sotheby expurgated this stanza after his first edition.

— *61* and *63*. These two very beautiful stanzas were also sacrificed by Sotheby in all but his first edition. Cf. Introduction, p. xxix. Adams equals the original in power and beauty of expression. All three versions in MSS I, II, and IV are alike. Adams hit his best form at the first try. Wieland has painted the passion of Almansaris in a way that is not revolting, but awakes our sympathy. Thus the temptation of Huon becomes all the stronger and his victory and fidelity more glorious.

— *64*, 8. *That can on him prevail, to act a traitor's part.* This is the reading of MS II. MS IV is obscure: "Of might to make him act a traitor's part," possibly brought about by an attempt to reduce the six-foot eighth line to five feet. This is one exception to the editor's rule, to use MS IV for this text. Obvious slips of the pen in MS IV, when verified by the earlier manuscripts, have of course been corrected, but also referred to in the notes.

Canto XII (Book the twelfth)

XII, *2*, 4. *lovely.* This is the reading of MSS I and II. By a slip of the pen MS IV writes "lively" (W. lieblicher).

— *5*, 5. *desire* (W. was Götter selbst gelüstet). This reading is found in both MS I and MS II. MS IV by a mistake in copying writes "admire."

— *6*, 8. *Asmodeus* (W. Asmodi). In Jewish demonology a destructive demon; in the book of Tobit said to have loved Sara and to have destroyed in succession her seven husbands; was banished by Solomon. In German lore called "Eheteufel," destroyer of marriages.

— *7*, 2. *An urchin sly* (W. Verführer). Rendered *seducer* in MS I (prose draft).

— *13*, 8. *in light that still grows clear* (W. bei immer hellerm Schein). The prose draft of MS I gives the literal translation: "in a light still growing clearer."

— *14*, 2. *Would choose for stolen pleasures when she pants.* A frequent case of inversion, made for the rime; would read normally: Would choose, when she pants for secret pleasures.

— *16*. This stanza was expurgated by Sotheby after his first edition. Possibly his well-done lines 8–9 antagonized prudish critics of his time:

> Charms lovelier far than those that whilome chang'd
> To swan, or milk-white bull, the form of Grecian Jove.

— *17, 5. Apelles.* A Greek painter of the fourth century B. C., the time of Philip and Alexander. His most famous picture was Aphrodite Anadyomene.

Titian. Great Venetian painter and colorist (1477–1576), famous for his portrayals of Venus, Danaë, Sacred and Profane Love, etc., etc.

— *26, 6. Iman's call* (W. sobald vom Turm der Imam ruft). The leader of the devotions in Mohammedan mosques. Cf. Canto V, 22, 3, and note.

— *29, 4. And I, unpitied.* W. "Wie gern erlitt' ich unbeweint Mein traurig Los!"

— *31, 7. Haply* (W. Hat ihm *vielleicht* ... ?). MS I gives a literal prose rendering of the original: "Has to him, perhaps, as a pledge that his sufferings will soon end, the good protecting Spirit himself sent this refreshment?"

— *34, 2. trump.* Poetical but obsolete form for "trumpet."

— *43, 5. kurdee* (W. Kurdé). The "Glossarium" explains the word as meaning a wide outside garment ("weites Oberkleid") of Turkish ladies. Rezia throws this over her night-dress. Sotheby, not having seen the "Glossarium" (cf. Introduction, p. xxxi, where this passage is given as one of the evidences proving that Sotheby used an earlier edition than that of 1796), mistranslates the word *Kurdé* with "girdle."

> W. Wirft, wie sie steht, im leichten Nachtgewande,
> Den Kurdé um, und eilt in vollem Lauf
> Des Sultans Zimmer zu,—
>
> S. Casts o'er her limbs a night-gown loosely spread,
> Bound by a *girdle* to her throbbing breast.

There is nothing in the original that might have suggested the embellishments of Sotheby's last line.

— *59, 4. Aga.* An officer placed over the odalisks and eunuchs. *Aga* was once the title given in Turkey to the chief of the janizaries.

— *67, 3–4.* Correctly translated by Adams, while Sotheby misses the point (see the last four words). Cherasmin speaks for himself only.

> W. (Wiewohl der Alte raspeln oder schanzen
> Für eine bess're Kurzweil hält).
>
> S. Though Sherasmin, who views the giddy ring,
> Think that to delve the dike, not weave the dance
> Were better pastime *for that roguish crew.*

— *68, 3. fills.* This reading is found in MS II. MS IV reads "stills," which is found also in MS II, but there it is crossed out and the more readily understood word "fills" written by its side.

> W. Und immer stiller ward's im weiten Reich der Luft;

XII, *68*, 4. *Cynthia's image.* W. "Schon sahen sie *den Mond* in manchem See sich spiegeln."

— *69*, 6. *Is not this spot the same?* A reference to the visions of their dreams.

— *74*, 1–2. W. "Jungfraun, die in Reihn Vor ihnen her den Weg mit Rosen überstreun,—"

— *87*, 5. *Döolin of Mentz* (W. Doolin von Maganz). *Maganz* and *Mentz* are equivalent to *Mainz*. Doolin von Mainz was the hero of an Old French epic revived by the Viennese poet J. B. von Alxinger (first published in Leipzig, 1787), written in imitation of Wieland's manner.

— *93*, 6–7.

> . . . The fairy queen descends
> Unseen, to aid her charming favorite, down,
> And every heart submissive to her bends.

The punctuation is that of MSS I and II. MS IV has a comma only after the word "unseen."

> W. . . . Die Königin der Feen
> Schmiegt, ungesehen, sich an ihre Freundin an,
> Und alle Herzen sind ihr plötzlich unterthan.

— *94*, 5–8. Adams closes the poem with characteristic fidelity to the original and skill in versification. All three manuscripts are alike.

> W. . . . Es stirbt der alte Groll
> In Karls des Großen Brust. Er schüttelt liebevoll
> Des Helden Hand und spricht: Nie fehl' es unserm Reiche
> An einem Fürstensohn, der Dir an Tugend gleiche!